DATE DUE

FE 10 '00			

DEMCO 38-296

Music and Musicians
in
Ancient Greece

Warren D. Anderson

MUSIC
and
MUSICIANS
in
ANCIENT
GREECE

CORNELL UNIVERSITY PRESS
Ithaca and London

First published 1994 by Cornell University Press.
First printing, Cornell Paperbacks, 1997.

Library of Congress Cataloging-in-Publication Data

Anderson, Warren D.
Music and musicians in Ancient Greece / Warren D. Anderson.
        p.   cm.
Includes bibliographical and discographical references (p.   ) and index.
ISBN 0-8014-3083-6 (cloth: alk. paper)
ISBN 0-8014-8432-4 (pbk.: alk. paper)
1. Music, Greek and Roman.   2. Musicians—Greece.
ML169.A66 1994
780´.9´.01—dc20   94-28507

Printed in the United States of America

⊖ The paper in this book meets the minimum requirements of the
American National Standard for Information Sciences—Permanence of
Paper for Printed Library Materials, ANSI Z39.48-1984.

Cloth printing   10 9 8 7 6 5 4 3 2

Paperback printing   10 9 8 7 6 5 4 3 2 1

R. P. Winnington-Ingram
DIS MANIBVS

Contents

Illustrations

Figures

Plates

Preface

The fifth century is the centerpiece of this study, but earlier periods, so often and so inexplicably neglected, receive extensive consideration. The decision to write about music and musicians rules out any but minimal consideration of philosophers and theorists: Plato and Aristotle appear only when their words can perhaps shed light on the nature and uses of the *harmoniai* or of the instruments on which they were played; so also for Archytas. Ethnomusicology has a voice here; selections and emphases differ from those chosen by M. L. West in *Ancient Greek Music,* though without a conflict of views.

My chief concern here is with the ways in which lyre and kithara, aulos and harp and percussion—sounding alone or joined with the human voice—had a place in Greek life. A negative corollary follows: for this inquiry, the prescriptions and descriptions provided by later theoreticians matter far less than what was once the heard, sounding reality.

How, then, can we grasp that fearfully elusive reality, at a remove of twenty-five centuries? No easy answer comes, but the effort is worth making. First and always, Greek literature must be consulted. Nothing can substitute for a command of the language itself, as some recent attempts by American scholars show all too clearly. A concern with philology will draw us into epigraphy and papyrology, into ancient history and the geography of the classical world. All these are givens; we must venture beyond them, to music history as well as to the discipline of ethnomusicology. Doing so means employing comparative techniques, which classical philologists have been slow to accept.

My approach is chronological. It begins with the Stone Age, when instrumental music first appeared. The archaic period, starting from the Cycladic statuettes of harpers and pipers, receives more attention than any previous treatment has given it. For those dark, mysterious centuries, we depend almost wholly on the evidence of ancient art.

Most of the black-and-white illustrations included in this book relate to this period and form the basis for my discussion.

In a previous book (*Ethos and Education in Greek Music*), a number of articles and extended reviews, and more than seventy entries for the *New Grove Dictionary of Music and Musicians* I have had the opportunity to present my thoughts on ancient Greek music. In the present treatment, I have chosen to avoid repetition of my earlier arguments whenever possible. I have also favored accessible reference sources, written in English, over the magisterial works that we so often owe to the immense diligence and thoroughness of German scholarship. No one who seeks a rapid overview of the subject could do better than to consult R. P. Winnington-Ingram's article in the *New Grove Dictionary* (7:659–72); my approach is a different one.

Thanks are due to the staff of the University Library of the University of Massachusetts at Amherst, especially its excellent Interlibrary Loan Services, as well as to the staff of Robert Frost Library, Amherst College. I recall with particular appreciation the interest and kindness shown by Pamela Juengling, head of the music library at the University of Massachusetts, and by Sally Evans, who was in charge of the music library in Buckley Recital Hall at Amherst College. I was much helped in the final stages of writing by the resources of Wilson Library and Ferguson Music Library, on the University of Minnesota's Twin Cities campus.

I also thank Basil Blackwell for permission to quote from Kathleen Freeman, trans., *Ancilla to the Pre-Socratic Philosophers* (Oxford, 1948). Permission to reproduce illustrations has kindly been granted by the Citadel Press, for figure 1, from Jack Lindsay, *A Short History of Culture* (New York, 1963); Harvard University Press, for figure 20, from my own work, *Ethos and Education in Greek Music* (Cambridge, Mass., 1966); the Museum für Völkerkunde (Berlin), for figure 21, from Ulrich Wegner, *Afrikanische Saiteninstrumente* (Berlin, 1984); the *American Journal of Archaeology,* for figure 22, from Nicholas B. Bodley, "The Auloi of Meroë," vol. 50, no. 2 (1946); Oxford University Press, for figure 23, from the *New Oxford History of Music,* vol. 1 (New York, 1957); the Museum of Fine Arts, Boston, for plates I and II; the Metropolitan Museum of Art, New York, for plates III and IV; the British Museum, London, for plates V, VI, and VII. Thanks are also due to Verlag Hans Carl for permission to reproduce portions of the musical examples in E. Pöhlmann, *Denkmäler altgriechischer Musik* (Nuremberg, 1970).

If the title of this book seems to echo that of the *New Grove Dictionary,* the resemblance is not chance: I use it as a tribute to Stanley Sadie. Amid all the responsibilities of his editorship, he responded at length to queries and comments about my entries, and with every appearance of leisure, over a period of years. I hope that I have learned from his genial wisdom.

Many others have helped my thinking. Offprints and counsel have come from Andrew Barker at the University of Otago, E. Kerr Borthwick, now retired from Edinburgh University, Miroslav Černý in Prague, Douglas Feaver, now retired from Lehigh University, Thomas J. Mathiesen at Brigham Young University, Lukas Richter at the Deutsche Akademie der Wissenschaften, Luigi Enrico Rossi at the University of Rome, Jon Solomon at the University of Arizona, and Martin L. West at Oxford University. If I differ with them at times, I am not the less grateful. I owe particular thanks to Andrew Barker, who pointed out much that was questionable, incorrect, or unclear in an earlier draft of this book. I have tried to acknowledge and incorporate many of his suggestions. At Cornell University Press, Bernhard Kendler has been an unfailing editorial resource, and Marian Shotwell as copy editor did much to improve the consistency, clarity, and formal correctness of my presentation in many portions of the manuscript.

My wife has borne with me the long process of bringing this book to completion, and out of her own delight in Greek poetry she has given unfailing encouragement. What I owe to her cannot be expressed here.

Finally, I dedicate these pages to the undisputed master of the study of ancient Greek music, the late R. P. Winnington-Ingram, whom I found kind and generous on many occasions and to whom for twenty years I have owed most.

WARREN D. ANDERSON

Amherst and Minneapolis

MUSIC AND MUSICIANS
IN
ANCIENT GREECE

{1}

From the Beginnings
to the Dark Age

Deep within the Trois Frères
cave, among the Stone Age sanctuaries of the Dordogne, the shaman
dances. A bison-headed figure on the rock wall, half man and half
animal, he has been dancing for more than ten thousand years. He
holds a special place in history, for he is the first known performer on
a musical instrument (fig. 1).

He plays a musical bow, related to the bow used today in southern
Africa by cattle herders.[1] The player holds one end in his open mouth,
which serves as a resonating chamber, strengthening the sound of
the plucked bowstring and varying its pitch. Bantu performers on the
musical bow can produce more than a half dozen harmonics, and the
instrument is capable of extended sequences. The refinements of this
present-day version, the *gora,* differentiate it from the one played by
the Trois Frères shaman, but it does not differ basically. Perhaps the
musical resources of Stone Age people were less rudimentary than we

---

[1] Trois Frères shaman: Sieveking and Sieveking 1966, 29, 203. The only detailed
general study of the musical bow remains Balfour 1976, first published in 1899; the
New Grove Dictionary of Music and Musicians contains scattered entries. Nettl (1964,
213) lists the varieties of this instrument that are found today in nonliterate societies;
the number is remarkable. See now Lawergren 1982b. Present-day use of musical
bows in Africa: Wegner 1984, 12–17. The Huli of Papua New Guinea combine it with
singing in the most highly developed of their art forms. For an understanding of the
capacities of this instrument, the analysis of Huli music by Jacqueline Pugh-Kitingan,
in Kassler and Stubington 1984, 97–99, is indispensable. The ritual bow in modern
shamanism among the Japanese: Blacker 1986.

Fig. 1. Wall engraving of a bison-headed shaman with a musical bow and animal quarry, Neolithic period, from the Trois Frères cave, Dordogne. (Reprinted, by permission of the publisher, from Lindsay 1963, 21.)

suppose. If the shaman is far indeed from Homer's bards, he is not unimaginably so.

Over the span of five millennia covered by the Mesolithic and Neolithic periods (ca. 8000–3000 B.C.), Homo sapiens became truly and distinctively human. According to Marius Schneider and René Berthelot, this transformation consisted essentially in acquiring the gifts of creation and organization. Already, as most believe, human beings had experienced the beginnings of symbolist thought. Moreover, they had passed through the animistic and totemistic phases of religious belief and the megalithic, lunar, and solar stages of culture.[2]

Berthelot founded his views on a study of the Far East. Schneider has attributed to megalithic European culture discoveries in which music has a significant part. As he maintains, the final stage of the Neolithic differed from what had gone before "in the preference it showed for static and geometric forms, in its organizing and creative genius (evolving fabulous animals, musical instruments, mathematical proportions, number-ideas, astronomy and a tonal system with truly musical sounds). . . . The entire cosmos comes to be conceived

[2] Cirlot 1962, xvii.

after the human pattern. As the essence of all phenomena is, in the last resort, a vibrant rhythm, the intimate nature of phenomena is directly perceptible by polyrhythmic human consciousness."[3] These theoretical musical achievements were to mark Greek musical thought from its beginnings.

Much that concerns the Neolithic will always be conjectural. We know nothing about the musicians of that period that would add to the extremely limited evidence of Paleolithic cave art. Since this evidence includes playing on a musical bow, there would seem to be no reason to place the advent of the instrument in Neolithic times (as Curt Sachs has done), especially since the musical version may predate the one used for hunting.[4] Paleolithic bone flutes did not have finger holes; their Neolithic counterparts did. However slow the later development of melodic resources may have been, the appearance of holed flutes could not signify more obviously an evolving tonal system.

The Bronze Age, a time of migrations, marks the beginning of Greek history. By 2000 B.C., Greek-speaking peoples had settled the mainland. The civilizations and areas of cultural transmission that furnish the great bulk of evidence about music were located generally to the east and south. In overlapping chronological order, they are the Cycladic (as early as 3000 B.C.), the Minoan (its central period 2000–1400 B.C.), and the Mycenaean (1600–1100 B.C.) civilizations. The Cyclades are the wheel-shaped group of small islands between Greece and Asia Minor; the single island of Crete, more distant and vastly larger, produced the Minoan civilization; and the closely related Mycenaean culture flourished in a few fortress cities of the southern mainland (the Peloponnesus), above all in Mycenae itself and in Tiryns. Evidence from adjacent nations and territories, principally Egypt, Cyprus, and the coastal regions of Asia Minor, is also of interest.

Among Bronze Age instruments, chordophones (stringed instruments) are represented by the lyre and triangular harp. The earliest known musical artifact from the Mediterranean-Aegean area is a Cycladic marble statuette from Keros of a seated harper (fig. 2). Accord-

---

[3] Schneider, quoted in Cirlot 1962, xviii.
[4] Priority of the musical bow: Schneider 1957, 57.

Fig. 2. Marble statuette of a seated harper, ca. 2700 B.C., from the Cycladic settlement of Cnidus (modern Cape Krio, south of Cos) in Asia Minor. (Reprinted from Aign 1963, 33, fig. 4.)

ing to the most recent study, it dates from about 2700 B.C., centuries earlier than had once been supposed. For the majority who agree that Greek-speaking peoples entered their new domains during the third millennium B.C., this piece may be seen as a portrait in stone of the first Greek musician.[5]

His instrument has almost the depth of a modern concert harp. At its highest point, the frame apparently incorporates a bird's head: a beak projects horizontally. Aesthetically, this harper is important because of his rapt air and the sense of inwardness that he conveys; technically, what matters is the instrument. Its shape offers a basis for the change from harp to lyre that took place during succeeding centuries. Greeks would never accept any of the numerous later types of harp as Hellenic. No Cycladic harp, moreover, demonstrably owes anything to Egyptian influence.

To judge from the surviving figurines, only men played the harp or

[5] Fig. 2: Aign 1963 (hereafter Aign), 33, fig. 4. Dating: Thimme 1977, 494. This English version of Thimme, edited as well as translated by Pat Getz-Preziosi, is more nearly up-to-date than the German original. Aign follows M. Wegner and others in disputing the authenticity of the statuette, now thoroughly vindicated by Thimme (495). The first Greek(?) musician: Renfrew 1972, 53. West (1992b, 327) describes the Cycladic civilization as "a non-Hellenic culture," like the Minoan, "with Anatolian affinities." For Frieder Zaminer (in Riethmüller and Zaminer 1989, 116), the question of whether there are connections with Greek music remains open.

the double pipes. The fact that they are portrayed as naked or nearly unclothed makes it unlikely that they were priests. Yet secular status need not have prevented them from taking part in religious ceremonies. Some connection with religion appears to be not only possible but almost mandatory; it is difficult to see why else these performers received attention. Originally, the rapt inwardness of the Keros harper may have been associated not with the musician but with the divinity in whose service he plays and perhaps sings. If so, what we encounter here—at the very beginning of the history of Greek music—is *enthousiasmos,* the indwelling of the divine. The bird's head that forms part of the harp frame would then be an acknowledgment of the bird as symbol of divinity. Its later connection with the lyre, and very possibly with Apollo, can be seen unmistakably in the Mycenaean palace fresco at Pylos, which shows a bird flying beside an imposing lyre player. Whatever the correct explanation may be, these statuettes of musicians prove that the Cycladic peoples assigned music a place of importance.

The decline of Cycladic culture coincided with the rise of Crete. The splendor of this island civilization, called Minoan after the legendary King Minos, characterized mainly its final period. Throughout their history, the focal point of the religion of the Minoans remained the same: a mother-goddess. Instruments and performers shown in Minoan art may relate to ritual occasions more often than we suppose.

From the Middle Minoan period (ca. 1850–1700 B.C.), we have a half dozen representations, seal impressions or graffiti, showing harps or what may be lyres (fig. 3).[6] Beyond question, it is a transitional sequence, ending with something very like a lyre. A pair of seal carvings show eight-stringed harps, each with two distinct sets of four parallel strings and with each set differently angled. Here the bird's head and projecting beak survive. They have shifted to a central position, as if the Cycladic harp had been tilted 90 degrees backward. After this they disappear, to be seen again centuries later on the Late Minoan concert lyre.

The two graffiti (fig. 3c) were found by Arthur Evans at Knossos. They are rough impressions, hardly more than outlines; yet these

[6] Fig. 3: Aign 35–37, figs. 6–11.

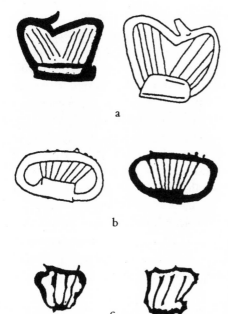

Fig. 3. Seal carvings and graffiti of harps or lyres(?), Middle Minoan, ca. 1850–1700 B.C. from Crete: *a* (left), from the Candia district; *a* (right), not assigned any precise location; *b* and *c,* from Knossos. (Reprinted from Aign 1963, 35–37, figs. 6–11.)

instruments do not look at all like harps. They appear to be lyres, and they have no more than three strings. Something remarkable is happening, or appears to be happening: within a century and a half, one basic type of instrument apparently becomes another. Moreover, this transformation takes place without any indication of significant foreign influence; commonplaces about the importance of such influence can no longer simply be accepted (see fig. 19).

The final period of Minoan culture (ca. 1700–1400 B.C.), more correctly called Minoan-Mycenaean in this phase, gives evidence of both simple and concert forms of the lyre. The lyre cannot have failed to grace secular as well as religious occasions in the atmosphere of spacious luxury at the Cretan court, where normal dress was a loincloth or a full-skirted dress that left the breasts bare. To recreate the scene, we have from Knossos a steatite seal impression. A woman holds a three-stringed "horseshoe" lyre as she dances and sings (fig. 4)—a light, simple affair, unskillfully drawn. The performer has a plectrum in her right hand, if the restoration can be trusted, and she holds it correctly. Clumsy though the draftsman was, he knew that it

Fig. 4. Seal carving of a woman performer with a horseshoe-shaped lyre, Late
Minoan, ca. 1700–1400 B.C., from Knossos,
Crete. (Reprinted from Aign 1963, 41,
fig. 12.)

ought to function as an extension of the index finger.[7] This is the first
evidence of its existence.

The so-called palace at Hagia Triada, near Phaistos, has yielded the
fragments of a painting on stucco that shows a lyre player (fig. 5). The
painting dates from about the period 1580–1510 B.C. The performer
wears a long robe; it flares outward slightly from the waist and has a
band going down the side. The lyre is by far the most magnificent
instrument that we have yet encountered. Its workmanship brings to
mind the splendor of the great fifth-century concert kitharas. The
arms curve gracefully inward, then recurve to form (seemingly) a
swan's bent neck.[8] We see what has happened to the bird's head of the
Cycladic harp.

B. P. Aign has restored the right hand by making the wrist turn
inward; but lyre players did not bend their right wrist thus, certainly
not when using a plectrum. If we ask what the painter intended to
portray, we do not have to look far for an explanation. Like countless
successors, this artist was concerned with representing the right hand

[7] Fig. 4: Aign 41, fig. 12. Plectrum: *plēktron,* literally "a beating thing," from
plēttein, "to strike, beat."

[8] Fig. 5: Aign 43, fig. 14. Swan-necked lyres: Vorreiter 1975, esp. pl. 22. Evans
(1921, 1: 836; cf. 1935, 4: 403 n. 1) is certain that the heads carved on the frame of this
instrument are those of gazelles (without the horns!), copied from an Egyptian example. They are not shown "clearly," as he claims.

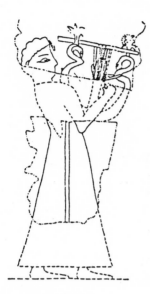

Fig. 5. Fragments of a painting on stucco of a lyre player with a concert instrument, Late Minoan, 1580–1510 B.C., from Hagia Triada, Crete. (Reprinted from Aign 1963, 43, fig. 14.)

at rest. He was the first to show how the Greeks normally played lyres or kitharas: that is, with the plectrum brought toward the body rather than away from it. He was also the first artist to bring before us a musician wearing what M. P. Nilsson calls "sacral dress." The stiffly hanging robe, with its distinctive lateral band, is worn by both men and women. In one instance, a goddess wears it. Nilsson draws the inescapable conclusion: "This dress is certainly not one for everyday life but is reserved for deities and officiants of the cult."[9]

According to one widely held belief, around 1400 B.C., invaders swept through Crete with the purposefulness and savagery of Vikings. From some period shortly before the raids, we have the last lyre player painted by a Minoan artist whose work survived them (fig. 6); it came to light during the excavation of a tomb near Hagia Triada. The lyre is an elegant affair, with spindle ends and what appear to be three or four inlaid pieces. Unfortunately, the artist was badly confused about the way lyres were played, and also about liturgical vestments. Nothing whatsoever supports the lyre in midair, except perhaps a double band. It runs over the performer's left shoul-

[9] Nilsson 1927, 136; sacral dress, 135. Evans (1928, 2: 721) sees oriental influence of a priestly nature in the Hagia Triada and Knossos robes of this type. He claims many Semitic parallels for the narrow vertical bands; see Evans 1935, 4: 403 and fig. 335. Fig. 6 (below): Aign 44, fig. 15.

Fig. 6. Fresco of a lyre player with a concert instrument, Late Minoan, ca. 1400 B.C., from the vicinity of Hagia Triada, Crete. (Reprinted from Aign 1963, 44, fig. 15.)

der and down the left side of his bell-bottomed robe. We know, however, that this band is a part of the robe, and a distinguishing mark of sacral dress. A lyre player who had to perform on a large instrument while standing used a supporting strap, later called a *telamōn*. Presumably the Minoan painter had some idea of the existence and function of lyre straps, but only a vague one.

This was not the end of his troubles. The performer's left hand comes into view from an impossible direction; it pinches a string in a way that can have no meaning; and the left arm is on the inner side of the instrument, another impossibility. The right hand holds a plectrum, and here at last the artist got something right: the plectrum is grasped in the proper manner—between thumb and forefinger, and parallel to the thumb.

In ancient Cypriote art, which reflects a bewildering mixture of foreign influences, not always assimilated, chordophones are represented first by a highly stylized harp from 1600–1350 B.C. From about the same period comes a representation of a lute player.[10] To find the lute appearing outside of Egypt so early surprises us; it will

[10] Aign 61, fig. 26; harp (cylinder seal impression, from Enkomi), 60, fig. 25. The lute is copied from an Egyptian instrument, according to Myres 1967, 273 (and now West 1992b, 79), but see Aign 61 n. 6. Fig. 7 (below): Aign 70, fig. 34.

Fig. 7. Bronze cup showing a symposium scene with a naked girl lyre player, ca. 600–550 B.C., found at Salamis, Cyprus. (Reprinted from Aign 1963, 70, fig. 34.)

not reappear among the Greeks for many centuries. The most unusual depiction of all comes from the earlier or middle sixth century, on a bronze cup (fig. 7). Clearly, the occasion is the *sumposion,* caught at an advanced and extremely relaxed stage. A man lies at his ease on a couch. Beside him, straddling an adjoining couch, a young woman is leaning back. The presence of a belt suggests that he wears a tunic; she is naked. She spreads her left hand upon the strings (not shown) of a lyre and may be damping them.

Far more staid is the girl with a lyre who has come down to us as a seventh-century terra-cotta (fig. 8).[11] She wears a massive headdress or bonnet; ruffles adorn the bodice and sleeves of her long gown. It would seem that we have here a Cyprian (in whatever sense) dressed and coiffed to the nines. The fingers of her right hand rest on the strings of a small lyre, very crudely and incompletely rendered. The general appearance of this lyre player suggests secular performance; but whatever the true explanation, no one would confuse her with the sprawling, naked sixth-century hetaera.

The great discovery relating to this period was made on the Anatolian mainland only a quarter century ago during the excavations at Old Smyrna, the modern Ort Bayrakli. It is a fragment of a mixing bowl (*dinos*) from the first or second quarter of the seventh century, the Late Geometric period (fig. 9). On it is painted a seven-stringed lyre—this in or very near the age of Terpander, who was credited with introducing just such an increased complement of strings, one

[11] Fig. 8: Aign 73, fig. 38; from Lapethus ("Lapithos," Aign), on the northern coast of Cyprus.

Fig. 8. Painted terra-cotta of a robed
girl lyre player, probably seventh century
B.C., from Cyprus. (Reprinted from Aign
1963, 73, fig. 38.)

that made available a scale (or scales) of six or seven notes.[12] As
evidence, the vase painting far outweighs the tradition. Here, at the
"right" time, are seven strings; here too are a plectrum and the thong
that tethers it to the base of the lyre. Although the artist (like so many
of his fellows) lacked a sound grasp of the nature of lyres, he has given
later ages one of the chief benchmarks in the history of Greek musical
instruments.

The final body of evidence comes from finds made on mainland
Greece and the nearby islands. Mycenaean civilization began two
centuries before the crippling, almost fatal blow that was dealt in 1400
B.C. The vital centers were its eponymous city, Mycenae, and Tiryns:
the two fortresses sit like dreadnoughts on the Argive plain. At the
plain's southwestern tip is the palace at Pylos, which goes back to
about 1300 B.C. The "throne room" contains a fresco, largely intact,
showing an elaborately robed figure who holds a swan-necked lyre
with five strings (fig. 10).[13] Known as the Singer, he is in actual fact
shown as silent; the name has its bardic sense. Nothing can be seen of
a plectrum or a supporting strap, although Cretan performers used
both during the Late Minoan period. The fresco depicts an instru-

[12] Fig. 9: Aign 77, fig. 42. The variation in dating: Aign 77 n. 1. Hexatonic or
heptatonic scale structure implied: West 1992b, 328.
[13] Fig. 10: Aign 80, fig. 44.

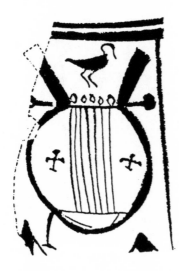

Fig. 9. Fragment of a mixing bowl showing a seven-stringed lyre, Late Geometric, 700–650 B.C., from Old Smyrna (modern Ort Bayrakli). (Reprinted from Aign 1963, 77, fig. 42.)

ment that is almost half the height of what would appear to be an exceptionally tall man.

His unusual height gives us a clue to the Singer's identity: throughout classical antiquity, gods were thought to be taller than mortals. Furthermore, he wears a full-length robe, decorated from midthigh downward with horizontal bands; it resembles ceremonial robes worn by male and female votaries, including musicians.[14] But the Pylos fresco contains a sign of divinity clearer than height or dress: this is the bird that flies beside the Singer. Thirty years before the Singer was discovered, Nilsson described a comparable scene, and his words apply here equally well: "The bird . . . is the embodiment of the deity, the form of its epiphany, and is added to the anthropomorphic representation to make its significance clear."[15] The fresco is the earliest representation of a lyre from the mainland of Greece or the nearby islands; it links Minoan musical culture with Mycenaean, one of the very few such links that we possess.

The end of Mycenaean civilization came in 1100 B.C. The four centuries that followed left no evidence concerning musical instruments: they are the so-called Dark Age of Greek music, and much

[14] Evans 1935, 4: 403 and fig. 335; cf. 1928, 2: 721.
[15] Nilsson 1927, 287. See Aign 81; cf. 46. Instruments certainly or probably known to Minoans and Mycenaeans: West 1992b, 327; Minoan influence, 327–28.

Fig. 10. Fresco of a robed figure of a divinity, perhaps Apollo, with a five-stringed lyre, Mycenean, ca. 1300 B.C., from Pylos, Messenia, in the southwestern Peloponnesus (the "Singer"). (Reprinted from Aign 1963, 80, fig. 44.)

else. In the second half of the eighth century, this darkness ended. From a variety of locations, chiefly in Attica, we have vase paintings of lyres. Almost every one is U-shaped—a bowl lyre—and has either three or four strings. This reduced compass has been seen as indicating a more restrained style of singing than the Minoans and Mycenaeans had employed. During the course of the seventh century, artists gained greater skill at portraying musical instruments; this period was one of especially notable development for the lyre. From around 700 B.C., we have the standing figure of a man who holds a five-stringed instrument (fig. 11) unlike anything seen previously. Its narrow arms angle outward, with no curve, from a small, circular sound chest inset with a tortoise shell. The true lyre, called *chelus* after the mountain tortoise, has made its appearance.[16]

By the middle of the seventh century, vase painters had begun to

---

[16] Fig. 11: Aign 99, fig. 64 (a reconstruction). Wegner (1949, 136, fig. 20, no. 7) shows this lyre as part of a series; his presentation serves to make clear its anomalous nature. In a letter concerning an earlier draft of this book Barker conjectured that these developments may reflect changes not in the actual design of the instruments but in the abilities of the painters and the conventions they observed.

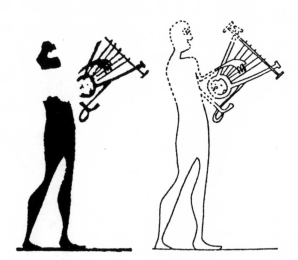

Fig. 11. Fragment (hydria) of a vase painting of a man with a five-stringed tortoiseshell lyre, early Attic, ca. 700 B.C., from Analatos. (Reprinted from Aign 1963, 99, fig. 64.)

depict a new type of lyre. It was taking on the characteristics of the large, elaborate instrument that most fifth-century writers were to call a *kithara*. An amphora fragment from Delos has preserved about two-thirds of a painting of a small but unusually handsome lyre (fig. 12).[17] It has the look of a much larger instrument. Seven strings, by now the canonical number, are set radially. The performer is playing as if he held a harp; clearly the artist did not know the correct hand positions.

An amphora dating to about 645 B.C. from Melos, the largest Cycladic island near the Greek mainland, shows a bearded and singularly unprepossessing Apollo, with the Muses following (fig. 13).[18] He holds a seven-stringed lyre, more advanced technically than anything we have seen thus far. The surface of the ample sound chest area has not only a string holder near the base but a bridge as well. With his left arm, Apollo raises the lyre high; the supporting strap that undoubtedly would have been used does not appear. Artists, it seems, were reluctant to show this highly practical aid. The god's right hand,

[17] Fig. 12: Aign 99, fig. 68. The reproduction in Wegner 1949, 137, fig. 20, no. 11, is more regular and more nearly complete than the original.

[18] Fig. 13: Aign 100, fig. 69.

Fig. 12. Fragment (amphora) of a vase painting of a man playing a seven-stringed concert lyre, ca. 650 B.C., from Delos. (Reprinted from Aign 1963, 99, fig. 68.)

crudely rendered, grasps a plectrum that is secured by a thong. The length of this fastening makes it evident for the first time that a wide sweeping stroke was possible and, presumably, normal.

From Athens of the late seventh century comes a small lyre, sturdy and well decorated (fig. 14).[19] Once again, both string holder and bridge are shown. The player (if indeed he is playing) spreads thumb and fingers over the strings in the approved position for damping.[20] Perhaps the painter did not realize that the spread left hand is meaningless in itself. The fact that the hand position here is too low gives this conjecture added credibility. We have seen that, over the long span of the pre-Hellenic centuries, lyres and lyre playing presented many problems for artists. By this time (625–600 B.C.), however, the instrument itself is fully developed in all essential features. It has become capable of undergoing the changes, and also the division into types and subtypes, that will characterize the great period of Greek musical culture.

The most primitive form of aerophone (wind instrument) is the pipe without finger holes. By itself, such an instrument offers very limited possibilities for making music. On the other hand, two or more such pipes could form part of a syrinx (*surinx,* "panpipes"), mentioned from Homer onward. Complications arise when double-reed pipes are wrongly labeled "syrinx" or "panpipes." We must think, from the beginning, in terms of the long history of end-blown pipes.

From the Early Cycladic period (3200–2000 B.C.), the island of Keros has given us not only the first possibly Greek performer on a

[19] Fig. 14: Aign 103, fig. 72.
[20] Aign (103) errs on this point.

Fig. 13. Fragment (amphora) of a vase painting of Apollo, with a seven-stringed concert lyre, and the Muses, ca. 645 B.C., from Melos. (Reprinted from Aign 1963, 100, fig. 69.)

stringed instrument but also the first to play on double pipes, later to be designated by the term *aulos*. The latter is a marble statuette representing a standing man (fig. 15).[21] Like the harpists, he is naked or perhaps wears a loincloth. He grasps two pipes, diverging but not set wide apart. Though neither bears any trace of finger holes, the spacing of the player's hands might suggest some kind of divided gamut; yet the difference may be nothing more than an accident.

We receive the impression of pipes that would in actuality have been a foot long at most—the approximate length of fifth-century auloi. They must owe their surprising thickness to the difficulty of working marble on such a small scale: the statuette stands only 20 centimeters high, slightly less than 8 inches. No revealing details tell us whether the instrument is a double flute (that is, end-blown), a double oboe like the Hellenic aulos, or perhaps a double clarinet.

At least six centuries pass before further evidence comes to light. On the famous sarcophagus from Hagia Triada in Crete, a performer dressed in a ceremonial robe plays on two long, slender pipes, held parallel (fig. 16).[22] If the usual restoration is accepted, they are the

[21] Fig. 15: Aign 34, fig. 5; see Thimme 1977, 66.
[22] Fig. 16: Aign 47, fig. 17.

Fig. 14. Fragment (pinax) of a vase painting of a man with a small lyre, 625–600 B.C., from Athens. (Reprinted from Aign 1963, 103, fig. 72.)

same length but differ markedly at the farther end, where the left-hand pipe curves upward in a large bell. Such pipes were known as *elumoi auloi* to fifth-century Greeks, who thought of them as Phry-gian.[23] They always were fitted with vibrating reeds held inside the mouth: that is, they constituted a type of double oboe. Whether the Hagia Triada pipes were fitted in this way is a question of some importance. We cannot pretend to see, much less count, finger holes on them, but the finger positions would seem to be compatible with the existence of a range of intervals as wide as those of a Hellenic double aulos up to about the year 450 B.C.

While reeds have always been notoriously fragile, the possibility of their presence in preclassical art may nevertheless be inferred. Two revealing signs are the angle of the pipes and the way they are held. End-blown pipes such as recorders are cut with a slit, like the flue of an organ pipe; they are angled quite differently from reed-blown instruments. The other chief early type is that of the vertical flute, played by blowing directly into the upper end; it is best known in the multiple form represented by the syrinx or bagpipe. Double pipes so seemingly advanced as those shown on the Hagia Triada sarcophagus can hardly have been vertical flutes. Another sign of an advanced stage is the use of a mouth band or *phorbeia,* not identifiable in Helle-nic art until the late seventh century.

Concerning pipes, whether double or single, Cyprus has left very

[23] Wegner (1949, 53) wrongly states that *elumoi auloi* first appear in Hellenistic and Graeco-Roman art. West (1992b, 91–92) usefully summarizes the place of "Phrygian" auloi in classical cultures; Bélis (1986) has examined all aspects of the instrument.

Fig. 15. Marble statuette of a standing man playing double pipes, Cycladic, 2200–2000 B.C., from Keros. (Reprinted from Aign 1963, 34, fig. 5.)

little evidence of any kind; we must look to the mainland and the related islands or territories.[24] The earliest significant depiction of the double aulos appears on a Proto-Corinthian vase dating from 640–630 B.C. The scene is remarkable, unmatched in Greek art. Before a massed group of shouting or singing infantrymen marches a piper, dressed only in a light tunic (fig. 17).[25] Head thrown back, he angles his pipes steeply upward. He wears a simple version of the *phorbeia,* here seen unmistakably for the first time. Slung from his right arm is the *subēnē,* a case made of fabric or leather in which aulos players, or auletes, carried their instrument.[26] A careful examination shows it to be a little shorter than the pipes. The artist has not erred: like modern flutes, auloi were often made in sections and taken down when not in use. Here both barrels have markings, inconspicuous but clearly visi-

[24] Thus we must ignore the wild claims of Schliemann, for whom three fragments could constitute "a marvellous Mycenean flute consisting of bone, baked clay, and stone" (1878, 77–79 and figs. 128, 129, 130a). See Aign 81, where "130x" should be corrected.

[25] Fig. 17: Aign 102, fig. 71. In n. 4, he corrects the statement by Wegner (1949, 56) that the *phorbeia* first appears in the early sixth century. Shouting or singing: see below, n. 27.

[26] The noun *aulētēs,* meaning "aulete" or "aulos player," first occurs in Greek literature a century later (Theognis 941).

Fig. 16. Sarcophagus painting of a performer on double pipes in a ritual scene, Late Minoan, ca. 1400 B.C., from Hagia Triada, Crete. (Reprinted from Aign 1963, 47, fig. 17.)

ble, to indicate the joints. So do those of the Hagia Triada piper, a point overlooked by Angelo Mosso and many later scholars.[27] As for the unusual angle of the pipes, no performer could have maintained such a stance for long without fearful strain, even with the mouth band. Either we are meant to see a moment of sheer bravura, or else the need to show opposed ranks of infantry close at hand left insufficient horizontal space for the normal playing position. With this splendid flourish, the testimony of early Greek art concerning pipers and their instruments comes to a close.

Among idiophones (instruments that produce sound through the vibration of their own materials), only one has any importance. It appears on a vase of black steatite from the Hagia Triada "palace" and dates from the last half of the sixteenth century. This justly famous work, known as the Harvester Vase, shows a man closely followed by three comrades; all four are open-mouthed, as if singing, chanting, or shouting (fig. 18).[28] He holds high a sistrum (*seistron*). Usually one thinks of this sophisticated descendant of the Paleolithic rattle as an Egyptian instrument. Fifth-century devotees of the goddess Isis brought it into Athens, and into Greek areas generally; it had always

[27] Aign's tentative suggestion (102 n. 3) that the markings represent finger holes perpetuates an old error.

[28] Fig. 18: Aign 42, fig. 13. Alan Lomax speaks of the "harsh-voiced, forceful style" of Amerindians throughout North America, whose unison singing is "roughly organized" and "hearty" (Lomax et al. 1968, 8). This is precisely the impression given by the central figures on the Harvester Vase.

Fig. 17. Vase painting of a military piper, Proto-Corinthian, 640–630 B.C., found at Veii, Italy. (Reprinted from Aign 1963, 102, fig. 71.)

been closely associated with her worship. The upper portion, sometimes oval but often (as here) rectangular, had one or more thin, horizontal rods of metal; normally there were two or three. These bore metal discs that clashed together when the device was shaken. On later specimens, the sides and top commonly have adornments such as the figure of a lion.

The instrument shown here has only a single rod and a pair of discs—the absolute minimum—with no ornamentation anywhere. By Egyptian standards, it can only be called primitive. Arthur Evans nevertheless did not hesitate to identify it as a sistrum, and with good reason: in both types of Minoan script he had found a variety of closely related signs, unquestionably pictographs illustrating different types of this instrument.

We must next try to determine the place of these instruments, the status of musicians at this early period, and the ways in which the music may have been performed. Cycladic and Late Minoan-Mycenaean representations suggest cultic origins for the lyre, similar to those of the aulos. Ancient artists regularly paid it more attention, however, and they show it in greater detail. It also differs from the aulos in having an early and strong connection with the dance. The triangular harp is found instead only during the earliest stage, in

Fig. 18. Relief carving on a vase ("Harvester Vase") of a man with a sistrum and three comrades, all singing, chanting, or shouting, 1550–1500 B.C., from Hagia Triada, Crete. (Reprinted from Aign 1963, 42, fig. 13).

Cycladic sculpture; thereafter, the lyre replaces it. The two instruments, which have a common origin, were differentiated in form and function from the Early Bronze Age onward. Ambiguous forms occur only when harp develops into lyre in a particular culture. In the history of both instruments symbolism may play a part, not easily determined. Several Western cultures have recognized a symbolic connection of harp and harpist with death; Greek tradition held Hermes to be not only the inventor of the lyre but also guide of souls (*psuchopompos*) on the journey to the lower world.

From earliest times, the aulos had a close connection with cult. It appears first as a tomb offering, in the Cyclades, and seems always to have served religion. Late Minoan art shows it in processions to the tomb. Moreover, the scenes on the Hagia Triada sarcophagus are not merely funerary: they record the process whereby the dead man was thought to become a god.[29] In Attic vase paintings of the Geometric period, auloi would become a regular part of the funeral rites for ordinary persons, who were neither heroized nor divinized.

Many points of evidence suggest the place accorded to musicians during these early centuries. Almost always they are given ritual status; the nonreligious aspects of ordinary life do appear, but a religious setting predominates. Minoan-Mycenaean art provides the musician with a context for the first time. The Cycladic figures, however splendid, are not figures in a landscape. Now a landscape has been added—not invariably, but often enough to give a sense of the whole.

[29] Nilsson 1927, 292, 378.

On the Hagia Triada sarcophagus, aulete and lyre player are taking part in a well-organized ritual act. Although they are evidently subordinate to the priestesses in a religion that still is matriarchal, the two performers wear sacral robes or tunics. Here, as in a few other instances, the wearer's gender cannot readily be determined; such sacral clothing might be worn by either sex.[30]

Cretan domestic cults, which probably were numerous, have left no evidence that relates to music except for the Palaikastro terra-cotta group, assembled from fragments. A woman lyre player and three women dancing with arms linked all wear the long, stiff robe required by religious custom. The other evidence from Palaikastro shows unmistakably that they are taking part in a ritual observance. Identifying them with Apollo and the Muses amounts to sheer fancy: the lyre player is a woman; she and her three companions represent mortals.

So with the Harvester Vase: the scene comes from everyday life; its earthy vitality cannot be matched in Minoan art. Whether speech or song, or perhaps something midway between the two, the utterance so vividly indicated by the gaping mouths must have been formal to some appreciable degree. It was rhythmized as well; use of the sistrum proves that. Apparently the occasion involved ritual of some kind. Whatever its nature, this bawling group of yokels and toughs brings us as near as we are ever likely to get to music making by common people in Minoan Crete. It is a wonderfully effective portrayal, worthy of being ranked with Breughel's "Peasant Wedding."

Plainly, the tall, majestic lyre player of the Pylos fresco does not come from everyday life: his bird epiphany marks him as a god. Some conjecture a connection with the theatral areas of Mycenae and Phaistos; a similar connection has been made with the Cretan dancing places that Homer mentions. Mortal musicians wear ceremonial dress as the rule and not the exception, to mark their status. Nilsson's definition of the sacral can include the robes of the terra-cotta figures from Palaikastro as well as those in the Hagia Triada and Pylos paintings. Whether he is Hermes or Apollo, the "Singer" of Pylos displays robes of unusual splendor; yet they do not have so liturgical an air as

[30] Aign 307, 309.

those of the officiants. He has been seen as the lyre-god in his capacity of divine patron of bards; we need not go so far.

Other signs besides dress may indicate whether musicians were accorded special regard. In certain instances at least, the lyre was (to use T. B. L. Webster's term) a "pedigree" instrument. The frescoes from Pylos and from the chamber tomb near Hagia Triada illustrate this, and the latter in particular prepare the way for the professional's instrument that Achilles plays in *Iliad* 9. Some of the facts might be interpreted as weighing against the likelihood of special status. Individual musicians are not usually set apart from the group. In the sarcophagus scene they carry out subordinate roles, and the aulete's function of providing music for rites at the tomb does not appear to differ perceptibly from that of auletes in the Hellenic period. The latter did not enjoy privileged status, even though their presence was all but indispensable.

The music of this early period embodies types of performance that would still be found in classical Greece. Any choral singing as accompaniment to the sacred dances would have been performed in unison, or at times in octaves.[31] The scenes on the Hagia Triada sarcophagus, along with other evidence, show a special kind of hero cult, one in which the dead became gods. Hymns or encomiums honoring the divinized mortal would have had their place, since forms of the divine cult were taken over for the celebration of heroes. So far as earthly things may have been allowed entrance into the liturgy of hero cult, we can conjecture sung accounts of the deeds wrought by the deceased. For these, our paradigms are of course the "glorious deeds of heroes" (*klea andrōn*), Achilles' theme when he sang to the lyre.

Singing to lyre accompaniment could also be a solo performance, even in pre-Homeric times; or it might take the form of responsories. The only lyre player in early art who may have been a singer (though not at the moment that the artist has depicted) is the august figure on the Pylos fresco. If he is indeed Apollo, we recall the extreme view of him as the patron of all solo singers to the lyre. If the figure is that of a mortal, this man evidently enjoys high esteem. He may be the first known kitharode and bard; certainly it is possible to view him as the

---

[31] The modern conception of harmony is, of course, irrelevant.

first court poet, a link with the courtly world that Homer describes. In the terra-cotta group from Palaikastro, the possibility of responses, such as a refrain by the three other women, is particularly strong. Homer uses the noun *molpē* and the verb *melpesthai* of simultaneous singing and dancing; how far this simultaneity applied to the Minoan-Mycenaean period can only be guessed at.

The "Dark Age" of early Greek history lasted from about 1100 to 900 B.C. or later; many would set the upper limit as late as 750 B.C. Bounding this time of upheaval was the eclipse of the Minoan-Mycenaean culture and the eventual appearance of the Homeric poems. Three aspects of the period concern us: the reflections of the time in the Homeric poems, the transition undergone by performers of poetry and music, and finally the nature of that music—the most profound mystery of all.

The *Iliad* and *Odyssey* may at times reflect the past in unexpected ways, by reversal or diminution, or by what is left unsaid. The Mycenaean king (*wanax*), who had been comparable with the gods, can no longer be discerned in Agamemnon, Menelaus, or Priam, chief monarchs of the *Iliad*. The title (*w*)*anax* has now become a generalized, stereotyped form; *basileus* has replaced it. *Basileus,* the usual Homeric word for "king," had denoted a lesser official at Mycenae. In the *Odyssey,* monarchical succession has become shaky and unclear. The main subjects of both poems also involve inheritance and change; and of these two, change is the more marked. The *Iliad*'s theme of siege appears in Minoan-Mycenaean artwork from Knossos, Mycenae, and Pylos. Now it undergoes adaptation: as Webster says, Agamemnon's vassals become the suitors of Helen.[32] In the *Odyssey,* accounts of a hero's exploits differ markedly, not simply from such early examples as the Gilgamesh story, but even from the ways of portraying glory in the tale of Troy.

The *Iliad*'s poet mentions no professional singers, although recent scholarship has rightly noted traces of their presence. The only nonprofessionals are Achilles and an unidentified youth who performs the Linos song. With the *Odyssey,* we enter another world. Professionals —court singers of varying status—dominate its music making. One

[32] Webster 1958, 291.

passage seems anachronistic: the reference to Agamemnon's leaving his wife under the protection of a bard may be thought more appropriate to "Dark Age" conditions.[33] Still, it shows a court bard entrusted with grave responsibilities.

Originally, such bards were solo performers. Court poetry, unlike choral lyric, could be adapted to the immediate celebration of specific individuals or events. If the singer was drawing on an extended epic poem, he limited his performance to a relatively small division of the whole work. Later would come the possibility of rhapsodes working in relays to present an *Iliad* or an *Odyssey* in its entirety. These specialists were professional reciters, and explicators as well, of the works attributed to Homer. They had become established figures by the time of the poet Hesiod, perhaps in the late eighth century. What we call Homer—meaning the decisive shaping of the two epics (our text is a much later version)—is now generally thought to have occurred not much earlier than Hesiod, and very possibly later.

We know little about "Dark Age" music.[34] Nothing has come to light that bears on the syrinx; there can be little reason to suppose change in an instrument that already has its rectangular Hellenic shape in Cycladic sculpture, a millennium before the fall of Troy. As for the aulos, the Late Minoan paintings of double pipes suggest a high degree of earlier development. Its popularity must have diminished, in proportion as cults of the "Great Mother" type—that of Cybele, for example—had to take second place to the worship of the Olympians, the lyre-god Apollo notable among them. Archaeological evidence concerning the lyre is somewhat uncertain. The lyre was more and more firmly established as the Hellenic instrument par excellence, the natural accompaniment for solo singing. No longer, however, did it accompany epic poetry: this was now recited or chanted by the rhapsode.

Concerning the vocal music of these dark centuries we are lamentably ignorant. Was it sung or chanted or intoned? If we knew the relevant meaning of *aeidein,* we should be far better off. At a minimum, *aeidein* denoted an activity significantly different from speech.

---

[33] *Od.* 3.267–71; Webster 1958, 121.
[34] West (1984) has assembled the evidence bearing on the nature of music in archaic Greece.

Certain uses of the voice occupy a border area between the two.[35] They are known in many cultures, and whatever is going on in the Harvester Vase scene may provide an example. The solo singing of Achilles and a youth's "lament" for Linos (*Iliad* 9 and 18) may illustrate this mediate form as well. A singing, shouting, dancing chorus provide a background for the Linos song; both singers accompany themselves on the lyre. Throughout the *Odyssey,* solo performances of epic narrative have lyre accompaniments.

Evidently choruses had a subordinate place. The traditional elements obviously were powerful, and these change only very slowly. Perhaps an independent role can be discerned in the *Homeric Hymn to Delian Apollo,* which some date to the same period as the *Odyssey* and the works of Hesiod. At any rate, we know that the festival of Apollo held on Delos goes back to the eighth century, and possibly farther. Lines 158–63 of the *Hymn* describe the choral songs of the Delian maidens. First they sing a prelude to the gods and chiefly, of course, to Apollo. "Great men and women of bygone times" are the burden of their hymn. Moreover, they "know how to imitate [or "reproduce," *mimeisthai*] the tongues of all men." This mimetic knowledge points beyond epic to other dialects, genres, meters, musical forms— even beyond choral lyric to lyric monody, the newly emerging art of the solo singer. It is a guidepost to the future of Greek literature and of Greek music.

---

[35] There is textual and metrical evidence for a distinction between the 2:1 ratio of long to short in the dactyl and the irrational 5:3 (approximate), which some believe characterized the singing of poetry in Homer's time. In some cultures, moreover, singers of epic may depart from the practice of repeating one simple melody: at times they use several, with subtle variations to take account of context and word accent. The Homeric singer may have employed such an approach. The comparative evidence from Hungarian (Bartók) and Jugoslav epic song is of particular interest on these points. (The preceding summarizes West 1992b, 135, 208.) List 1963 offers the best-known short treatment of borderline uses.

{2}

From Orpheus
to the *Homeric Hymns*

Orpheus of legend was a famed lyre player and singer. According to tradition, even after Thracian maenads had torn him apart, his severed head continued to sing and to utter prophecies. After he died his lyre gained significant status in itself, dedicated as a cult object or thought to have become a constellation. Yet, though traditional accounts of his life and death center on him as musician and singer, in actual fact neither the poems ascribed to Orpheus nor the diverse cult observances now designated as Orphism give music a prominent place.[1]

Neither Homer nor Hesiod mentions Orpheus; he does not appear in art or literature until the sixth century. But Greeks of every period took Orpheus to be literally a magician, an enchanter. West has rightly emphasized in a recent study of the Orphic poems that Orpheus was a shaman.[2] His power to charm the natural creation is mentioned by Aeschylus, and Euripides speaks of it many times. In addition, the *Alcestis* (357–62) makes clear that such gifts of enchantment marked Orpheus not only as a singer and lyre player but as a poet and prophet.

The question of his origin has occasioned much dispute. W. K. C. Guthrie speaks out against the formerly received opinion that he was

---

[1] Contra: *Oxford Classical Dictionary* s.v. Orpheus (M. P. Nilsson, J. H. Croon, and C. M. Robertson): "His fame . . . as a singer is due to the poems in which the Orphic doctrines and myths are set forth."

[2] West 1983, 4–6, 145–47, 162–63.

a Thracian: "The legend of Orpheus puts beyond doubt the strange circumstance that he was a Hellene living in Thrace, offering opposition to Dionysos in his own native land. . . . The earlier the evidence the more it lays stress on his being a Hellene and a worshipper of Apollo."[3] Webster suggests that the myth mirrors history.[4] Through alternative traditions, it connects Orpheus with Lesbos. According to one tradition, after the Thracian women had flung his head into the Hebrus, it was carried down to the sea and made its way to the island's shores. The other rehearses essentially the same story, this time about the lyre. Both show the musical skills of the renowned singer and lyre player reaching the coasts of Lesbos.

Taken in the context of music history, this myth is aetiological, and to a certain extent openly so: it provides a cause (*aitia*) for the Lesbian tradition of lyric poetry.[5] Yet aetiological myths may be grounded in history, and for this one Webster offers a purely historical basis. A people from central Greece settled Lesbos; in later times, they claimed descent from the Mycenaean lord Agamemnon. Greek tradition mentions a migration to Lesbos by way of Thrace. It is only a short step to the conjecture that the legend reflects this shift.[6] May Orpheus, then, have been Mycenaean? Robert Böhme has championed this view. Unfortunately, his work *Orpheus: Das Alter der Kitharoden* contains many inadmissible claims. The very title is a misstep, as Aign points out.[7]

Although Orpheus does not appear in either the *Iliad* or the *Odyssey* Homer does mention two mysterious musician figures, Linos and Thamyris. The reference to Linos occurs in a description of a vintage scene depicted on Achilles' shield; it tells us nothing about him.[8] Hesiod makes him the son of the Muse Urania and calls him "skilled in every kind of wisdom."[9] For range of ability as well as parentage, this account places him with Orpheus. During the Hellenic era, var-

---

[3] Guthrie 1956, 315–16.

[4] Webster 1958, 47.

[5] See Aign 264. His term *Kitharodie* hardly fits Sappho and Alcaeus; the distinctive barbitos is the instrument associated with both.

[6] Webster 1958, 47 n. 1, citing Böhme (see next note).

[7] Böhme (1953, 16–19) argues for a Mycenaean Orpheus; his claims have not won acceptance. See Aign 264 n. 4; his vast bibliography omits Guthrie 1956.

[8] *Il.* 18.569–72.

[9] Frags. 305–6 Merkelbach-West, 1 Evelyn-White.

ied traditions clustered about his name. He was celebrated as a master musician and composer, even as the inventor of music. But in the end, we do not know whether Linos was a real person. His existence may have been conjured out of a vintage song.

Thamyris is the only singer and lyre player who is mentioned as an individual with a name and a reputation in the *Iliad*, apart from the special case of Achilles. *Iliad* 2.594–600 describes how Thamyris, "that famous Thracian," was maimed by the Muses, who took away his skill at singing and playing the lyre as punishment for his boast that he could outdo them in song. This incident forms a small part of the long insertion in *Iliad* 2 known as the Catalogue of Ships. Most believe the Catalogue of Ships to be much older than the rest of book 2, older even than the *Iliad* as a whole. It has been dated to the late thirteenth or early twelfth century.[10] The itinerant bard therefore comes from a pre-Homeric past. He is not a dependent, or at any rate he is not presented as such, which means that he may be even older than the last great days of Mycenae and its civilization. The poet does not call him an *aoidos,* but in the *Iliad* that word occurs once only (24.720), clearly with the meaning "mourner." The details of the story told in *Iliad* 2.594–600 leave no room for doubt: Thamyris is the first identifiable bard.

In the *Odyssey aoidos* is used to denote the professional singer, with no other sense. We find seeming paradoxes associated with this figure: "I am self-taught [*autodidaktos*]," says Phemius, then adds at once, "and the god has implanted in my mind song paths [*oimas*] of every kind."[11] That is, bards combine the god-given gift of song with specific technical abilities. Most suppose that bards had independent status and should be included in Homer's list of *dēmioergoi* (*Od.* 17.382–86). Literally "workers for the people," these individuals travel from one community to another; they are called in because of their special skills. Yet it could not be more obvious that Phemius is a retainer. In the lines just quoted, he pleads with his newly revealed master for his very life.

The bard's song has sufficient impact to make even the iron-willed

[10] Thomas and Stubbings, in Wace and Stubbings 1969, 285.
[11] Use of *aoidos* as "bard" in the *Odyssey:* Schadewaldt 1965, 54–86; Werba 1940, 3–69. Phemius' double claim: *Od.* 22.347–48. Possible resolutions of the paradox: Dodds 1957, 10, 22 n. 63, 80–81, 95 n. 15–100 n. 20.

Odysseus give way to tears (*Od.* 8.84–92). Its catharsis, more commonly the release of joyful feelings, brings the singer affection, respect, and fame. Horace comments memorably that although there were mighty men before Agamemnon, they remain unknown because no Homer has perpetuated their memory.[12] If he erred, the underlying point nevertheless remains valid. In every age, poets have proclaimed the importance of poetry.

On closer examination, the majesty of the Homeric bard diminishes somewhat. We have noted that only in the *Odyssey* does *aoidos* mean "singer" as bard. According to a recent source, the portrait given there "is archaizing: what we are shown is the singer of the heroic age. His characterization as a free and honored individual reveals a tendency to idealize." The conclusion that such an approach "obviously" aims at the poet's self-aggrandizement does not necessarily follow, but the main argument has force.[13] Certainly, one does not look to find a Homer describing bards unfavorably.

The key phrase is "free and honored." Questions arise: How free, and honored to what degree? It is "under compulsion" (*anangkēi*) by the suitors that Phemius performs. Eventually this fact becomes an argument in his plea to Odysseus that he not be put to death. Both he and Demodocus respond to requests for this or that selection. Moreover, both are told to stop recounting a tale that has brought unhappy reminders; they are, in effect, rebuked. Obviously, they are in some sense dependents, subordinate though not servile. If we are to accept the idea of an archaizing description that harks back to the heroic age, we must illustrate it as Webster does—by the strangely Mycenaean incident of Agamemnon's entrusting Clytemnestra to a bard on his departure for Troy (*Od.* 3.267–68). In the world of the *Odyssey,* bards have no such status.

One more point may be added concerning the Homeric bard. He is no longer credited with extraordinary powers, for he has altogether ceased to command the role of shaman. No elemental force emanates from him; thus, for example, he cannot heal. In an inserted tale from the past, the young Odysseus is badly gored while on a boar hunt. His older companions recite an *epaoidē,* a "charm" to stop the flow of

---

[12] *Carm.* 4.9.25–28.
[13] Snell 1979, vol. 1, col. 982.73–78.

blood. The word occurs nowhere else in Homer, but this precise kind of charm is still widely known and credited.[14] At an earlier stage of culture—a point that men of the Homeric age had already passed—this would have been among the shaman's functions. In the *Iliad,* the story of the doomed overreacher Thamyris may afford a moment's glimpse of that earlier stage. It is, however, a cautionary tale. The bards of the *Odyssey* are retainers. They dare not displease their supposed betters, much less challenge the Muses, whom they repeatedly acknowledge as the source of their inspiration. What they sing and play receives praise as entertainment: like dancing, it is just the thing to add the final touch to a good dinner.[15]

Being an *aoidos* could have its compensations, certainly. For Phemius they were not obvious, but the great house on Ithaca has suffered abuse of hospitality and a consequent overthrow of good manners. In the dreamlike serenity of King Alcinoüs' palace, where courtesies are ceremoniously observed, Demodocus receives honor, deference, and praise. He lives apart from the palace, and he does not have the status of retainer so clearly as Phemius does.[16] Both bards are free of religious obligations: unlike the Minoan and Mycenaean lyre players, they take no part in any ceremony. Even the elaborate sacrifice to Poseidon in the *Odyssey* has only ritual cries for accompaniment. Now palace singers are secular: their audiences listen with

[14] *Od.* 19.457. Stanford, in his note on the passage, says: "Formed directly from *epaeidō* 'sing over', the noun refers to a blood-staunching spell chanted over the wound, a practice known in many parts of Europe. I have heard a circumstantial description of the process from a Russian cavalry officer who witnessed an immediate stoppage of blood from a sabre-wound in this way." A. B. Lord, in Wace and Stubbings 1969, 200, explains the magical nature of a Russian spell of this kind: it "abounds in *kr* alliterations, which suggest throughout the incantation the word for blood, *krov,* over which the singer wishes to obtain power."

[15] *Od.* 1.152: *molpē t' orchēstus te: ta gar t' anathēmata daitos,* "singing and dancing: for these are ornaments [or perhaps "accompaniments"] of the feast." As the separate mention of *orchēstus* shows, *molpē* here has the meaning that predominates not only in Homer but among the Attic poets. Frequently it is translated as "dance and song"; but this sense occurs only twice, in *Il.* 18.606 and in *Od.* 6.101 (where the reference is to rhythmic movement rather than to a dance).

[16] A. B. Lord, in Wace and Stubbings 1969, 183, points out that if Demodocus had been a retainer, his lyre presumably would have been ready to hand, and he could have dispensed with assistance from the herald. He seems instead to have been called in, as Jugoslav singers were called in by the local aristocracy of beys and pashas until 1919, as long as the Turks ruled the southern districts of Jugoslavia.

unmixed delight to a Rabelaisian tale of cuckolding among the gods themselves. In the descriptions of lyre players accompanying dancers, this secular side becomes still more visible. A. B. Lord writes of recording a Jugoslav singer in 1950: the performance consisted of several epic poems and also of "humorous songs and love songs for dancing," all sung to the bard's own accompaniment.[17]

Within Homeric society, it is only bards who can keep alive the memory of what individuals have accomplished—an overstatement, taken strictly, but only a slight one.[18] The bards themselves do not claim this; the individual does. It forms a defense against the aristocracy's tendency to treat them as one of the conveniences of life, something taken for granted. Homer is their master advocate: he loses no opportunity to burnish the honor of the singer's craft. At the same time, he acknowledges the restraints that society imposes.

Homer's bards aside for the moment, we must consider how the aulos and lyre and other instruments figure. In Homer, *aulos* means "tube" or "pipe." Only the outward appearance is taken into consideration, not the channel as such. Thus Odysseus' mantle has a brooch with two *auloi* that serve as tubes—that is, sheaths or grooves—for the pins that secure it (*Od.* 19.227). *Aulos* may even denote a "jet" of blood from a nostril, with no hollow interior or channel.[19]

The aulos as musical instrument therefore is named from its main element. In Homer, *aulos* appears with this sense only twice; and once at least the circumstances are suspect, for the reference forms part of *Iliad* 10. C. M. Bowra has said of this book that it "may well be an independent poem," and he speaks for many.[20] Moreover, the reference itself (10.13) concerns Agamemnon's amazement when he hears "the sound of syrinx pipes" (*aulōn suringgōn . . . enopēn*) from the Trojan camp. The compound *aulōn suringgōn* is a strange one; and elsewhere in Homer, *enopē* denotes the voice of men, especially

---

[17] A. B. Lord, in Wace and Stubbings 1969, 209–10. The performer accompanied himself on the *čemane,* a type of lyre with medieval antecedents, not on a *gusle* or *tambura.*

[18] Lomax, in Lomax et al. 1968, 134, remarks on the restraint and moderation of the epic poet, and also on his "leaning toward the specific and the explanatory style [which] remains the keynote of all learning thereafter."

[19] LSJ s.v. 2: "but in Od. 22.18 *aulos pachus* means the *jet* of blood *through the tube* of the nostril." One cannot have it both ways.

[20] Bowra, in Wace and Stubbings 1969, 46.

shouting, or the crying of birds. As W. Leaf noted, *suringges* recurs only in 18.526 and *auloi* only in 18.495 of the *Iliad*.[21]

Vase painters do not portray auloi at all until the end of the Geometric period, and then only twice. Further evidence (a pair of examples) does not come until about 700 B.C., the beginning of the early Attic style. Only thereafter does depiction of the aulos become common.

We must conclude that the instrument was barely recognized by singers of heroic poetry. In the heroic world it had no accepted place, certainly not in the world of the *Iliad*. The phrase *aulōn suringgōn,* with no connective, and the nonmusical usages demonstrate the fact that in Homeric poetry *aulos* designated nothing more specific than a pipe or tube, of whatever sort.[22] It had no separate, distinct use to refer to a musical instrument. Here *aulōn* is generalizing, *suringgōn* specific. The poet is describing panpipes.

Nevertheless, we have reason to believe that both aulos and syrinx formed a part of the culture described in the Homeric poems, and also of the later culture that brought this poetry to its highest point of development. The flute without finger holes is one of the oldest of all instruments; and the pre-Hellenic syrinx, like its successor, consisted of a group of such flutes, fastened together to make a rectangle. It is distinctively the herdsman's instrument, though it actually predates the pastoral stage of civilization. As Plato's condescending reference to it (*Rep.* 399d8–9) shows, the syrinx was never an accepted part of life in the polis, any more than it was part of the heroic life pictured in the *Iliad*.

When finger holes are bored in the barrel of a pipe, a new stage in the development of musical instruments has been reached; this first happened before the end of the Stone Age. Adding a second pipe with

[21] For Leaf (1900, 427, on *Il.* 10.13), these references constitute "an evident anachronism," a verdict that is less evident today. In 1900, the controversy over Homer involved many more separatists than unitarians. We are aware, as Leaf was not, of a syrinx player in Cycladic art, sculpted a thousand years before the fall of Troy. West comments that the aulos "goes unmentioned in various contexts where it might have been expected on the basis of later usage," for example, in connection with choral dancing (1992b, 82, 329).

[22] No connective: the following *te,* a connective very much like the Latin enclitic *-que,* links both nouns with the phrase that follows. This point has at times been overlooked.

finger holes marks a high culture, such as that of Minoan Crete. The double aulos on the Hagia Triada sarcophagus bears a remarkable resemblance to what is shown in Attic vase paintings during the sixth and fifth centuries. In the world of heroes, this aulos evidently gained no more acceptance than did the syrinx. Already, however, it had secured a place in civic life—the life of the city at peace, wrought on Achilles' shield (*Il.* 18.495). It was to have a role in the life of every city throughout the Mediterranean-Aegean region, one that it had no doubt been filling long before the Greeks sailed against Troy.

As already pointed out, vase paintings of the Geometric period tell us little about the aulos. Since double pipes were so slender, at this early stage of Attic art a single brushstroke represented each of the two. The angle at which they are held proves that they were not equipped with the recorder type of mouthpiece found on end-blown flutes. Instead, they had either a single reed or else a pair of reeds that vibrated against each other. They were placed in the player's mouth, not gripped between the lips as in the playing of the modern oboe.[23] Among present-day folk instruments, scarcely any have real affinities with the aulos; the reed-blown pipes of oriental musical cultures provide the chief exceptions. The modern clarinet does partially resemble the single-reed aulos; the recorder, which has no reed, does not. Even the comparison commonly made with the oboe can mislead us: almost always, it fails to take into account the position of the aulos's double reed. This exercised a great effect on control, and thus on the kinds of tone produced. The inner diameter, or bore, also affects tone. Oboes have a conical bore, whereas the bore of all surviving auloi is cylindrical.[24]

Apparently, the two pipes of the Homeric instrument were equal in length. One of the only two known vase paintings that constitute our evidence shows them to be almost half the height of the performer. If that was 5 feet, they must have been between 2 and 2 1/2 feet in length, roughly 60 to 70 centimeters. The other of the two auletes shown plays on short pipes. They are the length of his upper arm, and they measure distinctly less than a fifth of his height. This would give

[23] The term *auletēs*, "aulos player," is not a Homeric word, though *auletēr* (with the same meaning) occurs very early. Later we find the feminine equivalent, *auletris*.

[24] In a very few instances, ancient art does show auloi that have a conical exterior form. It is clear that they were the exception, not the rule.

a measurement of about 30 centimeters. All estimates based on figure drawing in Geometric art involve risk, since the parts of the body were not shown in true proportion. With that caveat, we may accept Y. Gerhard's estimates: 30 centimeters for the shorter and higher pipes, 60 for the longer and deeper ones.[25]

Throughout the history of Greek musical instruments, the pipes themselves normally were identical, or almost identical, in length, except for the "Phrygian" aulos. The length varied with the freedom that was to be expected of a musical culture in which absolute pitch was never allowed any normative role. We may conjecture that actual pitch was kept within reasonable limits by two factors: the restricted nature of the range that the voice can cover (seldom more than two octaves) and perhaps the capacities of the phorminx, lyre, or kithara.[26] The increase to a standard complement of seven strings would soon take place. In isolated instances, it had already begun: the Old Smyrna lyre is a witness to this. The musical forms mentioned in Homeric epic may also have limited what the aulos could do.

In the later of the two examples available to us, the Geometric-Attic vase painter shows an aulete accompanying a round dance—a scene that matches several of Homer's descriptions. Pipers for round dancing must provide lively tunes with a strongly marked rhythm. The young men of the peaceful city who were "whirling" (*Il.* 18.494) may have been performing such a dance; in any case, the same kind of accompaniment would have been required. Possibly *enopē* and *boē,* which describe the sound of the pipes, convey some suggestion of pitch and timbre. Elsewhere, Homer invariably uses both terms of shouts and cries, especially with the meaning "battle cry." There would be a natural connection, then, with pipe music of a high-pitched, strident, raucous nature.[27] Also, in *Iliad* 3.2–5 *enopē* is closely linked with *klanggē*. The latter refers to bird cries, or is associated

---

[25] Gerhard, in Snell 1979, vol. 1, col. 1556.17–18.

[26] The limits of pitch alteration on a reconstructed *chelus:* Roberts 1974, 85, 89–91; cf. 184, 189. Paquette (1984, 147) conjectures a viola tessitura.

[27] Affinities with the human voice are claimed for the sound of the modern oboe. During antiquity, similar claims were made for the aulos. In the section on music (book 19) in the *Problems,* á late work that has come to us from the school of Aristotle, the "similarity" (*homoiotēs,* a concept of some importance in his genuine works) between aulos and voice is twice mentioned as if it were an indisputable fact (19.43, 922a10–11, 15).

with them, five times in the course of the two epics. A single example, from the *Iliad,* will suffice: unlike the Greeks, who marched in silence toward the meeting on the plain, the Trojans "went onward with shouting and outcry [*klanggēi t' enopēi t'*], like birds" (3.2). Throughout this passage from the *Iliad,* the poet is mainly concerned to account for the diversity of languages among the varied contingents defending Troy. As a borrowing—an attempt to describe a kind of music not yet familiar at the time of the Trojan War—*enopē* could indicate high pitch and a sharp, abrupt, clangorous sound.

The case for the lyre proves to be quite different. No other musical instrument is mentioned as often in the poems attributed to Homer and Hesiod. Three passages in Homer (*Il.* 1.153, 2.600, 3.54) have *kitharis* or *kitharistus* for "lyre" or "lyre playing." Everywhere else in the Homeric epics, the term *phorminx* and no other designates the lyre.[28] Usually it is a concert instrument, associated with professional musicians. In these respects, it resembled the Hellenic kithara; but the phorminx of Geometric and early Attic art is U-shaped, with a rounded base. There are four strings, parallel or in a minor degree radial. To judge from Geometric vase paintings, its height was seldom less than 2 feet or much more than 3 feet.

Neither Homeric poem mentions the plectrum; vase painters do not show it until about 700 B.C. The mid–seventh-century *Homeric Hymn to Apollo* refers to it (185), and the later hymn to Hermes has three references (53, 419, 501). Moreover, we have seen it on very ancient lyres, such as the one from Old Smyrna (675–650? B.C.). These are contemporary with, or older than, the earliest period to which established versions of the *Iliad* and *Odyssey* could possibly be assigned. Although the seven-stringed Old Smyrna instrument was not a phorminx, its appearance in Ionia has great importance for the development of the whole lyre family. This event coincides with the floruit of Terpander, credited with adding a seventh string to the lyre.[29] Like Sappho, he was a native of Lesbos.

[28] Neither *lura* nor *kithara* occurs in the Homeric poems.

[29] So the *Suda*. The belief rests chiefly, if not entirely, on the poet's own supposed claim that he will scorn "four-voiced song" and instead sound "new hymns on a phorminx of seven *tonoi*" (frag. 1 Bergk, 5 Edmonds). Page (1962, 363) rejects these lines as not being the work of Terpander. See Anderson 1966, 44–45. It is at any rate reasonable to associate Terpander with the introduction of "the more elaborate flat-based instrument of the professional citharodes, which first appears in the seventh century" (Winnington-Ingram 1970, sec. 9.i). See Wegner 1968, 17.

Instrumental music as a wholly separate activity has no place in Homeric epic, except perhaps for the distant piping that surprised Agamemnon. It does have a subordinate place in the performances of Homer's court bards, Phemius and Demodocus. Both singers begin by preluding on the phorminx, an act expressed by the verb *anaballesthai*.[30] This form is the middle voice of *anaballein*, "to delay, put off" some activity. The meanings of the active may have carried over into the use of the middle, to describe a postponing of the sung or chanted narrative.[31] Possibly *anaballein* and the words that derive from it were applied to the voice no less readily than to instruments. For example, the *Iliad* describes Andromache's wailing with the adverb *amblēdēn*, a syncopal form of *anablēdēn;* this occurs before she commences her formal lament for the dead Hector.[32] So far as the two recognized bards of the *Odyssey* are concerned, however, *anaballesthai* denotes preluding, playing an *anabolē* (a post-Homeric term) on the phorminx.[33]

The nature of such a prelude can only be conjectured. Comparative evidence should not be cited when the analogies are specious. The *anabolē*, for example, has more than once been likened to the *alap*. In the classical music of India, the *alap* precedes the *raga*, providing an outline of the intricate explorations that are to follow. Such a comparison seeks to equate a highly developed modal and rhythmic complex with one of extreme simplicity.[34]

When Odysseus strings his massive bow, he is said to do so without apparent effort, "as a man who has expert knowledge of the phorminx and of singing easily stretches a string round a new *kollops,*

---

[30] Phemius: *Od.* 1.155, 17.262; Demodocus: *Od.* 8.266.

[31] Snell 1979, vol. 1, col. 754.34–35.

[32] In his note on the passage, Leaf (1900) interprets the reference as being to repeated sobbing; he follows a scholiast's misinterpretation. LSJ (s.v. *amblēdēn*) makes the same wrong choice. Monro, in his 1888 edition, had already seen the error; but he chose instead a basic meaning of *anaballein* ("to lift up") that has no relevance for *Il.* 22.476. For this passage, Snell (1979, vol. 1, col. 615.22) correctly has "einleitend, als Einleitung" ("introductory, as prelude").

[33] See also West 1992b, 205. The unnamed *aoidos* in Menelaus' great house (*Od.* 4.17) merely provides an accompaniment for tumblers. Nestor (*Od.* 3) apparently has no bard.

[34] Wegner (1968, 17) argues that preluding by a bard served to establish the mode; this lies beyond either proof or disproof. He may be correct in claiming that for Homer's singers the *anabolē* consisted only of a few touches on the strings to establish the tempo (1949, 73; he compares Schadewaldt 1965, 72).

making the (?)supple sheep gut fast at either end" (*Od.* 21.406–9). The simile tells us that this aspect of stringing a phorminx was done swiftly and easily, as a skilled archer strings his bow. The procedure referred to here is neither the initial fitting of a string nor its tuning. Rather, the poet is describing the method of fastening one end to the string holder and the other to the crossbar. The upper end of the string is wound around something called a *kollops,* and a new one at that.

Although vase painters often portrayed the *kollops,* the word seldom occurs in Greek literature. Fortunately, two fragments from lost comedies of Aristophanes reveal the fact that it could then refer to a piece of the thick skin on an ox or a hog, taken from the nape of the animal's neck.[35] Modern scholars repeat the explanation given in the twelfth century by Eustathius—that these napes were strips of skin, with the fat still on them, used to hold lyre strings fast to the crossbar. Eustathius gives little more information than the lexicographer Hesychius had supplied seven centuries earlier; but that little suggests his habit of illustrating the meaning of Greek terms from antiquity by the practices of his own time. If Eustathius was indeed drawing upon observation, his remarks have special value, for they have not been correctly understood; nor is it possible to understand them unless we follow his precedent and observe how the strings of present-day lyres are secured.

As found throughout central Africa, the instrument has leather wrappings on the crossbar. The strings are wound over and around these, crisscross fashion, and wooden pegs are inserted in the windings to maintain or alter the tension.[36] They form part of the lyre but are not built into it, not an integral component like today's tuning mechanisms. Pegs of the kind familiar to us were unknown before the Hellenistic period; yet the Lexicon gives "screw" or "peg" for *kollops* (see H. G. Liddell, R. Scott, and H. S. Jones, *A Greek Lexicon,* 9th ed. [Oxford, 1940]; hereafter LSJ). Clearly, the leather wrappings of the African lyre are the present-day equivalent of the *kollopes.* The fat is no longer left on; normally, in every age and every culture, those who prepare hides for softening or tanning scrape it off. If Eustathius was

---

[35] Aristophanes frags. 506, 646.
[36] Wegner 1984, 104, fig. 68 = fig. 21 here. For other evidence regarding methods of tuning, see West 1992b, 61.

right, if it did form part of the string wrappings on a Greek lyre, its purpose remains a mystery. Perhaps it was left exposed and thus came into contact with the wound string, making adjustment easier. Except for this area of uncertainty, the combined evidence of classical philology and ethnomusicology indicates that lyre strings are held in place today very much as they were during the eighth and seventh centuries B.C.

The strings of an instrument as modest in size as the phorminx would normally have a medium range of pitch. If a rough equation can be made with what Helen Roberts estimates for the sixth-century lyre and kithara, the gamut may have corresponded more or less to the octave e–e^1 (taking c^1 to indicate middle C), pitched comfortably for a baritone. Such a suggestion obviously runs counter to the belief that Greek instrumental accompaniments were higher than the vocal line. By now, this view ought to have been subject to closer criticism than it has in fact received. Where sources that might conceivably be dated to the classical period are concerned, the only support comes from the *Problems,* set forth by the theorists of Aristotle's school and their successors. In addition, what may have been true at some time (perhaps late) in the Hellenistic or Graeco-Roman period has no necessary validity for Hellenic times, let alone pre-Hellenic.

Singing could and did take place without the aid of a phorminx or any other instrument. Men joined in singing the paean (*paiēōn*), properly a hymn of thanksgiving for deliverance (*Il.* 1.473), sometimes a triumph song (*Il.* 22.391). In the single instance of the Sirens' unaccompanied song, we have the actual words (*Od.* 12.184–91). Attendants on a bride performed the *humenaios* or hymeneal song in a wedding procession (*Il.* 18.493); otherwise, mortal women do not sing together in Homer. For choral performance, unison was the unvarying rule throughout antiquity. When boys sang with men, they had to take the melody at the higher octave; the first references to this combination are post-Homeric. Harmony in the modern, Western sense did not exist. Throughout most of the non-Western world, it has not yet come into being except as an imported replacement for indigenous tradition.

Women, or any rate goddesses, sometimes would sing at their tasks when they were alone. A teenaged princess like Nausicaä might volunteer to do the laundry, with a good deal of help, and with girlish games afterward; the poet makes no mention of work songs. The song to accompany games, which does figure in this seaside jollification, is another matter. Both Circe and Calypso are singing at the loom when we first encounter them in the *Odyssey*. Through the extraordinary melodiousness of its vowels and liquid consonants, the Greek text conveys the tone color of lyric in both instances (*Od.* 5.61, 10.221). By Greek standards of vowel count, the single word *aoidiaous'*, "singing," contains seven vowels. A comparable effort to give the impression of lyric poetry informs the Sirens' song. By manipulating the placement of pauses and word beginnings, the poet suggests a rhythm based on the anapest (˘ ˘ -) instead of the dactyl (- ˘ ˘).

Besides the nameless youth who performs the Linos song, three men sing individually in the Homeric poems: Achilles and the court bards, Phemius and Demodocus. The playing and singing of Achilles seem a complete anomaly. He is not a bard, or for that matter an ordinary mortal; and so far as we can tell, this demigod sings for himself alone. He does have an audience of one, his companion Patroclus; but the poet makes clear that the giving of pleasure through music here is self-directed. The "dialogue of the mind with itself" can be heard on many occasions throughout the *Odyssey*. In the *Iliad,* it is less frequent. It occurs most strikingly of all in the scene here at 9.186–91: "And they found him delighting his heart [*phrena terpomenon*] with a phorminx, clear-toned, beautiful, richly ornamented, having a silver crossbar. He had gotten it from the spoils of war when he destroyed Eëtion's city. With it he was delighting his spirit [*thumon eterpen*], and he sang the glorious deeds of heroes [*klea andrōn*]. Patroclus sat across from him, alone and in silence, waiting until the grandson of Aeacus should cease from singing."

The occasion is Agamemnon's sending of a propitiatory embassy, and here we see Achilles through the eyes of the envoys. They have taken him by surprise: we are intruding upon a private moment. It is something meant only for the solitary pair: the man who is playing and singing, and the other—an extension of Achilles, his second self—who sits waiting in silence for the song to end.[37] One might well wonder why there should have been this need for privacy.

---

[37] Bowra (1930, 32) understands Achilles' singing to be improvisatory and (following the view of Drerup 1921, 47) sees Patroclus as a partner waiting to take over when his friend tires. Their song is thus "amoebaic"; he cites a modern parallel from Finland, described by Comparetti (1898, 70), "where pairs of bards improvised in turn

A part of the answer may be sought in Achilles' feeling of aliena-
tion. Possibly another part relates to a parallel known from so-called
primitive music, better called nonliterate music.[38] This performance,
like those in the *Iliad,* is strongly communal. Nevertheless, the individual may sing privately. This is done in secret, particularly because
in such societies singing has a special category: that of the private
song, which belongs to the individual, and to the individual alone.
Should the wrong person hear the individual's song, the consequences can be extremely dangerous for the singer.

The theme of the song is described in two words, *klea andrōn,* as if
no further comment were needed. The poet seems far more interested
in the phorminx: nowhere else, whether in Homeric epic or in any
later work, is a completed instrument—one not in the process of
being made—given so detailed a description. We quickly learn that it
does not belong to Achilles. An amateur, he handles it with something less than a professional's carefulness when he suddenly becomes
aware of the visitors and springs to his feet, still holding the instrument (194: *autēi sun phorminggi,* almost "lyre and all"). It has become
his possession by right of war, awarded in the division of booty after
"the city of Eëtion" was sacked—leaving, probably, a dead bard.
Eëtion's city, Thebe, was also the city of Briseis, another of the spoils
of war given to Achilles. Now Briseis has been taken from him by
Agamemnon. Achilles' consequent withdrawal from the fighting has
occasioned severe losses among the Greeks; it is the reason for the
present embassy.

The phorminx remains with him, a reminder of the taking of Briseis and therefore of its result: the *mēnis,* that slow-burning wrath
announced by Homer as the theme of his tale.[39] These are back-

---

with rapid alternation." In his final treatment of this question (1966, 442) Bowra
draws back from Drerup's interpretation. The supposed Finnish parallel is hardly
amoebaic as that term is normally understood. A. B. Lord, in Wace and Stubbings
1969, 182, gives the best short modern treatment of the modern singing of epic by two
men together. He adds instances from his own field work in Albania and Jugoslav
Macedonia, where this kind of performance proved unsuitable for any but short
poems.

[38] "Nonliterate" is preferable to "primitive" (which is "gradually disappearing from
the literature of anthropology and ethnomusicology") and also to "preliterate," which
implies "an evolutionary, inevitable sequence" (Nettl 1964, 6).

[39] We ought not, however, to interpret the phorminx as being an actual symbol of
Briseis. *Mēnis* is the first word of the *Iliad.*

ground resonances; the narrator's interest centers on the phorminx itself. The description of its clear tone, handsome decoration, and provenance creates the distinct impression that we have here a professional's instrument.[40] Yet Achilles knows how to accompany his singing on it; nor does anything about the narrative indicate surprise at his possessing musical skills.[41] How he acquired them is never stated. The familiar mythic tradition that the centaur Chiron taught him lyre playing does not appear in Homeric epic. The *Iliad* has no place for it; although the poem does bring before us two aristocrats who are in some degree musicians (the other being Paris), the relevant passages may actually be instances of anachronism.

However Achilles acquired his ability to sing and accompany himself, he has no didactic purpose in doing so. The envoys take care of that element as they remonstrate with him, especially when they cite as a warning the case of Meleager. The poet concerns himself with other matters. Before mentioning the "praise of heroes" he twice tells us, with the utmost possible explicitness, that Achilles was enjoying himself by playing the phorminx. In ten other Homeric passages, it is poetry to which the verb *terpein,* "to give pleasure," applies; here, a distinction is made. This is the first known aesthetic response to music in Western literary tradition, and it concerns the affective capacities of an instrument, not those of the human voice. The order of reference, with instrumental performance preceding singing, has a parallel in the kinds of word order found in references to preluding. All of these instances support the hypothesis that phorminx playing had a certain degree of independence. Concerning its nature we know nothing.[42]

The melodic nature of what Achilles may have played and sung can be usefully discussed only within the larger context of bardic performance. For over a century, discussion of the Homeric poems has centered on Phemius and Demodocus. During more than half of that period, comparative evidence has been taken from the practices of

[40] The use of *ligus,* "clear," may indicate high pitch here; this remains a debated point.

[41] Winnington-Ingram (1970) opens the article "Music" in the *Oxford Classical Dictionary* by noting that when the embassy came upon Achilles they "expressed no astonishment that a hardy warrior should seek relaxation in music of his own making."

[42] Roberts 1974, 169, sees it as "monotonous and austere."

singer-poets in other cultures who employ oral composition. As far back as 1925, classical philologists had protested against the introduction of this kind of evidence. Beginning in the following year, the whole controversy took on new life, thanks to Milman Parry's arguments for oral formulaic techniques as the structural basis of Homeric epic. The comparative element in his theory came from field study and from recordings of performances of epic poems, sung for him by Jugoslav bards. His concern with the two traditions has been continued by Lord, whose short work *The Singer of Tales* has now become very widely known. Like Lord's full-scale study, *Serbocroatian Heroic Songs,* this more accessible treatment contains only scattered comments on vocal melody and instrumental accompaniment.

A lack of interest in the role of music is common to most comparative studies of epic. For example, with his contributions to *A Companion to Homer* (1962), Bowra hardly advanced beyond the position he had taken more than thirty years earlier: that any melody to which the *Iliad* or *Odyssey* was sung must have been simple, consisting of repeated motifs. He finds parallels in Albanian and Russian epic poetry, as well as in Jugoslav. Such poems may occasionally be delivered in a monotone; at best, he concludes, the delivery must be called "really no more than recitative."[43] This conclusion would have astounded Béla Bartók, who provided the musical transcriptions for *Serbocroatian Heroic Songs* and did so with an agonizingly scrupulous precision, seldom if ever matched.

West has discussed the singing of Homer's poetry in a 1981 article that began a new era. The discussion is continued here, with contentions based as far as possible on known fact. One way of making progress is to use evidence, whether Hellenic, modern, or anything in between, that still seems relevant and enlightening after close examination.[44]

---

[43] Bowra 1966, 39; cf. his descriptions in 1930, 58 ("intoned or chanted") and in Wace and Stubbings 1969, 22 ("at the most intoned to a very simple chant"). See also n. 35 to chap. 1. Bartók's transcriptions (below): Nettl 1964, 41, 106.

[44] At the beginning of his dissertation on ancient Greek woodwinds (1960, 6) J. G. Landels would rule out any comparative evidence that does not come from a similar musical culture (1) showing the same general level of development, (2) exposed to the same influences, and (3) expressing taste and temperament such as those of the Greeks. Such requirements effectively rule out any comparison whatsoever. In addition, the specific arguments that are meant to support them contain misperceptions.

Throughout the Hellenic period, Homer's poetry was recited; it was not sung. Any attempt to provide musical settings was thought unusual, and literary historians took special note. To a fifth-century Greek, the singing of Homer would have seemed a strange idea. Yet the *Odyssey* contains many references to the presentation of epic or mythic narratives; and, as we have seen, the verb most often used is *aeidein*. The injunction *Mēnin aeide, thea*—"Sing, goddess, the smoldering wrath" of Achilles—opens the *Iliad;* it sounds the theme of the entire work. Moreover, *aeidein* reappears in Achilles' song of heroic deeds (book 9), and again in the wedding festivities that characterize the peaceful city, depicted on his shield (book 18). The question is whether it means "sing" as we think of singing or verges instead on prose, with a meaning something like "chant."

Concerning the text of the *Iliad* and *Odyssey,* it will be assumed first of all that the accent marks designate different levels of pitch. This starting point is obvious. Once past it, however, we find that almost everything is disputed—a truth that applies with particular force to the pitch levels. These were present in spoken Greek throughout the Hellenic and Hellenistic periods, although inscriptions of the time do not acknowledge them.

At the close of the third century B.C., according to tradition, an Alexandrian grammarian devised the system of accents. Three marks prevailed: strokes slanting to right or left—the acute and the grave, respectively—and a third, the circumflex, which consisted of these two combined. They are vocalic signs: within the sentence, they normally occur over a single vowel or over the second element of a diphthong. The Greek names *oxeia, bareia,* and *perispōmenos* are adjectives. They mean "high-pitched," "low-pitched," and (literally) "turned around" in the sense of a right-angled turn. The three terms modify an understood noun, *prosōidia.* This "singing [*aeidein, ōidē*] in accompaniment to [sc. words]" is what we call accent, from the Latin close equivalent *accentus* (*ad* + *cantus,* from *canere*). The terminology, therefore, is musical.

It would be worth a great deal if we could know the size of the interval within which these accents operated and their placing within that interval; but the knowledge is not available in any reliable form. Nothing at all was said until the time of Augustus, when Dionysius of Halicarnassus devoted a few words to the nature of pitch accent.

Even this brief mention is flawed by ambiguity on a crucial point. As a result, no one can be certain whether the writer intended to refer to (1) a total range of a fifth, in which the voice moved upward from the bottom note and went back to it, or (2) a fifth with a central level, from which the voice might vary upward or downward by approximately a minor third, as we today think of intervals.

W. B. Stanford adopted the first of these conversion systems, expressing in modern staff notation the opening line of the *Odyssey*.[45] The initial phrase appears in C major and 4/4 time as follows:

This illustrates the results of applying Dionysius' statement to the text of Homer without reservation or modification. It has been justly criticized for angularity; the real difficulties lie deeper. They come from a failure to consider either the complexities of sung pitch accent or the powerful constraints that the limitations of the phorminx imposed upon bardic performance.

The primary error is the assumption that in a tone language all pitches are sounded and are clearly differentiated. From this, another erroneous assumption follows, namely, that these same tone distinctions are observed, with equal precision, in singing. The companion inference—that instrumental accompaniments take some account of the distinctions—does not stand or fall by the validity of the other two suppositions; often it is correct. The two assumptions, however, are incorrect; and recent reconstructions such as Stanford's have been based on mistaken beliefs about the way tones are used.

The realm of pitch accents is not governed by an egalitarian democracy. Some pitches (indeed a good many) are clearly sounded, in accordance with their semantic status. These regularly modify the nature of neighboring pitches; thus, for example, a preceding third

---

[45] Stanford 1967, 158. West (1992b, 198–200) usefully summarizes many of the basic points concerning the relationship between accent and melody. For an ethnomusicologist's overview of the correlation between linguistic and pitch patterns, Nettl 1964, 289–91 is valuable. His rules for upward and downward movement (290) may be compared with those that Pöhlmann has drawn from his intensive study of the surviving examples of Greek music (1970, 140).

tone becomes a second tone. But many are "neutral" tones: they have a negative status, like that of the *praçaya* (multitude) tones of Sanskrit. Only under exceptional conditions is each syllable given its individual, unaltered tone: for Mandarin, the formal reading of a Confucian ode would constitute such an exception. The odes of the *Book of Songs* are not lengthy; there can be no parallel here with the hundreds of lines recited by a bard or rhapsode during a single performance.

Musical settings of Chinese texts show an undeniable relationship between spoken levels or contours of pitch and of melodic form. Nevertheless, that relationship is not absolute even in Cantonese opera, where the "vocabulary" of melodic equivalents for given pitches enables a singer to master long texts and give them vocal settings, all in an astonishingly short time. Any one of a half dozen or more factors may alter the equation. As for Vedic chant, the example that has been brought forward as a parallel to the singing of Homer does not match the Greek system of pitch accents.[46] Undoubtedly it is ancient; but the many proofs available from comparative philology, especially comparisons with Greek, confirm the belief that this type of chanting is "secondary," not original.[47]

We would welcome some revealing analogy derived from the performance of epic among other peoples, but it does not seem that any close parallel exits. Different cultures display individual methods of relating instrumental accompaniment to a sung text; whether some of these can reasonably be termed analogous is difficult to decide. Mentioning them at least prompts us to see Homer as not quite so isolated a phenomenon.

Comparisons with the *gusle,* a kind of fiddle used by Jugoslav bards, apply mainly to questions other than those of instrumental technique; this is because of the nature of the instrument.[48] Usually it has but one string, played with a bow, and an unfretted fingerboard. The player may add only a single note to that of the open string. Two more are very often employed, but seldom three; the total compass

[46] West 1981, 115. To cite only one of a number of discrepancies, the equivalents of the perispomenon (´plus`) appear as mere single notes.

[47] Vedic chant as secondary: Burrow 1973, 115.

[48] The only detailed discussion of the *gusle* is found in a posthumously published work written in Serbo-Croatian by Matija (Matthias) Murko, *Tragom srpsko-hrvatske narodne epike* (Zagreb, 1951), 322–35.

does not usually exceed a minor third. Within its limits, however, fingering can often be extremely rapid. The ring finger is not used.

On all these counts, the *gusle* differs basically from the Homeric phorminx. Ideally, the analogies that we are seeking ought to come from a people who play the lyre, and who sing or chant epic to its accompaniment. Northern and central Africa have lyre-playing tribes such as the Nuba, vividly described by Leni Riefenstahl (1974), but they do not have an epic tradition that they perform to the lyre. Neither, apparently, does any other people.

The performance of Japanese epic illustrates a technique that is, at the very least, intriguing. Here the epic material is the *Heike no monogatari* ("The Tale of Heike"), which commemorates a feudal period of savage fighting. The performance, done in the traditional manner, involves as accompaniment a four-stringed, fretted lute called the *biwa*. The player holds a large, triangular plectrum and employs a variety of strokes. Speaking of the role of the *biwa* and *koto* (a long zither) in ensembles today, William P. Malm says: "These instruments do not play the melody but rather use short stereotyped melodic phrases or arpeggios which, while influenced by the mode and the melody, function primarily colotomically [i.e., as section divisions] through the regular intervals between their entrances."[49] (In later Greek literature, we may compare the use by lyric poets of brief instrumental passages, inserted between strophe and antistrophe.) The *gusle* likewise avoids duplicating the main melodic line. Although it may frequently restate the melody, it always does so with a greater or lesser degree of alteration.

The text of the *Iliad* and *Odyssey* displays such virtuosity that readers might be excused if they imagine an age in which the resources of music had been comparably developed. The evidence, however, does not justify such an assumption. A phorminx had fewer strings (three as often as four) than its Minoan predecessors and smaller dimensions overall, though a larger sound chest had increased the resonance. West suggests that epic singers used a comparably limited scale such as a b c' e'. One can argue that a reduced number of strings does not necessarily indicate decline. Moreover, works of art from the Minoan,

[49] Malm 1967, 139. In colotomic structure, instruments mark the beginning and end of sections with recurring melodies or rhythms. This structure characterizes the music of Southeast Asia.

Mycenaean, and Geometric periods show considerable variation in the string complement. It is conceivable that more experimentation was going on than will ever become known.[50]

After the passing of the old "heroic" civilization, the age of bronze gave way to an iron age. Vase painting became Geometric, so called from the designs adopted from decorative motifs. These are commonplaces. So is the fact of a broad pattern of expansion eastward. Its consequences for Greek music receive little attention; yet they are momentous. Establishment of a Greek presence along the western seaboard of Asia Minor created the conditions that brought the *harmoniai* into being.

When all but isolated parts of the Greek mainland fell to the Dorians during the eleventh century B.C., Greek immigrants headed east, the only place where there was extensive, desirable, and attainable land. They went chiefly to the coastal plains of Asia Minor across from Greece, and also to the larger islands, such as Lesbos or Samos, which lay close to the Asia Minor coast. Three spheres of influence came successively into being: Aeolis (including the large island of Lesbos) to the north, Ionia (with Samos and Chios) in the middle, and Doris (with Rhodes) to the south.[51] Properly speaking, the name "Ionia" applied only to the central area; in time its use was extended to describe the Greek settlements along the entire western seaboard of Asia Minor.

It was a succession of mixed groups who settled that coast. When we make distinctions among them, the criterion must sometimes be geographical, sometimes ethnic. The general pattern of colonization stands out clearly enough, and its results have fundamental significance for the history of Greek music. Three areas bear the names of those Greeks who emigrated to them. With the names given to the colonists—*Aioleus* (plural usually *Aioleis*), *Iōnes* (plural; singular not in use), and *Dōrieus* (plural usually *Dōrieis*)—went the corresponding adjectives and adverbs. Two of the adjectives, *Aiolikos* and *Iōnikos*, are

---

[50] Vorreiter (1972) has shown that a decrease in the number of lyre strings may indeed be a symptom of decline (Mytilenean coinage, ca. 350–80 B.C.). The epic singer's scale: West 1992b, 328; number of strings on the phorminx, 52.

[51] This account follows the standard chronology, which has recently been called into question.

Hellenistic or later; the variety of adjectival forms, however, will seldom concern us.

It is the adverbs, especially those ending in *-sti,* that are useful for our inquiry. The Greek colonizers did not take over uninhabited land but had to settle in territories that belonged to native peoples. Two instances are relevant: the Achaeans and Aeolians established Aeolis in the demesne of the Phrygians, who had invaded Asia Minor from Europe two centuries earlier; and Ionia was made up of land belonging to the Lydians.[52] What brought about the coexistence of Greek and Oriental we do not know; we do know that the basic adverbs reflect it. Besides *dōristi,* there are *phrugisti* and *ludisti* as well as *aiolisti* and *iasti.*[53] Of these five, only the first could have referred to mainland Greece, and even that one case is not free from ambiguity.

If the sequence of usages given in LSJ is to be believed, some at least of these forms originally denoted a manner of speech, and the reference was later transferred to the idiom of musical terminology—specifically, though not invariably, to mode. The nature and dating of the references themselves, though, suggest a different conclusion. Only three come from authors earlier than Plato, and two of the three concern music; so does *phrugisti,* which appears first in Plato. *Aiolisti* is not attested before the time of Christ. Even *Hellēnisti,* "in Greek," occurs no earlier than the writings of Xenophon, born about 444 B.C., and of his younger contemporary, Plato. In the two categories under which the lexicon lists these "ethnic" adverbs, priority remains uncertain. The terms may have taken on musical meanings as quickly as nonmusical, or even more quickly. Furthermore, the application to music requires another field of reference, and obviously this must be song. It was from song, not from speech, that the Hellenic *harmoniai* derived their existence; and throughout the history of Greek music, they maintained a remarkably close connection with the sung text.

The noun *harmonia* appears in both the *Iliad* and the *Odyssey,* with the characteristic Ionic long *e* for *a.* It shows the capacity associated

[52] The old belief that *Aiolos, Aioleus* were shorter synonyms for *Achaios* appears to have been abandoned. The singular form *Iōn* occurs only as a personal name. Doris, original home of the Dorian people, was a tiny strip of territory near Mount Parnassus.

[53] *Iōnisti* is rare and very late. *Iaones* for *Iōnes* occurs once in Homer, *Il.* 13.685.

with agent nouns that have this type of ending: that is, it not only can express a process and the result of that process; it may also apply to objects that constitute or bring about the conditions prerequisite for the achieving of the result. Early epic usage goes no farther: *harmoniē* does not yet denote harmony, in any sense, as a condition. During this period, its special shade of meaning is likely to be the process or result of joining together different and perhaps opposing elements, so as to form a unity. When it applies to an object, it probably means "clamp," either the carpenter's tool or else a fastening of some sort for timbers (*Od.* 5.248, 361).[54] Here we need only note that there is unmistakable Homeric evidence for a wholly concrete use of the term.

The *Iliad* furnishes an abstract use, in the plural as in the *Odyssey*.[55] Hector is making a stand against Achilles and parleying with him, before their fight to the death. He proposes that they swear by their respective gods that the victor will return the body of the slain man. The gods, he adds, are to be "watchers over the agreement" (22.255: *episkopoi harmoniaōn*). The positive aspects of such a compact—which Achilles, replying, mentions only in order to dismiss them—create the strong impression that it usually had as objects peace and friendship.

We are left with two conclusions. First, *harmoniē* denotes a literal or figurative joining together of diverse elements, so that they in some sense fit together. Second, Homeric poetry already begins to convey an awareness that this fit, of whatever kind, may in fact be considered "fitting" and therefore a source of pleasure (*Od.* 4.777). As yet the term has no connection with music. Both the *Iliad* and the *Odyssey*, however, present it in contexts that favor the establishing of such a connection. Its beginnings are auspicious.

Epic may not provide answers to the baffling questions of how, when, and where the Hellenic *harmoniai* came into being, but answers are hinted at here and there in early elegiac, iambic, and lyric poetry. These genres represent the chief kinds of shorter poem. The practice

[54] Blümner 1969, 2:306, *harmonia* as "clamp" in woodworking; 3:99, 139, *harmonia* as "clamp" or "joint" in stonemasonry, and also *diatonikos* in stonemasonry. LSJ gives only a musical meaning. See Mader, in Snell 1979, vol. 1, col. 1323.30–31: *harmonia* as the "mortise and tenon" type of joint in shipbuilding (cf. *Od.* 5.361).

[55] Homeric poetry has no instance of *harmoniē* in the singular.

of composing such works may have been at least as old as the making of epic poetry. In form and tone, they are obviously closer to folk song. They differ from it no less clearly: the earliest surviving specimens honor the gods or the city-state; later, the poet's individual nature makes itself felt. The proper term here, however, is not "poet" but "poet-composer," for throughout every period of Hellenic history until the closing years of the fifth century the creator of any text intended for singing created the melody and accompaniment as well.

Before turning to other genres, we must take note of two figures, one historical—the Boeotian epic poet Hesiod of Ascra—and one who belongs at least partly to legend—Olympus the Mysian. Two of the poems that make up the Hesiodic corpus are taken to be by Hesiod: the *Works and Days* (*Erga kai hēmerai*), in effect a farmer's almanac, and the *Theogony,* an account of how the gods came into being. Both have Homer's meter, the dactylic hexameter, and much of his diction. They differ from the *Iliad* and *Odyssey* in that the author deliberately and continually sets forth his views, especially his concern with day-to-day tasks (*erga*) and with ethical obligations.

In this so-called didactic form of epic, the bard is an avowed teacher. Little room remains for a concern with music: the two poems contain only a single reference to instruments, *Theogony* 95. Song gets more attention, usually when Hesiod invokes or mentions the Muses. They themselves are marvelous singers, he asserts, and skilled dancers as well. They bestow on men the gift of "lovely song"; Hesiod treats beauty and truth as synonymous.[56] One who has received this power can make men forget heaviness of spirit by singing to them "the glorious deeds done by men of former days."[57] We cannot easily miss the similarity to Homer; yet the emphasis on an ethical-social function for music, the view of it as anodyne, represents a marked difference. Here, moreover, the bard's subject is not merely the mighty deeds of heroes but "the blessed gods" as well. Now the

[56] Yet the first thing that Hesiod's Muses declare about themselves is their ability to express falsehoods resembling truth (*Theogony* 29). H. J. Rose (1960, 62) resolves the paradox with the conjecture that Hesiod "is declaring himself the representative of a new school of poetry" concerned not with doubtful heroic legends but with facts. Dodds (1957, 81) suggests that the Muses here may be hinting "that the true inspiration of saga was petering out" in the kind of "mere invention" discernible in the later portions of the *Odyssey.*

[57] *Theogony* 100: *klea proterōn anthrōpōn;* cf. *Il.* 9.189: *klea andrōn.*

hymn has taken on importance; and this accords with the early date of several *Homeric Hymns,* each assigned to a god.

The Muses, Hesiod tells us, are also the divine patrons of "bards and kithara players" (*aoidoi kai kitharistai*).[58] The competitive, agonistic factor now emerges. Presumably, this constitutes the element of truth in the stories about his entering competitions. We also see emerging the rhapsode (*rhapsōidos,* literally "stitcher of songs"). Bards have become professionals, recognized as such. Eventually they are to be reciters of Homer, and at times of Hesiod's own works.[59] The received view has been that when Hesiod tells how the Muses on Helicon bestowed their inspiration by placing in his hands "a shoot of olive," he is epitomizing a transition from kithara-playing bards to rhapsodes who held only a staff—from singing or chanting to recitation.

West has given strong reasons for questioning the first part of this assumption. He conjectures a transitional period, perhaps quite lengthy, during which the kithara may still have had a place. It is true that the Jugoslav *guslar* has sometimes performed without a *gusle,* and on occasion without even a staff.[60] The distinction drawn between bard and kithara player remains puzzling, but it does not invalidate West's contention. Neither does the unsupported claim of the late writer Pausanias, who associates Hesiod with the later stage, that of recitation without musical accompaniment.[61]

Olympus the Mysian was thought to have been active around the close of the eighth century. Ancient sources describe him as a Phry-

[58] *Theogony* 95.
[59] Plato *Laws* 658d6–8. West (1978, 63) identifies Plato's "rhapsodes" with the *sophistai* mentioned by Isocrates in *Panathenaicus* 18: they were rhapsodes in that they recited the poems attributed to Homer and Hesiod, Sophists in that they added a commentary. See above, n. 18, for Lomax's claim regarding the style of the epic composer; with this we may compare E. A. Havelock's claim (1963) that the Homeric poems constituted a total paradigm of the society described in them.
[60] West 1981, 115. Murko (1919, 285) found that, instead of using a *gusle* or *tambura,* singers might beat time with any of a number of objects, or even on the shoulders of a small child. Later (1929, 10–11) he comments on the inaccuracy of the literary term *guslar,* meaning properly not "singer" but simply "player on the *gusle.*" A good many of the singers, he points out, do not accompany themselves on the *gusle.* In a posthumously published work he devotes a brief chapter to epic poetry without instrumental accompaniment (*bez instrumenta*) (1951, 340–42).
[61] Paus. 9.30.3.

gian, a master aulete and composer of both epic and elegiac poetry, but famous above all for the auletic nomes ascribed to him.[62] Three centuries later, Aristophanes spoke of these works for solo aulos as well known, and in the following century both Plato and Aristotle praised their ethical power. According to Aristotle's pupil Aristoxenus, Olympus was believed to have "invented" the Lydian *harmonia* and the enharmonic genus (most often with two quarter tones and a ditone making up the tetrachord).[63]

These last claims show how the Greeks regarded their own musical history. They were ready, sometimes overly ready, to see foreign influences at work. They also insisted on identifying a *prōtos heuretēs,* a "first discoverer," for anything thought significant. The supposition that there once existed a virtuoso aulete and composer called Olympus does not go beyond the bounds of possibility; but if we concern ourselves with this, we are missing the point. For Hellenic Greeks, and for those who came after them, the name "Olympus" represented a means of grouping under a single, immediately identifiable concept certain important and incontestable aspects of the early development of Greek music. The common denominator becomes evident at once. Phrygia, the Lydian *harmonia,* aulos playing, and solo aulos music (thought by later Greeks to mark the beginning of their instrumental music): these patently reflect the early, dimly recalled importation into mainland Greece of new or supposedly new instruments, scales, and forms of composition. Greek writers knew that the innovations had come from Asia Minor, particularly from Phrygia, around 700 B.C.

The shorthand designation for all this was "Olympus." His name represents not only oriental influence but, far more important, the new symbiosis between a hellenized Ionia and the Greek mainland. The individual figure of Olympus, like that of Orpheus, remains shadowy, far closer to myth than to any credible reality. The new age of Greek music had to emerge from what he symbolized: relation-

---

[62] The recent attempt (Michaelides 1978, "Olympus") to distinguish between two figures bearing this name, one legendary and the other historical, has no warrant. Winnington-Ingram's brief comments with regard to Olympus (1970, sec. 10) provide a corrective; see now also West 1992b, 331.

[63] Aristoxenus: ps.-Plut. *Mus.* 10–11, 1134f-1135a; 15, 1136c; cf. 29, 1141b; 33, 1143b.

ships between East and West, between the colonies founded in Asia Minor and the homeland from which the colonists had come.

According to legend, the aulos and the Phrygian *harmonia* had been discovered by the Phrygians Marsyas and Hyagnis, while the particular contribution made by Olympus was the auletic nome, a ritual work for aulos alone. *Nomos,* which may basically denote what is habitual, refers to usage, custom, law, or melody. It does not occur with reference to music until the close of the seventh century. For later Greeks, it denoted a traditional melody or melodic form, widely known and widely venerated. Poets were still ascribing certain auletic nomes to Olympus in the late fifth century. At the very least, he seems to stand for the infusion of some lasting strength at the initial stage of a native musical tradition.

As the beliefs about Olympus celebrate the role of the aulos during the "Dark Age" and afterward, so the *Homeric Hymn to Hermes* tells how the precocious godling, while he was yet newborn, fashioned the first tortoiseshell lyre. The poem is not early; it may come from as late a period as the opening decades of the sixth century. The description of lyre making is straightforward as far as it goes, with several unusual details. In part at least, it appears to be an attempt to describe a "primitive" lyre, though the undertaking has perhaps been compromised by the inclusion of sophisticated touches. A précis and partial translation of the central passage (4.20–56) follow.

> No sooner had Hermes leaped from the womb of his mother, Maia, than he sprang out of his cradle and made for the cave where Apollo's cattle were kept. As he entered it, he came upon a mountain tortoise (20–24); the encounter seemed to him a good omen for his rascally enterprise (30). He promised to make the creature a singer in death, and this promise he proceeded to fulfill. When he had reduced it to an empty carapace, he "cut reed stalks to the proper length and fixed them in place, running them through the shell along the back; and all around [the front] he stretched cowhide. . . . Then he inserted the arms, fitted a crossbar onto the pair of them, and stretched [over it] seven strings made of sheep-gut.[64] When he had made it, . . . he tested [each string]

---

[64] Arms: *pēcheis* (50), the correct technical term for the arms of a lyre. Originally they were the horns of an animal. The term for these, *kerata,* is rightly avoided here: Hermes has not yet stolen Apollo's cattle!

in turn with a plectrum. Under his touch, the lyre made a fearful clatter. The god sang melodiously to its accompaniment, trying improvisations, in the manner of young men at festivals who taunt each other."

The work involved in making a modern reproduction of a tortoiseshell lyre confirms that the author of the *Hymn* has described the essentials of the process rather well.[65] The function of the lengths of reed (47: *donakas*), which may not be immediately apparent, is to support the stretched hide surface. This instrument appears to have a certain kinship with the seven-stringed lyre shown on a fragment found at Old Smyrna; and probably it was from the less distant parts of Asia Minor that the practice of using additional strings came to the Greek mainland. The author of the *Hymn* first calls Hermes' discovery a *chelus,* literally "tortoise" (53, also 242); but he goes on to speak of it as a *phorminx* (64), *lurē* (423), or *kitharis* (499, 509, 515).[66]

Though Hermes might be called the first musical prodigy, he proves to be something less than an instinctive master of the lyre. Naturally, and very properly, mastery is reserved for Apollo; it has been well said that in his case "the learning was immediate."[67] The poet has neatly brought out the contrast between the two. Unfortunately, his intended effect may be lost when an editor (Hugh G. Evelyn-White) or translator (Apostolos Athanassakis), unaware of the original intent, follows an incorrect reading. But the same, or almost the same, formulaic phrases referring to a performance on the lyre describe both gods here; and Apollo is given little opportunity to display his new skill (499–503; also 509–10, which is not formulaic). As the subject of this hymn, Hermes continues to have the leading role. In the course of his playing, which becomes increasingly less clumsy and more confident, points of technique emerge. Even with a master performer, a plectrum on gut strings produces a sound that we, unlike the Greeks, do not find particularly pleasant. Should it be used inexpertly, the resulting rattle and clatter can be fearsome (54:

[65] Roberts 1974, 76–91. Plumley (1966) gives an exemplary account of the building of a *tanbur,* the Sudanese bowl lyre.

[66] Wegner (1949, 38–39) discusses the difficulties involved in using the term *chelus.*

[67] Allen, Halliday, and Sikes 1980, 341, on *dedaōs* (510).

smerdaleon). This same passage contains the first reference to impro-
vising lyrics (55). The lyre may figure later in the poem as well, since
amboladēn (425) could refer to preluding.[68]

The story of Hermes' discovery may be an old Arcadian myth,
mentioned in the second century A.D. by Pausanias; this hymn gives it
an archaizing treatment.[69] The account contains many references to
the way a lyre is held and carried. Greek literature has nothing comparable, and they reveal details that are missing from the rather for-
malized depictions provided by vase painters. Even the aulos makes a
brief appearance: Apollo, before he is given the lyre, speaks of con-
sorting with the Muses. Their concern, he declares, is dance and song
and "the loud, lovely sound of the aulos" (451–52). A poet who
considered the double reed pipes newcomers to the Greek mainland
would hardly have made them the original instrument of the Muses.

Finally, the poem is charming and unique for the encomium with
which Hermes prefaces his gift of the lyre to Apollo. He calls it
suitable for banquet, dance, or revel, "a source of delight both by
night and by day. Whoever makes inquiry of it skillfully . . . , to him
it speaks and teaches him every manner of thing that pleases the
mind, since it is easily played with gentle (?) touch and shuns painful
drudgery. But if anyone out of ignorance begins by making violent
inquiry of it, for him it sounds nothing but false and random dis-
cords" (482–88). Taken as a whole, the speech constitutes the first
encomium of this kind, and one of the most beautiful. It begins the
long tradition of the lyre as boon companion and giver of delight, a
tradition still alive in German lyric poetry of the nineteenth century.
But it also portrays the instrument as teacher, and this, regrettably
perhaps, is a path not taken: here the tribute stands alone.

Save for Achilles, the amateur, none of the musicians whom we
have seen are figures of power. The rest fill modest places in their
societies, beginning with the Cycladic harpers. These figurines served
as grave offerings, a fact that suggests that the actual musicians were
retainers. Although a later lyre player or aulete might wear distinctive

---

[68] The adverb *amboladēn* is usually translated "in the manner of a prelude." On
anaballesthai, apparently used of instrumental preluding in Homer, and on the adverb
amblēdēn, see above, n. 32.

[69] Wegner 1949, 37.

and often handsome robes, such clothing is sacral. Those who wear it are providing the accompaniment required for the proper performance of a rite. During it, they have importance; their status apart from the ceremonies remains unknown.

Secular music makes an early appearance. In Homeric epic, singing to one's own accompaniment has an accepted place of honor. Hesiod's version of didactic epic seems to signalize eventual abandonment of the phorminx, or concert lyre, as a means of accompanying this genre. Attention turns to the *lura,* the lyre proper, although at first its designation under that name is not firmly established. Another genre now comes into being, or perhaps we ought rather to say that it makes its first recorded appearance. This new genre, lyric poetry, has strong associations with the kithara, Hellenic successor of the phorminx, as well as with the smaller, simpler *lura.*

{3}

Early Lyric Poets

Lyric poetry was by definition accompanied.[1] The instrument was sometimes the lyre, and at other times the aulos; we cannot always be sure which was employed in a given instance. The two earliest extant lines of lyric poetry present just such a problem. They date from 750 B.C. or not much later, and are part of a processional hymn attributed to Eumelus of Corinth. To sing it, a male chorus was sent from Messenia in the southern Peloponnesus to Apollo's festival, held on his sacred island of Delos. Pausanias quotes the two lines: "For he of Ithome took pleasure in a Muse / pure and wearing the sandals of the free [or "of freedom"]."[2]

[1] Whether elegy, lyric's companion form, had an instrumental accompaniment in ordinary use is disputed. It seems that auloi might be played on ceremonial occasions. West (1974, 12–14, 18–19; 1992b, 25) argues that the aulos commonly accompanied elegiac verses at symposia and revels; so Huchzermeyer 1931, 29. Campbell (1964) reviews the evidence, coming to a different conclusion; compare his treatment (64) of Theognis 239–43 with West's (1992b, 25). Iambic poetry was seldom accompanied.
At first glance, references to music making in both lyric and elegy may seem to indicate how a given poem was performed, but they do not actually reveal anything. Campbell (1964) has demonstrated this carefully and at length for Theognis and other writers. See also Archilochus frags. 120, 121 West (= 76, 77 Diehl, Edmonds): the poet describes himself as leading off the paean "to the sound of the aulos" (*pros aulon*), though Athenaeus 180e quotes this line to illustrate his statement that *exarchein* is a term peculiar to lyre accompaniment. Apparently we have here the exception that tests the rule. On *exarchein* and the origins of tragedy, see Arist. *Poet.* 1449a11. The only significant contribution concerning music making comes from Ion of Chios, who competed as a tragic poet at Athens 450–425 B.C.
[2] Paus. 4.33.3. West (1992b, 15n.8) questions whether Delos had such importance nationally as early as the eighth century. He conjectures that the lines "may go back to

Ithome (*Ithōmē*) was a Messenian citadel just north of the capital, Messene itself. When these lines were composed, the freedom of all Messenia was endangered. The people of Ithome worshipped Zeus Ithomatas as their patron; they had celebrated him with a yearly festival, a musical competition now evidently interrupted.

In later times, at least, an aulete furnished the accompaniment for a processional. It is conceivable but unlikely that on this occasion a kithara was used by the poet-composer. At Sparta a century later, around 630 B.C., the poet Alcman was to speak of Apollo as playing the aulos. Together with lyre and kithara, it had a place in the ritual and social usages of this age. As yet it had neither gained general recognition, nor had it suffered any consequent hostile reaction of the kind that would come in the fifth century.

"Muse" in the lines quoted by Pausanias is "music"; in a comparable substitution, Plato was to use "lyre" (*lura*) of poetry accompanied on it.[3] What matters is that this couplet, from the shadowy beginnings of Greek lyric, shows a poet-composer characterizing music through the language of moral and political ideals. His words take us into a world profoundly different from that of Homer or Hesiod. Music now has certain acknowledged associations; they will remain with it throughout the classical period. Concepts of modal and rhythmic ethos can grow quickly from such a seedbed.

Considered from a broader perspective, as a moment in the history of Greek music, Eumelus' processional deserves more than passing notice. The great yearly festival at Delos was one of the chief cultural events of the Aegean world. The island became a meeting place for Greeks from Ionia as well as from the mainland and the many islands. A cosmopolitan gathering, it was made still more so through the presence of skilled professionals in music. These men cannot have failed to learn from each other. On a more modest scale, the same would have been true of the chorus members; for nonprofessionals who appeared at such a gathering must have undergone hard training. We may conjecture that they went back to their homes and accustomed observances with a larger consciousness of singing and playing. A part of this new realization was awareness of common ele-

---

the time of the Messenian revolt from Sparta, *c.* 660." The dating does not affect the significance of these lines for the history of Greek music.

[3] Pl. *Leg.* 809c4, e6.

ments, actualized or potential. Out of this experience a common musical language developed rapidly among Greek-speaking peoples. Distinctive local traits were gradually eliminated, and eventually virtuosic excesses began to be displayed.

Until the fourth century B.C., the entire process was carried on without a single musical setting being preserved in written notation. The Greeks remembered, or thought they remembered, various melodies hallowed by tradition. One type, the *skolion,* had a continuing life, thanks to the singing customary at men's drinking parties. Another, the *nomos* or nome, kept a hold on the popular imagination and at the same time became a highly developed art form, cultivated by professionals and performed in competitions at the national games. There were many others. The characteristic common to all these melodic types was their general nature. Singers and instrumentalists applied them to a wide range of circumstances—and apparently to a variety of texts as well, in the case of *skolia.* The poet-composer on the other hand, composed for a specific occasion; he felt no need to insure the preservation of his work, especially since the text remained dominant. Nothing like a score existed. Written systems of notation did come into being, but it is not clear that they were earlier than the East Ionic alphabet on which they are chiefly based. This alphabet was officially adopted at Athens only in 403 B.C. The entire question is much disputed.

Except for the lines from Eumelus' processional, written evidence for the history of Greek music first appears in the sixth and seventh centuries B.C. As J. B. Bury pointed out, this period "is inevitably distorted and placed in a false perspective through the strange limitations of our knowledge. For at that time . . . the cities of the western coast of Asia Minor formed the most important and enlightened part of the Hellenic world, and of those cities in the days of their greatness we have only some disconnected glimpses. . . . The false impression is produced that the history of Hellas in the seventh and sixth centuries consisted merely or mainly of the histories of Sparta and Athens and their immediate neighbours."[4]

In point of fact, what we do know or can reasonably infer about the music of poet-composers from their poetry helps to right the balance.

[4] Bury 1945, ix.

Nevertheless, it remains true that credible data from this time are rare. One would not think so, reading the claims that Hellenistic and Graeco-Roman commentators so confidently advance for the founding fathers of Greek music. But such claims represent wishful thinking that seeks to satisfy a number of aims, above all the creation of an aetiology adequate to account for changes in instruments. Moreover, local traditions were uncritically embraced, and received Graeco-Roman views on music were read back into a far-distant past. For knowledge of that past, nothing was surely available other than the *Iliad* and the *Odyssey,* together with a few references to singing and dancing in the genuine portions of the Hesiodic corpus. We cannot tell, however, the nature or extent of the poetic or other evidence, now lost, that may also have existed in antiquity.

The materials to be considered here are principally the relevant poetic texts. Not infrequently, real or imagined textual problems complicate the study of these texts. Even more puzzling are the frequent ambiguities. Thus the nouns and suffixes *chordē* and *-chordos, tonos* and *-tonos,* may refer either to notes or to strings. One encounters also the tendency to state a point by indirection through the use of metaphor and, often in the case of Old Comedy, through double entendres. These may follow each other with confusing rapidity. Often they involve an obscene level of reference, which the Victorians ignored or euphemized; not even such excellent and forthright scholars as K. J. Dover and J. Henderson have adequately revealed the subtext. Still, the texts are essentially all that we have. When we go outside them—in part because of these very problems—the written word must be our point of departure.

For practical purposes, Greek lyric begins with Terpander, a native of Lesbos. The date of his birth may be earlier than the Ithomaeans' visit to Delos, in 730 B.C. The early historian Hellanicus, a contemporary of Herodotus, states that he won a victory (surely as kitharode) in the musical competition at the first Carneian games held in Sparta, which took place during the 26th Olympiad, 676–673 B.C.[5] With his arrival, Sparta first became notable for music. This era of cultural preeminence was the most striking result, among many, of musical influences from across the Aegean. The musicians of Lesbos, which

[5] The sources are Hellanicus and the Carneian victor lists cited in Ath. 635d.

lay only a few miles off the Ionian coast, were receptive to innovations from the inland regions of Asia Minor, especially from Phrygia and Lydia. Pindar reflects their attitude. Terpander, he maintains, "invented" the barbitos, a lyre with unusually long strings, upon hearing a similarly low-pitched instrument "at the feasts of the Lydians." There is no need to accept the belief itself. Writing two centuries later, Pindar was merely passing on a tradition that he had no occasion to question.[6]

One of the half dozen surviving fragments generally accepted as the work of Terpander may deal directly with a major development in the capacities of the concert lyre: "We will cease our liking for four-voiced [*tetragērus*] song, and make new hymns sound in your praise on a seven-toned [*heptatonos*] phorminx."[7] We today are aware that lyres with seven strings had been played more than half a millennium before Terpander; he was not. Knossos and Pylos formed no part of the world he knew, a world in which the traditional phorminx usually had four strings. The vase painting of the Old Smyrna lyre, with its unmistakable complement of seven strings, comes from the very period of Terpander's floruit. It corroborates the poet's claim— without, of course, making him the first to use a seven-stringed instrument. In this instance, facts outside the poem establish the meanings of *tetragērus* and *heptatonos*, which in themselves are ambiguous.[8]

Now that the appearance of a seven-stringed lyre has been attested

---

[6] Pindar frag. 110a Bowra, 125 Schroeder. Innovations in music credited to Terpander: West 1992b, 330.

[7] Terpander frag. 6 Campbell. Page (1962, 362) does not believe that any fragments of Terpander's lyrics have survived, with two possible exceptions (*PMG* [*Poctae Melici Graeci*] 697, 698). Neither is the one discussed here.

[8] All of the foregoing depends on the assumption, usually made, that Terpander's statement is a general one. While this seems the most likely interpretation, it cannot simply be taken for granted. The late geographer Strabo, who preserved these two hexameter lines (p. 618 Kramer), did make the assumption. West (1971, 307–8) has suggested that they may instead refer simply to a shift from a melodic type (*nomos*) requiring four notes to another that required seven. He remarks that ps.-Plut. *Mus.* 4 1132d ascribes to Terpander a *tetraoidios nomos*, taken to mean "a nome of four notes" (so LSJ, where the chapter reference should be 4, not 2). But this definition is conjectural and unconvincing: *-aoidios* ought not to refer to notes, and it does not appear with any of the other numerical prefixes. Much more probably it denotes an *aoidē*, "song" in the sense of "section," and the true parallel is with *-kephalos* (head) in the well-known *nomos polukephalos*, a composition having many sections.

both in art and in poetry, it is time to raise the question of scales. And so we must attempt to go back to the tuning of the simpler, Geometric phorminx. West has conjectured that its four strings gave varying sequences that incorporate the incomplete scales listed by Aristides Quintilianus, who proclaimed their extreme antiquity (without offering proof) and identified them with the *harmoniai* discussed in the *Republic*.[9] There is another possibility: the four strings might have sounded the boundary notes of the two four-note sequences, much later called tetrachords, into which the full heptachord (seven notes) or octave was divided by theoreticians. This framework bore the designation *harmonia,* a term with many meanings. Within an octave scale beginning on A, it would have consisted of A–D and E–A[1]. The concept existed, at any rate, as a part of Pythagorean theory. Whether it fulfilled a more practical role remains unknown; thus far we have no evidence that early scales were built on tetrachords.

Seven strings are another matter. Why seven and not eight?[10] The smaller number might represent a scale that lacked the higher octave note; or it might be one that had this note but omitted some other. On the first possibility, the "framework" *harmonia* would consist of conjunct, not disjunct, tetrachords: not A-D E-A[1] but A-D-G, interlocked on D.[11]

Hellenic theorists proposed the second possibility, a gapped scale, both for Olympus and for Terpander.[12] To the former they ascribed the "invention" of the enharmonic genus. If we begin on E, this would give the sequence E *E* F A B *B* C E[1]. (The use of italics represents a rise in pitch of about a quarter tone.) Two notes are

[9] West 1981, 117–18, highly speculative (see now West 1992b, 328); Aristid. Quint. *De musica* 1.9, p. 18.2–10 Winnington-Ingram (hereafter W-I in references) (followed by a listing of the *harmoniai* sequences in Alypian notation). Pl. *Rep.* 398e1–2, 9–10, 399a3–4 (quoted by Aristides).

[10] For the sake of brevity, symbological factors are left out of account here. See Cirlot 1991, xviii, 210, 240, 257, 302, 333 (on seven); cf. 172, 193, 233–34 (on eight, which has far less significance as symbol).

[11] The term "tetrachord" must not be read back into the thinking and practice of Hellenic musicians. In this connection, it may not be mere coincidence that vase painters sometimes show the strings of a lyre or kithara in what appear to be two groups consisting of four and three, with the larger group nearer the performer's body. See Paquette 1984, 146.

[12] Aristoxenus is taken here as the source for ps.-Plut. *Mus.* 11 and 28. For a later and more circumstantial account, see ps.-Arist. *Pr.* 19.32, 920a14–18.

added, *E* and *B;* two others, G and D, are omitted. Supposedly, Terpander added the upper octave note to the ancient *harmonia* and was the first to do so but omitted another note so as to keep the number of strings at seven. The absent note was *Tritē,* "Third"; it is the third one as we count upward from the central note, *Mesē* or "Middle."[13]

To illustrate the connection between *andreia* and *mousikē,* Plutarch cites two lines of Terpander as rightly associating manly bravery with music.[14] Sparta, says the poet, is a place "where the spearpoint of the young men and the clear-voiced [high-voiced?] Muse both flourish." By way of introduction, Plutarch mentions the poetry of the Spartans and their use of aulos marching tunes when troops went into battle. Normally, "music" will render *mousikē* well enough in a writer of the first century A.D., but not here. The poet is describing the salient aspects of Spartan culture in his day—and, of course, under his influence. Although valor in war comes first, "the Muse" is linked with it and complements it.[15] *Mousa* here stands for music and poetry in all their manifestations, as essential cultural expressions of the city-state.

The process of laying the state's foundations is completed in the second line: *Dika,* "Justice," flourishes among the Spartans along with martial spirit. From Hesiod onward, the poets personified justice; Aeschylus even credited it with an altar. In Terpander, the reference has a public sense, as a code of civil law; it also has a military sense, to be found in the "broad streets" of Sparta.

Justice is also "champion of noble deeds" (*kalōn epitarrhothos ergōn*). The epithet here, *epitarrhothos,* comes from the Homeric poems, where it regularly describes gods who come to the defense of men in battle. Homer does not use *kalos* (noble, excellent) of deeds, as his successors so often do. Yet in the *Iliad* the word that Terpander uses here, *ergon,* denotes almost exclusively what is accomplished by war. Having inherited the vocabulary of epic, Sparta's poet has made it

[13] Winnington-Ingram (1928, 85) has suggested that "the complete diatonic series was known comparatively early, and used concurrently with less complete scales," perhaps non-Hellenic.

[14] Frag. 6 Edmonds, cited in Plut. *Lyc.* 21. Page (1962, 363; note on *PMG* 698) questions the attribution to Terpander.

[15] The particles *te . . . kai,* which link two nouns closely, show the intimate connection between *aichmē* and *Mousa.* Edmonds's "both . . . and," however, is too strong. Smyth 1968, p. 667, sec. 2974, warns against this translation; cf. LSJ s.v. *te,* A.I.1.

describe the civil as well as the military dimensions of his adopted city. Moreover, he has done so with such skill that the two almost fuse into one. This is not the Sparta that our awareness of later Greek history has made familiar. It is real nonetheless, the first center of musical activity in Greece.

About forty years later, the impression so briefly given by Terpander recurs, expanded to a remarkable degree, in the lines of another outsider who brought his skills to Sparta, the poet Alcman. One tradition makes him an Ionian from the great Lydian capital, Sardis. Late writers credit him with little in the way of musical advances; he seems to have been a continuator rather than an innovator. Terpander's comparison must be in his mind when he says: "To play the kithara admirably / rivals [skill in wielding] the steel."[16] In the original, the line order is reversed, so that a climactic emphasis falls on the mention of expert musicianship. As Basil Gildersleeve suggested, the use of definite article with infinitive in *to . . . kitharisdēn,* "to play the kithara," may have its old overtone of contempt. A message would thereby be conveyed to the poet's critics: "This expertise on the kithara that you hold in such low esteem is worth as much as any mastery of weapons."

Alcman is noticeably less specific than his predecessor about the virtues of war. When he speaks of excellence in music, however, he is more specific. This was to be expected, if the late accounts of Sparta's musical history have any credibility. According to them, its first epoch (*katastasis*) began with Terpander; thus he came into a culture centered on military ideals. During the decades that followed, a second epoch was established. So far as we can tell, it had no one leading figure, but instead a succession of skilled musicians, among them the Cretan Thaletas (or Thales) of Gortyn, the Arcadian Clonas of Tegea, and the Ionian Polymnestus of Colophon. We have no poetry by any member of this second group; Alcman was not accounted one of them. Various sources do credit them with having introduced new rhythms, melodic types, and genres. At times, the information is simply misinformation: for example, Clonas was said to have created the first processional. Much of it can only have been

---

[16] Alcman frag. 7 Campbell, *PMG* 41. For *herpei . . . anta,* Campbell (1982b, 219) mentions "confronts" as a possible rendering, but this seems difficult. As he says, Scaliger's conjecture *rhepei,* "prevails," offers an easier solution.

conjecture, produced when the commentator went beyond what would have been obvious from the texts, or even from a mere list of titles.[17] Yet after we have weighed it with all due skepticism, this late comment still seems a fundamentally credible remembrance of a period when poetry and music alike were undergoing rapid development.

It was a time when Sparta did not instinctively reject anything new. The aulos, no novelty there, achieved prominence and showed versatility for the first time under Terpander's successors, especially Clonas. A traditional melodic pattern with or without words, the *nomos* now appeared as a composition sung to aulos accompaniment —the *nomos aulōidikos*. The adjective distinguishes it from the nome performed as an aulos solo, the *nomos aulētikos*. We speak of such nomes as aulodic or auletic. The auletic form was thought to have originated with Olympus. In other words, it had existed from time immemorial. The author of the pseudo-Plutarchian treatise *De musica* devotes a great deal of space to it, and one can hardly doubt that it held a place of honor from a very early period.

Finally, the late accounts of this second notable age of music in Sparta begin to mention briefly mode and genus. Both are said to have been employed or actually invented by Polymnestus, twice identified as a composer of auletic nomes. The *harmoniai* are the basic ones—Dorian, Phrygian, and Lydian; a separate reference to "the *tonos* now called Hypolydian" occurs.[18] Along with this we find a puzzling mention of two intervals, the *eklusis* (three quarter tones) and the *ekbolē* (five quarter tones), known to Graeco-Roman theorists as characterizing the enharmonic genus. The reference merits notice as one more indication of the importance of the aulos, the only instrument on which microtonal intervals could instantly and easily have been produced.

Such was the musical scene of which Alcman became a part. The second epoch at Sparta did not end with him. In the pseudo-Plutarchian *De musica* many others are named, but Alcman is not

[17] The sources are mainly late Hellenic or Hellenistic—Heraclides Ponticus and Aristoxenus, in the pseudo-Plutarchian epitome—but they include as well the fifth-century historian Ephorus, an encyclopedic and well-respected scholar. Clonas, processionals, and the aulodic nome: West 1992b, 333.

[18] Ps.-Plut. *Mus.* 8, 1134b; 29, 1141b. The (presumably) close relationship between Lydian and Hypolydian: Winnington-Ingram 1968, 13 and passim.

mentioned in connection with it. In fact, in the entire *De musica,* he receives no more than a few lines. Though he may have come to Sparta from Lydia, he bears a Greek name: *Alkman,* also *Alkmaōn* in the manuscripts, is the Doric form of the Ionic *Alkmeōn.* His origin may have been either Ionia or the Aeolian territories. He is one of the very few early poets from whom we have appreciably more verse than testimonia. The latter give the impression that he was able to profit from the many and significant reforms carried out by the pioneers, his predecessors or near contemporaries.[19]

Accordingly, Alcman speaks of both principal instruments in a more technical manner than anyone before him. The compound *hupaulein* occurs, for playing an aulos accompaniment. There is also a reference to an aulete who played "a Phrygian tune Cerbesian," that is, from Cerbesus. The added epithet baffles us, but the poet assumed that his hearers would know it. This suggests an audience with some sophistication in musical matters, as does his reported mention of three auletes with Phrygian names.[20]

He identifies himself not with the aulos but with the kithara. It is lyre playing that he singles out as an embodiment of Sparta's musical culture, worthy to be matched against bravery in war, whereas Terpander had spoken in general terms of "the Muse," much as Eumelus had done. Alcman describes himself as *kitharistas,* "kithara player," and perhaps as *hageochoros,* "chorus leader." In the extant fragments of his poetry, he makes hardly any reference to kitharas or lyres; and he merely mentions that puzzling stringed instrument (if such it was), the *magadis.*[21] It was nevertheless as kitharist—and as kitharode,

---

[19] Bowra (1961, 20) speaks of "a burst of musical innovation and invention" that prepared the way for Alcman; Greek name, 18.

[20] *hupaulein: PMG* 37b, 87b Page. Cerbesian aulos melody: *PMG* 126, in Strabo 12.8.21, p. 586 Kramer. The identification of *Kerbēsion* as a tribal name by Kramer is mere conjecture; so the Latin *Berecyntia (tibia),* used as a colorful synonym for *Phrygius,* is derived from the Greek *Berekuntos,* a mountain in Phrygia that was sacred to Cybele. Barker pointed out in a letter that retaining the MSS reading *to* could make possible the translation "a Phrygian tune, the Cerbesian [one]"—"the one from Cerbesus." Phrygian auletes Sambas, Adon, Telos: *PMG* 109, cited in Ath. 624b.

[21] Alcman: *PMG* 38.2, 48, 101. The reading *hageochoros* is a conjecture, omitted in LSJ and not recognized by Page. For line 84 in the Louvre *partheneion (PMG* 1), Campbell and Page (whose text Bowra follows), however, have *kai telos. chorostatis.* The *chorostatis* is "the conductor and leader of the chorus" while the singing is going on (Bowra 1961, 49). Not found elsewhere, the term refers to Hagesichora, described

necessarily—that he trained a chorus of wellborn girls. He speaks of himself in different ways, sometimes directly, sometimes through a third-person reference, or by having others speak of him. The last of these methods comes into play when he appears as kitharist, in a one-line fragment. His speakers identify themselves: they are the maidens of his maiden songs (*partheneia*).[22]

A single example of this form has been preserved, the so-called Louvre *partheneion*. The text goes on at some length, though it is incomplete and mutilated, and at times it deals with music. "I am a girl," the singer declares, "but I scream to no purpose like an owl from the rooftop," though she longs to please the goddess—Artemis, or possibly a divinized Helen—at whose festival the choral and orchestic competition is being held. What follows shows that the self-criticism has to do with tone quality. Through contrast, it prepares the way for praise of the chief dancer and singer, Hagesichora.[23]

Seldom acknowledged, this factor of vocal timbre complicates any attempt to grasp the nature of ancient Greek song. The fragment in which Alcman claims to know the *nomoi* of all the birds—meaning their characteristic songs—may be relevant. This claim seems closely related to another: when he combined words and music, Alcman declares, he "strung together" the cries of partridges.[24] To name these birds he uses not the usual term *perdix* but *kakkabis,* which suggests a clattering torrent of musical speech. Also, the immediately preceding adjective *geglōssamenos* clearly was intended to convey more than the vague meaning "tuneful," which the lexicon gives for this very instance. Nor is there any reason to accept J. M. Edmonds's statement that the poet is "jestingly praising the choir at his own expense." Artemis Orthia was assuredly a bird-goddess, and the members of Alcman's choir compare themselves to birds (the owl or swan) or

---

earlier (*PMG* 1.44) as *ha klenna choragos,* "the celebrated chorus leader." The role of the leading girl dancer as a kind of assistant director helping the choregus, who provided aulos accompaniment, is discussed in Calame 1977, 1:137; on *chorostatēs,* 1:105 n. 27.

[22] *PMG* 38.

[23] Comparison to an owl: *PMG* 1.85–88. On Hagesichora, see above, n. 21.

[24] Bird song: *PMG* 40. The cries of partridges: frag. 39.3 Campbell, Page. The text is not wholly certain in either instance.

actually take the name of a bird (*peleiades,* "doves"; also the Pleiades of the night sky).[25]

In one of his most poignant lyrics, the poet tells his maiden choristers: "My limbs can no longer carry me."[26] He longs passionately to be a *kērulos,* a bird of spring that fearlessly skims the wave tops with the halcyon. This bird, far better known, is a creature of fable; the Hellenistic anecdote about young halcyons bearing the aged ones on their backs in flight must be deemed no less fabulous. The lines of Alcman that it introduces do nothing to substantiate it. They do offer grounds for a reasonable inference: in early Sparta at least, composers of choral lyric were dancers as well as singers. They taught by example, until the weakness of age kept them from taking an active part in performances.

Here the meter is the six-foot epic line; but the four verses, which are complete, contain not a single spondee. The purely dactylic form, which cannot be found even in the *Homeric Hymns,* suggested to Bowra that possibly "these lines were sung in a more true sense than were the Homeric Hymns, which may have been merely intoned or even recited."[27] Melodic complexity can hardly have characterized Alcman's preludes, for dancing singers must not be expected to cope with a demanding vocal line. It is both possible and reasonable, however, to conjecture the stirring of a feeling for modality in a period of such new and intense musical activity. Whatever its precise nature, Dorian music must have exerted a natural predominance in Sparta, greatest of the Dorian city-states. Alcman's predecessor, Thaletas of Gortyn, had come from the region of Crete colonized by Dorians; he took a leading part in the city's second epoch of musical growth.

Alcman himself says nothing to indicate that he was such a leader. Apparently he used and enjoyed innovations already introduced by others. While the result charms us with a mood of happiness that no other lyric poet ever matched, it tells us little about music at Sparta. The clues that he offers principally concern vocal quality. He values a clear tone, high-pitched and also enchantingly sweet. This charac-

[25] On *Peleādes* (1.60), see Campbell 1982b, 205, and Bowra 1961, 56–57. "No part of the poem," says Campbell, " . . . has been more diversely construed."

[26] *PMG* 26.

[27] Bowra 1961, 25.

teristic of high pitch he renders through two closely related adjectives, *ligus* and *liguros*. Homer had often used them; the second occurs twice in *Odyssey* 12, describing the song with which the Sirens, as Circe claims, "bewitch" mariners. For Alcman, these deadly singers are goddesses; and in singing no mortal, not even Hagesichora, may command equal respect. The Muse herself is called not only *ligeia* but a *ligeia Seirēn*. A separate epithet, *meligarus,* literally "honey-voiced," expresses the sweetness of tone achieved by his choristers.[28]

Alcman's unusual interest in the quality of the singing voice provides hints of what his maiden songs may have sounded like. To go farther might seem flatly impossible; yet perhaps a way can be found in the accounts given by the ethnomusicologist Alan Lomax and his associates in *Folk Song Style and Culture* (1968). Their research, carried out with remarkable thoroughness and precision over a worldwide range of examples, confirms the presence of a strong mutual relationship between the two components of the work's title. One aspect of this relationship involves tone and the attitude that the culture takes toward premarital sexual activity on the part of women. Where very strict sanctions are applied, as in the south of Spain, vocal delivery is "piercing, high-pitched, squeezed, [and] narrow." Where such sanctions are mild, as in the extreme north of the same country, choirs produce a fresh, relaxed sound (viii; see further 194–97). More broadly, a contrast appears between the central and eastern European style, with its well-blended polyphony and clear vocalizing, and that of the Mediterranean area, where we find florid solo singing and high-pitched, nasal delivery (101). "Mediterranean Europe," say Lomax and Edwin E. Erickson, "the ancient center of the Greco-Roman metropolis, . . . shares as much of the Old High Culture as it does that of Europe" (96). Wellborn Spartan girls in Alcman's day unques-

---

[28] The *ligurē aoidē* of the Sirens: *Od.* 12.44, 183. Alcman: 1.98 Edmonds *siai* (Laconian, for *theai*), "goddesses," of the Sirens; 8.1 *Mōsa ligeia,* as in Terpander 6.1; 14.1, the Muse as *ligeia Seirēn;* 50.2, *lig'* (*ligu*), adv. with *aeidesthai,* "sing." In frag. 82, *ligukorton* (*kor-* for *kro-*) is used of a stringed instrument—not necessarily the lyre. The mention of *hendeka,* "eleven," in PMG 1.98 is taken by West (1992b, 224) to refer to the Sirens, representing ideal notes. Accordingly, he interprets it as being actually a veiled reference to a combination of tetrachords. But the meaning of this passage is much disputed: see Campbell 1982b, 211, for a summary of the problem. On Terpander 6.1, see Smyth 1963, 170; he cites many references for *ligus* and several for *liguros.* In his view, both terms denote a high pitch. *meligarus:* PMG 26.1.

tionably lived under strict constraints, which their singing may well have reflected. This conjecture could apply to other cultural and musical contexts—to Sappho and her circle, and indeed to many other situations. Its relevance to the Louvre *partheneion,* however, may be particularly worth considering.

If we have made the correct textual choices and interpretations in dealing with this poet's Louvre maiden song, it may be said to show his use of an assistant chorus-trainer. The separate dactylic prelude acknowledges his physical weakness, which may have been the cause. According to a well-known anecdote, Sophocles abandoned acting because his voice lacked sufficient strength. Albin Lesky rejects the story as aetiological. "In reality," he contends, "the increasing demands on the actor's technique enforced this separation of function."[29] The case may have been much the same for Alcman. It would be an indication of the sophisticated nature of musical life at Sparta during that remarkable interim of pleasure, enjoyed in peace, between a period of war making and one of economic austerity.

Much information, important but often difficult to fix with precision, has come down to us concerning a poet-composer who achieved prominence several decades after Alcman. This remarkable figure was Arion, from the city of Methymna on Lesbos. Herodotus calls him the most eminent kitharode of his day and the first known composer of dithyrambs, choral hymns to Dionysus. According to the historian, Arion gave this type of poetry its name and taught it to choruses at Corinth; there he passed most of his life, except for a profitable concert tour of Italy and Sicily.[30] Johannes Diaconus, a commentator of unknown date, notes a statement from a source far older even than Herodotus, the *Elegies* of Solon. On any reckoning, the man who founded Athenian democracy in 594 B.C. must be counted among Arion's near contemporaries. Johannes states that Solon ascribed to Arion "the first performance [*drama*] of tragedy (?)."[31] Both Pindar and Aristotle link Arion and Corinth with the origins of dithyramb and tragedy.

---

[29] Lesky 1966, 273.

[30] Arion as performer and composer: Hdt. 1.23; his concert tour, 1.24.1. Arion as kitharode and his supposed connection with the origin of the dithyramb: West 1992b, 339.

[31] Pickard-Cambridge 1962; text and translation, 98; discussion, 99–100.

It would not be useful to go into the endlessly disputed problems associated with these other references. We may conjecture that Arion gave some degree of formal shape to the ritual cries that constituted the *dithurambos* known to Archilochus. Thereby he furnished the early composers of Attic tragedy with models of choral lyric, the first to come out of the Peloponnesus.

Herodotus describes the great singer performing a well-known kitharodic nome, the *nomos orthios* (high-pitched), when he was about to be killed at sea for his wealth. Certain details receive emphasis: he dressed himself completely in his singing robes, and after he had sung and played the nome through from beginning to end, he leapt into the sea still wearing them—a weight that would drag down any swimmer. But a dolphin brought him safe to land: the happy ending is the most familiar part of the story.[32]

What concerns us here is something that may have gone unnoticed: the solemn, even ritual nature of the kitharode's actions. At times, Greeks of later centuries associated the "high-pitched" nome with a sense of exaltation. That sense pervades the incident; Herodotus, who did not usually treat professional musicians with respect, takes care that it should do so. One cannot dissociate from the telling some factor, however elusive, of ethos. Other nonliterate cultures, including that of the North American Indian, are familiar with the performance of a death song in full regalia; for the Greeks, this story captures a rare moment.[33]

Like Terpander, Arion came originally from Lesbos, where both the dialect and the music of the Aeolian peoples attained their highest, most distinctive form. We know of no contributions to the island's cultural life by these poet-composers. In this respect, they contrast strongly with two fellow islanders, Alcaeus and Sappho, active around 600 B.C. Both were aristocrats (he certainly, she probably), and political change—defeat, exile, triumphant restoration—affected the lives of both. Politics never enters Sappho's poetry; for Alcaeus it was a natural theme, one among many.

[32] Hdt. 1.24.2–6.

[33] No parallel will be found until the later fifth century: the characters of tragedy utter a lyric lament in the face of death. Such laments are characteristic of Sophocles and especially of Euripides; in Aeschylus' *Agamemnon,* Cassandra's interchanges with the chorus foreshadow them.

All four show how choral lyric, which spoke with a public voice, had yielded to monody (*monōidia,* literally "singing alone") and to the expression of individual feeling during the seventh century. For the first time (as many believe), we have the sense of listening to a specific person, when we read the savage diatribes and unrestrained laments composed by the Parian poet Archilochus around the middle of the seventh century.

Even in choral lyric, the seeming divisions among speakers throughout Alcman's maiden song were a surprising innovation. By the century's end, however, solo song was becoming established as an independent subgenre of lyric. Two factors aided its growth: the strength of folk song on Lesbos and (as it seems to us, at least) the willingness of its educated, aristocratic poet–composers to draw upon that strength. Ionia, only a few miles away, apparently did not exert such influence.

D. A. Campbell usefully summarizes the differences between these two kinds of lyric: "Solo song, or monody, differed from choral lyric poetry in the less formal circumstances of its performance, in its metrical form and in its language. Whereas the units of choral poetry were the long strophe, antistrophe (repeating the rhythm of the strophe) and epode, and the metrical patterns were complex, solo song used short repeated stanzas and simpler metres; and the monodists for the most part composed in their own dialect, Aeolic in Sappho and Alcaeus, Ionic in Anacreon, whereas the writers of choral lyric used an artificial language with a strong Doric element."[34] Campbell also emphasizes the convivial element in the poetry of Alcaeus. Most of it, he believes, was sung and played at the symposium. Both Sappho and Alcaeus are associated with the low-pitched barbitos; Alcaeus, however, mentions it only once, as "having a share in the symposium" (*pedechōn sumposiōn*). Similarly, the old terms *kitharis* and *kitharizdein* occur only once in his extant verses, as does the name of the many-stringed *pēktis* (Aeolic *paktis*), traditionally credited to Sappho.[35] Poet–composers who were lyric in the literal sense of that

[34] Campbell 1982a, 1:x; on the convivial element (below), x.

[35] References to music in Alcaeus: *pedechōn sumposiōn* 70.2 Campbell, Lobel-Page (hereafter L-P); *barmos* 70.3 Campbell, D12.3 L-P; *kitharis* 41B.15 Campbell, B9.15 L-P; *kitharisd[ein* 38B.3 Campbell (erroneous interpretation as "lyre"), B6b.3 L-P; *p]aktidi* 36.5 Campbell, B4.5 L-P.

term had no need to labor the obvious by calling attention to the lyre. Alcaeus says nothing about the technical aspects of performance or poem; such matters do not seem to have interested him.

Alcaeus' passionate concern with fighting and political power contrasts with Sappho's quiet life, which occasioned comment even in antiquity. She is famous for the privateness of her emotions, and at times an intimate setting will call forth some mention of music: "Abanthis, I bid you take the *paktis* and sing of Gonggula, the lovely one for whom desire once again flutters your heart."[36] As a woman, however, she did not have the opportunity to create poetry for the *sumposia,* which so often provided Alcaeus with an occasion— sometimes even for political verse. This fact must be taken into account when the range and nature of her themes come under consideration. The situation had one paradoxical result: her poetry could celebrate public festivities, through epithalamia for real or imagined weddings. A late papyrus lists the first lines or opening phrases of ten such wedding odes. Four have to do with music: "[Sing of] the bride," "When songs [please?] the mind," "Hearing a clear [*liguran*] song," and "Laying aside the lyre."[37]

Many of Sappho's best-known and most charming poems are epithalamia; yet the one detailed account of music making connected with a wedding does not come from this category. It forms part of a long, well-preserved description of the joyous preparations made at Troy while Hector and his groomsmen were bringing Andromache from Thebae. Aulos, kithara, and clappers (*krotala*) are mentioned. Maidens sing a "holy song," and men raise the "high-pitched nome" (here *orthion,* for the more usual *nomos orthios*) to Apollo, while the older women utter joyful ritual cries.[38] Most of these details come from Homer; clappers and high-pitched nome, however, do not, and the aulos appears but once in the two epics, as an alien intruder.

Elsewhere among the generally fragmentary remains of Sappho's poetry, musical terms occur now and again, but they have little or no

---

[36] Sappho frag. 22.9–12 Campbell, 9–13 L-P. In line 11, . .]*ktin* must be *paktin*.
[37] Sappho frag. 103.5, 9, 10, 12 Campbell, p. 84 L-P.
[38] Music in wedding preparations: Sappho frag. 44.24–26, 31–34 Campbell, 2 L-P. *krotala:* according to LSJ, first in *Homeric Hymn* 14.3 ("To the Mother of the Gods"); probably later than the present passage and the one other occurrence in Sappho frag. 214C.7 Campbell. *nomos:* in Alcman, but with *orthios* first here.

context. In an isolated phrase, "voice" has *aiolos* for its epithet. The term expresses rapid movement, and Homer invariably gives it a literal meaning. The present usage, not acknowledged in the lexicon, is new. It will show this figurative sense during the fifth century and for a long time afterward, from Aeschylus to Theocritus. Sappho calls the lyre *chelus* and *chelunna*, "tortoiseshell," as well as *lura* and *kitharis;* these are single references. She mentions the *pēktis* twice but leaves us no nearer certainty about its nature. The term *barbitos* does not occur in her extant poetry, possibly (as Andrew Barker suggests) because the name was applied to the long-armed lyre only later. Like Alcaeus, she prefers *ligus* and *liguros* over any other adjectives, to convey the quality of musical tone.[39]

At one moment, and at that moment only, Sappho's relationship with music comes alive. The rhetorician Hermogenes illustrates a precept of style by her words "Come, divine lyre, (?)speak to me and find a voice." He adds that she questions the lyre and receives an answer; thus we know that the full text went beyond the splendid echo in Horace. Sappho's attitude accords perfectly with the Attic *skolion* in which the singer wishes he were a lyre, adorned with ivory, that handsome youths would carry in procession.[40]

There is no evidence that the Sicilian poet Stesichorus of Himera (active around 530 B.C.) apostrophized the lyre, but when he invokes the Muse at the beginning of a long poem, he does treat it as if it were a medium of the sung text: "Come, clear-voiced Muse, begin the song [*Age mousa ligei', arxon aoidas*] . . . and give utterance [with your] lovely lyre." Among the few surviving fragments of his poems, one has relevance for our inquiry. It comes from his *Oresteia*, another long narrative. "Such commonly told tales," he says, "must we sing of the lovely-haired Graces [*Charitōn damōmata kallikomōn*], as we deli-

[39] *aiolos: aiolon phōn*[Sappho 213C, col. iii.5 Campbell. References in Campbell and Lobel-Page: 118.1 *chelu dia;* 58.12 *philaoidon liguran chelunnan,* which despite Campbell does not mean "song-lover, (player) of clear-sounding lyres" (LSJ mistranslates *chelunna* as "sound-board"); 103.12 *themena lura[n;* 44.24 *aulos* . . . *[kitharis]* t' or *[magadis]* t',* where one or the other is virtually certain. *pēktis:* 22.11–12 Campbell *laboisa* . . . *pa]ktin* (see above, n. 36); 156.1 Campbell, L-P *polu paktidos adumelestera,* "sweeter far in sound than a (?)lyre"; cf. 44.24 *aulos* . . . *adu[m]eles. ligus, ligu-* in compounds, *liguros:* 30.8, 58.12, 70.11 Campbell (cf. 10 *choron*), 71.7 (uncertain), 103.10.

[40] Sappho frag. 118 Campbell. Attic *skolion:* 14 Edmonds, *PMG* 900.

cately [*habrōs*] devise a Phrygian tune, / at the coming of spring."
Closely linked with this is an incomplete line, " . . . when in the
season of spring the swallow sounds her cry [*keladēi chelidōn*]."[41]
"Tune" here translates *melos;* it reveals nothing about modality. But if
the poet is referring to the Phrygian *harmonia,* the ethos here attributed to it differs sharply from the usual one.

In this partial line, Stesichorus established a light, joyous mood
wholly appropriate for a spring song. He has placed the adverb *habrōs*
at the close of line 2, before the mention of spring's coming, to
reinforce what that second line conveys. Like the adjective *habros* and
the noun *habrotēs,* the adverb expresses particularly the luxuriousness
and delicacy attributed to oriental cultures, including that of Ionia and
the adjoining inland territories. Although Greeks often used forms
based on the *habr-* root pejoratively, such was not necessarily the case;
it does not seem to have been the case here. This *Oresteia* was perhaps
composed for a spring ceremony at Sparta. Clearly, the poet designed
it to fit a Spartan view of myth. The work that resulted differed
greatly from the trilogy that Aeschylus presented a century later.
Noting the "air of gaiety" in the present lines, Bowra contrasts it with
"the gravity of Pindar or the Attic tragedians" in telling the story.[42]

Stesichorus' *Oresteia* was a large-scale work, and the mention of a
Phrygian tune suggests that it was sung to an instrumental accompaniment. "We may presume," says Bowra, that the instrument was
the aulos. There is no evidence to support this and no reason to
suppose that anything other than the kithara was used. West distinguishes Stesichorus, "a singing poet," from the kitharodes, who sang
verse written by others. As he notes, the lines from the opening of the
Oresteia are proof of this. The "Phrygian tune" he identifies with the
nomos Athēnas, the "nome of Athena" that Pollux mentions.[43] It was
sung to the kithara. The better-known nome of Athena to which the
pseudo-Plutarchian treatise *De musica* refers had aulos accompaniment.

[41] References in Stesichorus: 47, 37, 38 Edmonds, *PMG* 101, 35, 34. Since chi was
pronounced *k'h*, a pattern of alliteration links the second and third of these fragments.
Also, the similarities between *keladēi* and *chelidōn,* in *k-l-d* consonantal structure and in
initial vowel, might be thought to suggest mimesis of bird song. Louis Delatte (1938,
24, 28) unwarrantably assumes that *melos* in 37 means "mode."

[42] Bowra 1961, 115. He there translates 37.2–3 as "when the spring comes delicately
on" and renders *Chariton* as "Muses."

[43] Bowra 1961, 115; West 1971, 309–10; Poll. 4.66.

Unlike the Ionian epic that kitharodes recited or intoned, Stesichorus' sung epic employed meters chiefly of a dactylic nature rather than the standard, unvarying hexameter. For West, musical considerations partly explain the resulting restriction on the substitution of a long syllable for two shorts. It responded to the convention, observed until the later decades of the fifth century, that a syllable might be set to one note and one note only.[44] Two main inferences are made concerning melodic structure: where two short syllables alternate with a long, they were sung on the same note; where they do not alternate, each was sung on a different note. To judge from Stesichorus' metrical practice, the first of these methods was not employed at the beginning of the period or larger metrical unit; within the period, a certain amount of variation could be found; and there was a tendency toward melodic phrases between four (- ⌣ ⌣ -) and ten (- ⌣ ⌣ - - ⌣ ⌣ - ⌣ ⌣ -) syllables in length, with a preference for seven (- ⌣ ⌣ - - ⌣ ⌣ -).

There has long been controversy over the meaning of the proverbial question "Don't you even recognize 'the three [ta tria] of Stesichorus'?" The question appears in the Byzantine lexicon known as the Suda, along with the statement that Stesichorus wrote all of his poetry in triads—strophe, antistrophe, epode. The repeated mistranslation of ginōskeis as "know" has hampered the search for the "three." Important new fragments of Stesichorus' poetry have been discovered in our time, and recent finds continue to bear out West's statement in 1971 that major works by this poet have in fact exemplified the AAB pattern of triadic structure.[45] He summarizes the method of presentation thus: "The performer sang a sequence of melodic periods, with lyre continuo. A group of such periods made up a melodic whole, which, when it was complete, was repeated; and then a different melody (with similar rhythms) followed, giving the feeling of rounding-off in a still larger unit." The pattern itself is older, and "may be regarded as . . . traditional . . . in Greek melodic structure."[46]

The view that Stesichorus was a composer of choral lyric—a claim that the testimonia do not make for him—was voiced without hesita-

[44] West (1971, 311) says: "Each syllable was sung on a single note."

[45] Davies 1982 is an example. For more on the triadic structure of these long works and the inferences to be drawn concerning their melodization, see West 1992b, 339.

[46] West 1971, 312.

tion by Lesky in 1966.[47] In the second edition (1970) of the *Oxford Classical Dictionary,* Bowra committed himself only to the extent of saying: "He wrote in the traditional language of choral lyric."[48] By now, Stesichorus must be recognized as primarily a solo singer to the lyre who performed epic narratives. He was not a kitharode, as some commentators have labeled him, for he did not sing the works of others, works composed in dactylic hexameters. He created epic, using a variety of dactylic meters; thus ⌣ ⌣ – as well as – ⌣ ⌣ may begin the period, the first in strophes and the second in epodes. This is a lyric way of setting epic subject matter. It seems to have originated not in Ionia but on the Greek mainland, possibly at Sparta. Stesichorus brought it to the northern coast of Sicily and made it famous.

During this same period, southern Italy too had a poet-composer with unusual gifts, Ibycus of Rhegium. There is a late story that, while traveling by chariot on the way from Catana to Himera in Sicily, Ibycus fell and broke his wrist; the accident made him play the lyre "out of tune" (*apōidon*)" for some time.[49] Although this last claim is suspiciously vague, the truth of its substance need not be doubted. An itinerant bard, like any solitary traveler, risked mischance; and short of death or grave injury, the most serious would have been loss of one's ability to sing or to play the lyre properly. We recall the fate of Thamyris in the *Iliad*.

Ibycus did not remain in Sicily. He became a resident singer at the court of Polycrates, tyrant of Samos, and there turned to poetry of a markedly personal and passionate nature. Since his verses contain no mention of music, speculation must be based on metrical evidence. This evidence has long puzzled those who, like Bowra, take triadic structure to be an unmistakable mark of choral lyric. "The paradox of [Ibycus'] style," Bowra rightly observes, "is that certain of his poems . . . cannot be choral poems and seem to be amatory monodies." The impression is strengthened by the meter, "with its rows of dactyls." Only one conclusion is possible: "Ibycus, indeed, seems to have broken down the conventions of poetry by treating its different kinds as all very much the same thing."[50] A bold assertion, it might

[47] Lesky 1966, 151.
[48] S.v. Stesichorus.
[49] Himerius *Orations* 22.5.
[50] Bowra 1961, 282–83.

make us wonder what comparable sorts of enterprise were shown in the choice of mode (or modes?) and in the shaping of the melody. On this last point, metrical analysis of the kind that has been applied to Stesichorus' verse could perhaps prove helpful.[51] Concerning Ibycus' use of instruments we know nothing, beyond the obvious fact that he sang to the kithara. Stories that would make him the "inventor" of the *sambuca* do not merit consideration.

A fellow singer at Polycrates' court, Anacreon of Teos, is unusual among musicians of this early period in that he was wholly Ionian. He also seems more aware of himself as a musician, and especially as an instrumentalist, than any predecessor or contemporary. Excerpts from four fragments of his poetry give an idea of his liveliness and charm:

I have been draining a cask of wine, and now I delicately pluck the
    strings / of a beautiful *pēktis* as I serenade my beloved.
I pluck a twenty-stringed *magadis* [?in the Lydian mode].
Who turns his heart back to the delightful time of youth, and then dances
    to the music of the tender half-bore pipes [*hēmiopōn . . . aulōn*]?
I saw Simalus in the chorus holding a handsome *pēktis*.

The supposed references to "tunes" (*melē*), to the term "lyre maker," and to the lyre itself range from uncertain to highly unlikely.[52]

A half century after Anacreon's death, Critias called him *philobarbitos* in a hexameter tribute that Athenaeus quotes at length. In this same poem, and in the same phrase, Critias also speaks of Anacreon as an antagonist of the aulos (*aulōn antipalon*); but in context the intended sense would seem to be much more one of rivalry than of hostility.[53] We have seen that he speaks of the half-bore pipes in a kindly enough manner. According to Athenaeus' paraphrase, Pos-

[51] I now believe I erred in having formerly accepted Bowra's belief that the poetry of Ibycus contains the first known use of triadic structure; see the *New Grove Dictionary of Music and Musicians* 9:5, s.v. Ibycus. Alcman may well have come to Sparta from Lydia, but at best this is probable rather than certain.

[52] References to instruments in Anacreon: *PMG* 373–75, 386. Tunes: *PMG* 402. Both Campbell and Page read *logōn* here; *meleōn* was supplied by Blass to fill a lacuna. "Lyre maker": 387 Campbell, 42 Page. Both follow the ancient lexicographer Pollux in reading *muropoios*, "perfumer." Lyre: 121 Edmonds, omitted by Campbell and Page; Edmonds states that the line may be the work of "a later Anacreon."

[53] Critias: Edmonds 1964, 2:128; omitted by Campbell; cited in Ath. 600d.

idonius (a philosopher and polymath of the first century B.C.) declared that Anacreon referred to three "melodies" (*melōidiai*): Phrygian, Dorian, and Lydian.[54] He used only these, Posidonius adds.

Although Anacreon seldom speaks of himself in any but a deprecating manner, the Teian is the most appealing poet whom we have encountered, and at the same time the most sophisticated one. He lived in an age of *turannoi,* rulers whose coming to power had occurred outside the regular procedures of succession. His talent first took him to the court of an exceptionally powerful tyrant, the Samian Polycrates. Then he was invited to Athens, where Hippias and Hipparchus, the sons of Pisistratus, were managing the affairs of state. They welcomed poet-composers, and brilliant artists came to their court—Ibycus, Simonides, and Lasus, as well as Anacreon.

These men cannot have failed to be familiar with every innovation in music. At first sight, it would appear that references in Anacreon's poetry, and in statements credited to him, provide information not previously available; and this impression is valid in some degree. A possible description (the text is corrupt) of the *magadis* as twenty-stringed does add to our knowledge of a mysterious instrument—if indeed the term describes an instrument. Anything with this complement of strings must be a harp rather than a lyre. Also, the poet's words at least partly fit later claims that the *magadis* was a triangular harp that had ten sets of strings tuned in octaves. Further, they establish the fact that both *magadis* and *pēktis* were played with the fingers (*psallein,* "pluck") rather than with a plectrum. The use of *habrōs,* "delicately," with *psallein* seems typical of this thoroughly Ionian poet.

It is puzzling that his friend should have been holding a *pēktis* while a member of a chorus. Two implied points may be suggested: the instrument was small enough to be carried easily, and Simalus was providing the accompaniment. Finally, any technical information about the double aulos is precious. Unfortunately, the meaning of *hēmiopos* ("half-holed" in some sense) remains uncertain. On the traditional explanation, such pipes had three finger holes instead of six; this seems unlikely. Perhaps the adjective refers to half-covered finger

---

[54] Posidonius: Ath. 635c; Edmonds 1964, 2:134; omitted by Campbell; cited in Ath. 635c. "Dorian" was not in Athenaeus' text here; see below, n. 56.

holes, since partial obturation is a well-known means of altering the basic scale of any pipe. Later writers equate these *hēmiopoi* with the *paidikoi* (boys') auloi in Aristoxenus' catalogue of pipes with differing gamuts—thus the instrument accompanying boys' choirs? This does nothing to clarify *hēmiopos,* however.

Such additions to our store of knowledge or reasonable conjecture are welcome, if modest. They hardly compare with the possibilities concerning modality. It would be astonishing to find a sixth-century writer—even one who may have lived on until 488—using a technical musical term that ends in -*isti,* meaning "in the [Lydian, etc.] *harmonia.*"[55] In extant Greek literature, as we noted, these terms do not occur before the last decades of the fifth century at the earliest. More often, a fourth-century writer provides the first recorded instance. In fragment 19, *ludisti* must be rejected. So must Posidonius' account of the "melodies" Anacreon mentioned. Though late writers employed a variety of terms as synonyms of *harmonia, melōidia* was not among them. It occurs first in Euripides; soon Plato gives it a more precise sense. Within his own system of terminology, Aristides Quintilianus carefully distinguishes between *melos* and *melōidia. Melos,* however, seems the most likely candidate for what eventually appeared in Athenaeus' text as *melōidia.* The confused state of that text provides another reason to feel doubt, as does the patness of the Dorian-Phrygian-Lydian combination of modes, often read back into the work of early poets.[56] It may be worth noting that Posidonius has a reputation for style not matched by substance.

In the *Thesmophoriazusae* of Aristophanes, the poet Agathon displays effeminate traits. When he attempts to justify his way of dressing, he cites as precedents Ibycus, Alcaeus, and Anacreon. They "spiced the *harmonia,*" he claims, and "wore a headdress and moved with a mincing Ionian step."[57] The verb here, *chumizdein,* can only have meant "spice" or "season"; no other instances are known. Ac-

---

[55] The obvious exception, and the only one, is *iasti.*

[56] The order—*Phrugiou* followed by *Ludiou,* with *Dōriou* inserted between them—is not the usual one. Anacreon could hardly have been a resident singer at Athens without using Dorian, so that supplying *Dōriou* cannot be termed an error; but the original claims made by Posidonius are difficult to determine. West (1992b, 341) appears to accept this tradition limiting Anacreon to the three customary *harmoniai.*

[57] Ar. *Thesm.* 162, 941.

cording to the lexicon, the figurative use in this lone instance refers to making a rough *harmonia* smooth; but nothing in the text or context convincingly supports this interpretation. Aristophanes several times treated the modes as comic material, subjecting them to puns or extravagant metaphors. Here he must be borrowing a term from cookery (always important in Greek comedy, Old or New) to suggest the addition of exotic elements—scale steps or melodic figures, or both.

The context does show the oriental nature of this exoticism. Wearing the *mitra* suggests Persia, the stock example of luxuriousness, but Agathon's womanish movements are Ionian. What he says, accordingly, can apply only to Anacreon at best. Yet in point of fact he is being made to indict himself: the historical Agathon had an excess of good looks, and he was thought to have complicated the music of his tragedies with chromaticism and excessive ornamentation. The Aristophanic Agathon is only too ready to claim predecessors, however improbable; to take his claims seriously would be the greatest absurdity of all.

Lasus of Hermione, active around 525 B.C., is the last eminent sixth-century poet. He survives in poetry only through three lines that began a hymn to Demeter.[58] There he speaks of himself as "lifting up a honey-voiced Aeolian hymn in the deep-sounding [*barubromon*] *harmonia*"—or, as usually translated, "in the deep-sounding Aeolian *harmonia*." The final phrase does not readily lend itself to interpretation, since we do not know what is being designated by the "deep [*baru-*]" of *barubromon*. Lasus may be referring to the range typical of the long-stringed barbitos, particularly associated with the Aeolic poets. Greek musical culture did not recognize absolute pitch, nor had it yet adopted any system of written notation. Accordingly, in the absence of clear and unshakable literary evidence we cannot settle such questions.

During his own time, Lasus' reputation came chiefly from his dithyrambs; he continued to be famous for them long afterward.[59] Such renown lends credibility to the statements in Graeco-Roman and Byzantine collections that he used dithyrambic rhythm and

[58] Lasus I Edmonds, *PMG* 702.

[59] Aristophanes mentions Lasus in the *Wasps* (1410). During the late classical period his name was borrowed, always a clear indication that one has arrived.

"movement" (*agōgē,* which is more precisely "tempo") in other types of composition. If the assertions are true, his innovations gave impetus to the earliest stages of a movement that would grow ever stronger throughout the fifth century. This was the tendency in art music to exploit the capacities of the aulos (greatly expanded during that period) at the expense of the kithara and even of the voice. Like other early figures who shaped a native musical culture, he was remembered by most fifth-century Greeks with a surprising degree of respect and affection. It appears unlikely that he would have escaped their criticism if he had initiated radical and unsettling changes.

Lasus has another claim on our attention; it is one for which a fair amount of support exists. The evidence begins with Aristotle's famous pupil Aristoxenus and cannot easily be dismissed. Taken as a whole, it suggests that Lasus was the first musicologist. The *Suda* makes him the author of the first treatise on music: probably this goes too far. In the latter decades of the sixth century, such a work would have been most unusual. Yet later generations honored his thought; at times he was even counted among the *Hepta Sophoi,* the Seven Sages. Whether or not any written formulation existed, we may well conjecture that Lasus did theorize about music, and that his beliefs were remembered for centuries. He represents a significant stage in the development of Greek music, the stage at which it became conscious of itself. With that consciousness, musicology came into being.[60]

[60] Perhaps with greater caution than is necessary, West speaks of Lasus as having "aroused new interest in the history and theory" of music (1992b, 350).

{4}

Fifth-Century Lyric Poets

The careers of several poet-composers we have already encountered extend into the fifth century and begin to indicate some aspects of its music. Another such figure is Simonides of Ceos (556–468 B.C.). His lyrics show strophic arrangement, along with a noticeable increase in line length. This greater elaborateness may be ascribed to Lasus of Hermione, his contemporary and rival. The pseudo-Plutarchian work *De musica* maintains that Lasus, taking as a model the ampler resources of the aulos, altered the nature of melodic composition by using more notes and also more "scattered" ones. Theocritus was to describe Simonides as playing a barbitos, the long-stringed "Dionysiac" lyre.[1] Probably the Alexandrian poet was misled by a seeming association between two facts. On the one hand, Simonides enjoyed phenomenal success as a composer of dithyrambs, choral hymns to Dionysus. On the other, where one would have expected the aulos to be closely associated with the god and with his companions in the revel, the barbitos was found instead.

With wonderful vividness, Simonides acknowledges the power attributed to early music, embodied in the shaman figure of Orpheus: "Birds without number hovered over his head, and at his lovely singing, fishes were leaping straight out of the blue water." A fragment

---

[1] Ps.-Plut. *Mus.* 29, 1141c. West (1992b, 343) suggests that Lasus may have introduced into vocal music the semitone division in the enharmonic genus. Theoc. 16.45.

from a victory ode bestows on Apollo the epithet *chrusophorminx,* "god of the golden lyre." This was to be echoed in the famous phrase that opens Pindar's *First Pythian: chrusea phorminx.* Another scrap of papyrus, part of a victory ode or paean, seems to mention *donakes,* "reeds," of the type chosen for panpipes. *Donax,* then, may simply mean *surinx.* The supposed reference to an instrument called the *Molosson,* "Molossian," was tacked onto a fragment by the late anthologizer Athenaeus; there is no other authority for the term.[2] To the best of our knowledge, no such instrument ever existed, although LSJ cites this passage as fact.

Two lines that may not be by Simonides describe the satyr Marsyas, who discovered the double reed pipes and challenged Apollo to a musical contest. We see him placing the restraining bands of the *phorbeia* (literally "halter") on his cheeks: "With flashing bright gold he bound the . . . sides of his shaggy head, and his arrogant mouth [he bound] with straps knotted at the back [*opisthodetos*]." No vase painting of the *phorbeia* brings it before us with greater vividness. Again, in a prose paraphrase of a Simonidean original, the Muses are said to make a special effort to "sustain the melody" (*to melos teinousi*) when Apollo leads off the dance. The presumed original of the phrase would have resembled Aristophanes' use of *enteinesthai,* applied to a traditional *harmonia.* For the first time, a writer shows interest in turning the leaden technicalities of musical practice into poet's gold. A hint of Simonides' innovativeness as a melodist may be found in the famous fragment of twenty-seven lines from a poem about Danaë cast adrift in a chest with her infant son Perseus. Throughout most of the fragment (7–27), she is speaking to the child. Line 9 has what would normally have been *knōsseis,* "you are drowsing"; Simonides lengthens the initial syllable into a short-long dissyllable, *knoōsseis.* The melodic line was bound to reflect this and may have accentuated it.[3]

---

[2] Orpheus' song: 51 Edmonds, *PMG* 567. Epithet of Apollo: *PMG* 511, frag. 1a.5. Reeds: *PMG* 519, frag. 56.3. "Molossian": 88 Edmonds, omitted in *PMG.* Athenaeus 181b added the words *to d' organon Molosson,* "and (they call) the musical instrument Molossian" (said of the accompaniment to a wedding dance), to the third fragment quoted by Plutarch in *Quaestiones convivales* 9.15.2. The use of *organon* is highly suspect; if genuine, this would be the earliest known occurrence by a good half century.

[3] The *phorbeia* described: 115 Edmonds, omitted in *PMG;* Edmonds states that "the ascription is doubtful." LSJ, on *opisthodetos,* credits the passage to the third-century

The fifth century saw the accustomed forms of lyric in decline. Choral poetry was still to attain incomparable power, with the victory odes of Pindar. On ceremonial occasions, choruses continued to perform hymns of one sort or another, not only as part of a liturgy but often competitively; love of competition marked Greek music making from the beginning. After the close of the sixth century, however, the lyric portions of drama increasingly took over both choral song and monody or actually replaced them.

Controversy and uncertainty surround the name of Pratinas of Phlius, who gained his reputation at Athens. The view is taken here that he was a lyric poet. Only recently has this come to be considered a respectable position; it continues to be debated. Concerning the tragedies ascribed to Pratinas, we have nothing beyond late claims. Stronger evidence, some of it from his own verses, connects him with the beginnings of the satyr play and with two nondramatic forms, the hyporcheme or dance song and the dithyramb. Precise distinctions cannot be made among the terms *ta saturika* (plural), *huporchēma,* and *dithurambos.* This is especially true of evidence from the close of the sixth century and the beginning of the fifth—just the period when the satyr play had taken on established form.

In the case of Pratinas, we can argue from the content and tone of a long fragment quoted by Athenaeus.[4] The fact that he introduces the work as a hyporcheme (dance song), while modern opinion favors calling it a dithyramb, does not greatly matter. The singers may or may not be satyrs. Possibly they constitute a semichorus and indirectly berate another semichorus, not quoted: we are unable to say. The invective, however, becomes unmistakable at once, in lines 1–3: "What is this uproar? What are these dance measures? / What outrage [*hubris*] has come upon the altar of Dionysus, filled with clatter? / Mine is Bromios, mine; it is I who should raise the shout, I who should raise the clatter." The first line contains a barrage of dental consonants, including the *t* of *thorubos* when the theta is pronounced correctly, and it has a startling preponderance of short syllables (only

elegiac poet Simmias. The Muses' singing: 8 Edmonds; Himerius *Orations* 16.7 has *to melos ekteinasai;* cf. Ar. Nub. 968. Melodic innovation: *PMG* 543.9. See West 1992b, 201; he, however, gives ♪⌣ ♩ as the equivalent when a tied note cannot be assumed.

⁴1 Edmonds, *PMG* 1:708; cited in Ath. 617b–f.

-reu- is long): *Tis ho thorubos hode? ti tade ta choreumata?* The very sound registers an extreme of indignation.[5]

Almost at once, the singers make clear what has roused them to this protest. The *hubris* of their rhetorical question in line 2 has been committed by the aulos, through ignoring the fact that "it is song that the Muse has established / as queen" (6–7). The aulos must "go second in the dance" (7: *husteron choreueto*): this is no more than right for a "servant" (8). It should be willing to confine its area of command to reveling and beating tattoos on house doors, the sort of thing that young men do when they are drunk (9–11).

The chorus now begin to address player and instrument, aulete and aulos, as a single entity. Personification has already been established; the need at this later stage is to introduce technical musical criticism made palatable by imagery and diction, both seemingly dithyrambic —that is, with polysyllabic, ornate diction. Pratinas manages this; at the same time, he stays clear of the sexual double meanings with which comic poets were to deride musical innovations. He introduces a sequence of three polysyllabic adjectives, each freshly minted; they culminate in *paramelorhuthmobatan,* "going counter to melody and rhythm" (14).[6] The chorus now appeal to Dionysus as lord of the dithyramb: "Pray heed to *my* Dorian dance and song [18: *choreian*]."

When he introduces his citation of the text or partial text of Pratinas' complaint, Athenaeus calls it a reaction against hired auletes and chorus members taking over the dancing floors. In their performance, he explains, the chorus accompanied the aulete instead of the other way round. Athenaeus' reference to hiring has no warrant: auletes had regularly been hirelings or slaves—Pratinas uses the word *thēs,* "serf." As for the chorus, it was not made up of professionals until late in the fifth century. Athenaeus speaks out of Hellenistic and Graeco-Roman assumptions, and they have led him astray. His main point stands: the poem protests against a state of affairs that has permitted auletes to dominate choric performance, when they ought to be providing an accompaniment for the sung text. It is not a blanket condemnation of

---

[5] "One might guess," says Campbell, "that the song was preceded by a dance with noisy aulos accompaniment in parody of Lasus or some other" (1982b, 404).

[6] Campbell's "striding across melody and rhythm" (1982b, 405) is more literal. In a letter, Barker suggested "stepping *in* rhythm contrary to melody" as a possibility; this seems a less natural interpretation.

the aulos. Yet the poet does condemn misuse of the instrument, whether real or supposed; and so vigorous a counterattack mounted so early surprises us.

As part of their closing appeal to Dionysus, the chorus urgently call on him to note the "flinging about [*diarrhipha*] of hand and foot (16–17)." The indignant *ēn—idou*, "just look!" which prefaces their description suggests that they are attacking such dance figures as unsuitable, if not downright sacrilegious. The suggestion that *dexias*, "(right) hand" (16), refers to rapid finger movements on the aulos has little merit; the aulete had a separate place from the dancers, whose gestures contributed importantly to the total effect of the performance. At the very end, these singers call their dance and song distinctively Dorian. Granted, opposition has been set up between "Dorian" and "Phrygian"; but one cannot assume a reference to modality. Through the early decades of the fifth century, such terms as *Dōrios* clearly included a number of elements besides the melodic.

Like their successors, poet-composers at the turn of the century increasingly use ethnic names and the term *harmonia* itself, rather than some indirect equivalent. Two fragments of Pratinas' lyrics illustrate both tendencies:

mēte suntonon diōke
mēte tan aneimenan
[iasti] mousan, alla tan mesan neōn
arouran aiolizde tōi melei.
Don't go on pursuing either the severe or the dissolute
Muse [*iasti:* in Athenaeus' text; Page rightly deletes it], but instead [by?]
   plowing your field up the middle
Aeolize in your melody.
prepei toi pasin aoidolabraktais
Aiolis harmonia.
What is proper, certainly, for all boasters[?] in song
Is the Aeolian *harmonia*.[7]

Athenaeus, who quotes both fragments, separates them only by the remark that in the second one Pratinas speaks "more clearly." This

---

[7] 5 Edmonds, *PMG* 712a, b; cited in Ath. 624f–625a. Lesky (1983, 36) speaks of Pratinas as favoring "Aeolian harmony"; but the fault may be that of his English translator.

may be wishful thinking: he is citing texts to support the views of Heraclides of Pontus on modality. Yet the poem quoted first was composed, as its accompaniment was composed, for an audience not of musicologists but of nonspecialist Athenians. Many of Pratinas' hearers had studied lyre playing and the singing of traditional short poems when they were schoolboys. By taking part in music making at dinner parties, they had kept these skills alive. If we ask what would have come across to them from the lines preserved by Athenaeus, the answer may be represented reasonably well by the translations given above.

The surface meanings of Pratinas' advice would have been recognized at once as sexual. Modern commentators do not acknowledge this. The same critics have all pointed out double entendre in the complaint of *Mousikē* preserved from Pherecrates' comedies. Music herself there appears on the stage, a bedraggled creature who claims to have been repeatedly and innovatively raped by poet-composers prominent in the "New Music" movement. Comic effect was meant to be derived from double meanings. At the level of immediate apprehension, these were obscene. They were also witty: technical musical terms or descriptions of musical malpractice make their presence felt underneath the surface, often very close to it.

Deliberate linking of music with gender distinctions and sexuality characterizes nonliterate cultures today, as in the remote past. When Pherecrates made it part of his comedies at Athens, during the second half of the fifth century, he was following an example set many decades earlier; for the language of Pratinas' poem carries a heavy charge of sexual significance. The use of *diōkein,* "pursue," by Sappho to denote amorous pursuit illustrates an erotic meaning that had been a part of the vocabulary of lyric poetry for a century. *Suntonos* and *aneimenos* often described persons as being harsh or morally lax, respectively. The fact that the Muse (*mousan*) is in every sense the object of pursuit emphasizes her real identity as the personification of *mousikē.* Athenaeus' *iasti,* literally "in the Iastian (Ionian) idiom," is an intrusive gloss. With few exceptions, the use of ethnic adverbs ending in *-isti* (*-asti*) to denote music rather than language comes later than the start of the fifth century, and usually a good deal later. Moreover, the occurrence of *iasti* here would not fit with the technique of indirection that so clearly marks the rest of the poem.

This indirect approach continues with *arouran*. The noun denotes a tilled or arable field; but so early a writer as Theognis, active around 540 B.C., uses it of a fertile woman. *Nean*, "to plow," must surely have a sexual level of meaning; LSJ wrongly takes Pratinas' usage to be merely metaphorical. So, in a line famous for its callous vulgarity, Creon in Sophocles' *Antigone* remarks that the wombs of other women besides the doomed princess are "available for plowing." *Aroura* describes the incestuous relationship at the center of the *Oedipus Tyrannus*, and in other passages the poet speaks of furrows or of plowing with the same purpose, namely, to refer to sexual intercourse. Athenaeus actually quotes two lines from Pratinas that are seldom noticed, "not plowing [*arōn*] land that is already furrowed [*aulakismenan*], / but instead searching out unspaded ground."[8] In quoting them, he probably changes their reference, which may well have been sexual; here Pratinas is speaking perhaps of virgin soil, certainly of musical innovation.

Mesan, "middle" or "the middle (part) of," is neutral. It must take its sense from whatever opposed limits have been suggested by *suntonon* and *aneimenan*.[9] According to LSJ, *aiolizdein* here means "to play in the Aeolian mode"; yet the editors give *suntonon* an ethical sense rather than a musical one for its occurrence in Pratinas's poem. They cannot be correct on both counts, and internal evidence suggests that *aiolizde* refers, on the surface, to behavior. Some decades later, Sophocles was to employ this verb to express the rapid shifting to and fro of an equivocating speaker. The term is now equated with Homeric *aollein*, "to turn," used of turning a blood pudding on a spit. Something like this may bring us nearer to a sense of the effect that Pratinas wanted.[10]

The related noun *aiolisma* occurs with the genitive *luras*, "of the lyre," in a satyr play by Sophocles; but even here the reference is not to the Aeolian mode. Presumably the poet is speaking of the quick

[8] Theognis 582; West places the poet's floruit a century later than is usually supposed. Soph. *Ant.* 569; *OT* 1211, 1256–57; cf. 1485, 1497. Pratinas: *PMG* 710; cited in Ath. 461e. The participle *arōn* is from *aroun; aroura* is a derivative.

[9] As Barker points out (1984a, 282 n. 105), *suntonon* could be describing some particular variety of Ionian music; but this, although possible as syntax, does not seem to fit the larger design of the poem.

[10] Soph. frag. 912 (the fragment cannot be dated); *Od.* 20.27.

succession of notes rather than the "varied tones" (so LSJ) of the lyre. Underlying these terms we see the adjective *aiolos,* which first of all describes rapid movement—in Homer that of horses, or "wriggling" worms or wasps or snakes—and then what is changeful or variegated in hue. Even when Aristophanes couples it with a noun from the vocabulary of music, *aiolos* retains its general sense: it does not become technical.[11]

The same must be said of *aiolizde,* if the interpretation proposed here of Pratinas' strategy throughout this intriguing poem has any validity. Its surface meaning remains elusive; in terms of music, it constitutes a periphrasis. The adverb *aiolisti,* which would pose no metrical problems, nevertheless is avoided. It will not appear in surviving Greek literature for another five centuries. After the exhortation to "Aeolize," the poem ends with *tōi melei:* be Aeolic "in your song." This phrase contains no double meaning. Except for *mousan,* it is the only unequivocal portion of the four lines, and the only word that cannot refer to anything but music. It produces the effect almost of a surprise ending: Pratinas has managed to maintain his structure of double meanings for all but the concluding phrase.

The phrase *tōi melei* serves as a direction: it is as if the poet were saying: "At one level, my poem should be understood in terms of music." His lines ought not, however, to be mistaken for technical exposition. Probably *suntonos* at times meant "high-pitched," and its opposite, *aneimenos,* could mean "relaxed in pitch" or "low-pitched" by the early years of the fifth century—this much we can hazard. What must be kept out of the picture is the formal scheme of which Plato gives us odd bits and pieces. His offhand presentation of it in the *Republic* and in other dialogues has profoundly influenced our sense of the meaning of such terms as *suntonos, chalaros,* and *aneimenos.* A hundred years, perhaps more, separate him and Pratinas. During that time, Greek music acquired a formal structure, doubtless realized far more in theory than in practice.

This structure did involve an interrelated series of "modal" scales; its Aeolian component will not fit Pratinas' image of a middle position. For the fourth-century theoretician Heraclides of Pontus, whose

---

[11] Soph. *Ichneutae* 319; Ar. *Ran.* 248. *Aiolos:* Dyer 1964. In Telestes, *PMG* 806.3, the reading is uncertain. It appears, however, to be part of a reference to music in any case.

views the lines quoted by Athenaeus are meant to support, *harmoniai* reflected national traits. The poem that we have been considering does seem to be based on ideas of national character reflected in music. As Heraclides describes them, the Aeolians were neither dour nor dissolute, but instead good-tempered and given to speaking their minds. Here amiability provides a mean between the severe and the dissipated, while frankness of speech does not seem to fit anywhere, having no extremes to play against. Yet Athenaeus cites two verses that center on this very quality, after his interjected comment that they are a clearer expression of Pratinas' meaning. We have translated the second quotation, following the word order, as "What is proper, certainly, for all boasters(?) in song / is the Aeolian *harmonia*."[12]

The last two words of the Greek text, *Aiolis harmonia,* contain surprises. If they do indeed belong to Pratinas, we may have the first use of either term to refer to a mode. It depends on whether, at this early stage, *harmonia* can be limited to modality, which cannot be assumed. In the case of *harmonia,* this would be an occasion of some importance. The words come somewhat baldly after the immediately preceding adjective, *aoidolabraktais,* even if the first quotation is left out of account. A similar compound with *labr-* prefixed, the noun *labragorēs,* occurs in Homer.[13] It characterizes a man of empty and pretentious speech, even as *aoidolabraktēs* describes a certain type of singer. "Boasters," like Edmonds's "braggarts," misses the mark. What Pratinas describes is not a vaunt, like the *beot* of the Anglo-Saxon warrior, but a thoughtless, hasty outpouring—off the top of one's head, so to speak. It may be prompted by officiousness or by self-importance.

The half dozen lines of Homer, which have *labreuomai* twice, culminate in a flat statement: "It is not at all proper for you to be an empty talker."[14] *Prepei,* the impersonal verb of obligation in Pratinas, closely parallels Homeric *chrē.* Now, however, the particular reference has been redirected to the sung word rather than the spoken. It

[12] *PMG* 712b; cited in Ath. 625a. The text may be a single line; usually it is printed as two (three, in Page).

[13] *Harmonia* as "mode": Pind. *Nem.* 4.46 (*Ludia harmonia*); this ode can hardly be placed earlier than about 470 B.C. Compound with *labr-: Il.* 23.479; cf. *labreueai* in 474, 478.

[14] *Il.* 23.478–79: *oude ti se chrē . . . labragorēn emenai.*

provides one more indication that conditions have now come to favor some systematic formulation of views on musical ethos. It does not indicate the actual achievement of any particular system; for if the two quotations in Athenaeus are connected (as most assume), Aeolian cannot function as a mean in the second one.

At the fifth century's beginning, and throughout its early decades, terms for types of melody appear in poetry: Pratinas mentions an Aeolian *harmonia*, Pindar a Lydian. The one speaks of means and extremes, and of behavior; the other, as we shall soon see, speaks of music's profound and symbolic power.

Surviving poetry from the opening decades of the fifth century is still lyric. The Boeotian poet Corinna, whose dates are in dispute, makes a proud claim for Tanagra: "The city greatly rejoices in my clear, light cry." The last three words cannot adequately capture *ligourokōtilēs enopēs,* a densely packed phrase. The compound adjective is (or pretends to be) apologetic: *kōtilos* in late writers describes the kind of music that we call "light." *Enopē,* like *liguros* or *ligus,* goes back to Homer. He uses it to mean "outcry" (of grief, or often in battle), but also to mean the "sound" of reed instruments. Corinna applies *ligouros,* "clear, sweet," to Myrtis, another woman poet.[15] The term occurs in the course of a reproof, delivered because Myrtis, although a woman, had contended with Pindar. Yet Corinna herself did the same, reportedly. According to Plutarch, she actually took the Theban poet to task when he began to compose. She charged him with having emphasized melody, rhythm, and ornamentation at the expense of mythic content. The story of the reproof, often told, derives no support from her extant poetry.

Wilhelm Crönert's conjectural restoration *melpōsa] meli,* "hymning in song," certainly fits the context.[16] The limited evidence that we have noted suggests an interest in referring to song with special vividness, and also with precision. In this latter respect, Corinna belongs

---

[15] 1.5–6 Edmonds, *PMG* 655.5; 11.1 Edmonds, *PMG* 664a.1; *Il.* 10.13; Plut. *De glor. Ath.* 4, p. 347f. Campbell (1982b, 363, on Theognis 241 *sun auliskoisi*) comments that *ligus* and its compounds "were often, but by no means exclusively, used of high-pitched notes." He adds that the basic meaning of *ligu-* may be "penetrating." Lesky (1966, 178–80) shows that a fifth-century dating is possible.

[16] 33 Edmonds, *PMG* 654.i.21, ii.15. Page lists *meli* as an interlinear gloss. The nature of the gloss, however, indicates something like *melpōsa* (Crönert's conjecture).

to the century just beginning: she is a storyteller above all else. Presumably she wrote lyrics of a personal sort, as a single extant line may indicate, and we must especially regret their failure to survive.[17] So far as the musical elements of lyric composition are concerned, Plutarch's well-known anecdote reflects an attitude typical of her time. It is that rhythm and melody come second to the text; making them prominent therefore involves artistic misjudgment, just as an emphasis on poetic ornament does.

The story told by Plutarch (if it can be believed) has interest chiefly for what it reveals not about Corinna but about Pindar. It would afford a unique glimpse of him at the outset of his career. The young poet may or may not have emphasized form at the expense of content; according to Plutarch, he did pay a noticeable amount of attention to the musical setting. At all events, such attentiveness marked the mature Pindar, known because of his victory odes. These have survived almost complete. Pindar wrote in all the other lyric forms, but we have the results only in scattered fragments. A few relate to music; none of them tells us anything about it that differs greatly from what can be found in the odes. Almost invariably, the odes celebrate the victor in one of the many kinds of competition, including musical, that made up the Greek national games.[18] The type eventually received its own designation, *epinikion* (from *nikē,* "victory"); the English calque is "epinician."

Of Pindar's forty-eight extant epinicians, thirty-eight have a triadic metrical structure. The meter broadly followed one of several patterns; the detailed working out of the scheme differed for each poem. Within the antistrophic odes, each triad consisted of the following

[17] 41 Edmonds, *PMG* 657.

[18] For the recent view that the odes were monodies, see Heath 1988 and also Heath and Lefkowitz 1991 (bibliography at 173 n. 1), and for the opposition Carey 1991; further details in West 1992b, 346 n. 80. Morgan (1993) seeks to reconcile the two opposing camps; everyone concerned grants the impossibility of certain knowledge. Webster's claim, with which many agree, is presented here. In his view, the victory celebration was regularly provided with two choral odes, one sung at the competition site and the other in the victor's home city. The former, he conjectures, would have been sung by friends and supporters, who "could cope at short notice with the rhythms of Pindaric odes, which make us blench" (1973, 168). We may doubt whether such amateurs could have managed not only the text but grand orchestic maneuvers of the kind usually credited to those who performed the strophe-antistrophe-epode sequences in epinicians and in tragic choruses. Surely these would have required a professionally trained chorus.

parts: a stanza, the strophe, followed by a second stanza, the anti-strophe, and then a third, the epode. The antistrophe duplicated the strophe metrically; the epode differed from both. *Strophē, antistrophē,* and *epōidē* mean "turn," "counterturn," and "after song," respectively. Taken literally, they refer to the movements of the chorus members as dancers. Our interest, however, centers on the chorus as singers, and on the instrumental accompaniment. In question are the nature of the melody and, above all, its relationship to the speech melody of Greek.

Whether the pattern of normal accentuation acted as a constraint, and if so to what extent, cannot be prejudged; the matter may lie beyond our knowing. Yet the duplication of strophe by antistrophe remains indisputable: only minor variations were admissible in strophic responsion, as this metrical repetition is called. The sequences of long and short syllables, then, had to match very closely. The same could not have been true of the pattern of tonic accent, since the words were different. A few still argue for some significant degree of correspondence between word accent and the contours of the melody to which the words were set. They do not seek to prove their case from Pindar; a comparison of matching lines will show why.

Olympian 2 celebrates the victory of Theron, tyrant of Acragas in Sicily, whose driver had won the chariot race. Pindar memorializes the event in 100 lines, five sets of strophes and antistrophes followed by epodes. The opening line of each strophe and each antistrophe consists of eight syllables. These have the following accentuation (*A* stands for acute, *G* for grave, *C* for circumflex, *U* for unaccented):

	Syllable	1	2	3	4	5	6	7	8
Line	1	U	U	U	A	U	U	A	U
	8	U	A	U	G	U	G	U	C
	21	A	U	U	C	C	U	A	U
	28	A	U	U	U	G	U	A	U
	41	U	C	U	U	C	U	U	G
	48	U	U	A	U	G	G	U	G
	61	A	U	G	A	U	U	U	A
	68	A	U	U	A	U	U	U	G
	81	G	A	U	U	C	U	A	U
	88	U	G	G	A	U	U	C	U

The totals for each of the eight syllables are the following: (1) A 4, G 1, C 0, U 5; (2) A 2, G 1, C 1, U 6; (3) A 1, G 2, C 0, U 7; (4) A 4, G 1, C 1, U 4; (5) A 0, G 2, C 3, U 5; (6) A 0, G 2, C 0, U 8; (7) A 4, G 0, C 1, U 5; (8) A 1, G 3, C 1, U 5.[19] No poet-composer could have taken close account of this extremely diverse array if he was also concerned with preserving the nature of the melody to which line 1 was set. One of these alternative procedures was followed; we do not know with certainty which one, and the possibility of a compromise (something similar has been conjectured for the Homeric bard) cannot be entirely ruled out.

If Pindar's music remains beyond our knowing, a few of its characteristics can perhaps be conjectured. He was composing at a time when few challenged the primacy of the text, and he himself held strongly conservative views. It is possible, then, that he fitted the melody of a given work to the word accents. *Olympian* 2 opens with the splendid phrase *anaxiphormingges humnoi,* "hymns that are lords of the lyre." Only one other poet-composer spelled out more clearly this difference between master and servant, as we shall see, and the gain was at the expense of poetry.

About his melodies Pindar says little. In *Nemean* 4, he speaks to his lyre, using (as he customarily did) the old Homeric term: "Sweet-sounding phorminx, weave out to its end / in the Lydian *harmonia* . . . a song." Nowhere else does he describe a mode with one of the ethnic names that had come into common usage since the colonizing of Asia Minor. Of *Pythian* 2 he says: "This song [*melos*], like the wares of the Phoenicians, / is being sent with an escort over the gray sea. / [It is] Castor's tune on Aeolian strings: of your kindness, / greet it with favor for the sake(?) of the seven-stringed / phorminx." To *Kastoreion* (69) was a *nomos,* a nome or traditional melody, used to celebrate victories in horse or chariot races. Pindar speaks of the *Kastoreios humnos* in *Isthmian* 1; and in *Olympian* 1, he says of Hieron: "I must crown / him with the horseman's nome / in Aeolian dance and song."[20] Here *hippios nomos* (horseman's nome) evidently means

---

[19] In a letter, Winnington-Ingram commented that he had once undertaken the same sort of experiment. The result, he reported, was "six of one and a half-dozen of the other."

[20] *Nem.* 4.45; *Pyth.* 2.69–71 (not a proof of the existence of notation, as some suppose); *Isthm.* 1.16; *Ol.* 1.100–103. Castor's nome was played on the aulos when Spartans marched into battle, according to the unsupported statement in ps.-Plut. *Mus.* 26 1140c; echoed by Poll. 4.78, with no mention of the aulos.

Castor's melody; we shall be returning to the significance of this fact. "Aeolian," previously of the lyre strings, now is applied to the *molpē,* which here (as often) refers to song alone. *Harmonia* does not appear; neither does *tropos,* literally "turning," which does occur twice in the Olympian odes.

The words of *Olympian* 14.17–18, "for I have come . . . / singing . . . in the Lydian trope," are puzzling. Late writers on music use *tropos* interchangeably with *harmonia* or with *tonos,* "pitch scale." As their hesitant phrasing shows, they really do not know what it was supposed to mean. Although LSJ translates it as "mode" for this passage, such precision is not warranted. Pindar speaks in *Olympian* 3 of a "shining new trope" (*neosigalos tropos*). The adjective, apparently his own coinage, seems intended to emphasize creativeness: here, it promises, are *carmina non prius audita,* "songs not heard before." The earliest literal uses of *tropos* occur in two passages of Herodotus; both refer to the many turns or directions taken by winding trenches or channels.[21] Both, however, were written more than forty years after *Olympian* 14. From this we see how quickly *tropos* lost its literal sense and took on figurative ones. The fate of *harmonia* may be compared: Homer already has a (nonmodal) figurative usage along with a literal one. Barker has suggested that Pindar may have used the term without reference to music, simply as "way"; this is possible.

The general shape of Pindar's metrics and many of its details have now been perceived, after a long history of misunderstanding and arbitrary interpretation. Yet if the task has become easier, it still is not easy, nor can it be. As the authors of a recent manual on metrics point out, "Our ignorance of the musical tradition militates against setting up hard-and-fast schemes. In all of Pindar's poetry, it is the strophe rather than the period which counts as the complete unit."[22]

According to metrical classification the poems of Pindar, like those of his contemporary and rival Bacchylides, normally consist of either of two schemes. Some have the Aeolic meters associated with Sappho and Alcaeus; others combine dactyls (- ⌣ ⌣) with combinations of long-short-long (- ⌣ -), adding syllables that may be either short or long. This latter scheme is the fearsomely named dactylo-epitrite, the

---

[21] Confused use of *tropos:* Michaelides 1978, 344. The *neosigalos tropos: Ol.* 3.4. First literal uses: Hdt. 1.189.3, 2.108.3. Presumably the term in its application to music originally described the "turning" of a melody upward or downward.

[22] Halporn, Ostwald, and Rosenmeyer 1963, 40.

meter most characteristic of Pindar; both he and Bacchylides employ it frequently in songs of praise. Its basic unit is - ᵕ ᵕ - - ᵕ ᵕ - | - | - ᵕ - | - |; here the pairs of vertical lines enclose added syllables. The few poems that are neither Aeolic nor dactylo-epitrite have metrical schemes that are based on the iamb (ᵕ -) or that combine iambs with dactyls. Pindar elaborates all four of these schemes with remarkable diversity.

Students of Greek music have at times attempted to align metrical fact or conjecture that bears on Pindar's poetry—meaning in almost every instance the odes—with his use of terms that refer, or may refer, to music and the dance. One strong hope has been to gain insight into his choice of *harmoniai*. This prompted August Boeckh to see a parallel between dactylo-epitrite meter and Dorian modality, a parallel that does not exist. Four or possibly five passages, three at most from the odes and two from fragments, use *Dōrios* or *Dōrieus* in a musical context. The suspect instance comes from *Pythian* 8, thought to be the last, or among the last, of the odes. At the close of the first epode (20), the victor returns to his city "wreathed . . . with a Dorian ode." The word rendered as "ode" is not *melos,* much less *ōidē,* but *kōmos.* This last term occurs frequently after Homer in the works of many poets and prose writers, with several possible meanings. Usually the sense required is "revel," but the reference may instead be to the celebration with which a victor in the national games was greeted by his friends. Finally, *kōmos* at times denotes the epinician itself, composed for the occasion. Richmond Lattimore's rendering "with a song in the Dorian strain" suggests a musical context that *kōmos* does not have. Nor does *Dōrieus* provide such a context; elsewhere in the poet's works it occurs only as an ethnic term.

Previously Pindar had used the form *Dōrios* instead, most often in references to music or dancing. In the first antistrophe of *Olympian* 1, he bids himself "take the Dorian phorminx from its peg." Unfortunately for Boeckh's theory, this famous ode is one of the Aeolic poems, not a dactylo-epitrite. Its opening declaration "Water is best," *Ariston men hudōr* (aptly inscribed on the walls of the Pump Room at Bath), taken with the following *ho de,* represents a metrical sequence straight out of Anacreon (ᵕ - - ᵕ ᵕ - ᵕ -): this is the glyconic, the basis of Aeolic meter.[23] A recent translator, G. S. Conway, declares that

[23] *Dōrios:* In Bowra's index, *Nem.* 5.47 should be 5.37. Dorian phorminx: *Ol.* 1.17–18. The glyconic as Aeolic: Halporn, Ostwald, and Rosenmeyer 1963, 30.

"the music to which this Ode was set was in the Dorian 'mode.'"[24] It would be pleasant to trust his assumption, but one thing has become clear: dactylo-epitrite meter and Dorian modality do not necessarily coexist.

We noted that the opening strophe of *Olympian* 3 contains the poet's claim to have invented, with help from the Muse, a shining new *tropos*. Grammatically, and perhaps musically as well, this is subordinate to the immediately following claim (5–6) of "fitting into a Dorian sandal the sound / that gives splendor to the revel," *Dōriōi phōnan enarmoxai pedilōi / aglaokōmon*. Literally and also in the metrical scheme, *pedilon*, "sandal," which may stand for *kroupezdai* (a clapper device fixed beneath the aulete's foot), takes the place of *pous*, "foot." *Olympian* 3 is a dactylo-epitrite, and the poet has plainly identified its rhythm as "Dorian," a term still synonymous at times with "dactylo-epitrite" in modern handbooks. Although the verb *enarmottein* came to have a specifically musical sense, here it denotes that fitting of one thing to another that forms the semantic base of all words (most notably *harmonia*) deriving from the *ar*-root. The literal use suits the image, and Pindar had no choice of intended meaning. *Enarmottein* used in a musical sense would necessarily have referred to the sung melody, set in a certain *harmonia*, which is described so briefly by *phōnē*. Pindar elects to characterize this "voice" or "sound" only by a reference to the distinction that it brings to the celebration. "Dorian" here has everything to do with meter and nothing to do with modality. While the mode may indeed have been Dorian, neither the text nor the choice of meter tells us anything one way or the other.

In its original form, fragment 180 reads . . . *Aioleus ebaine / Dōrian keleuthon humnōn*. Literally, and in the Greek word order, this is " . . . Aeolian entered upon / a Dorian pathway of hymns." Boeckh supplied *aulos* at the beginning, and this has been accepted; it is no more than a possibility. Presumably Boeckh was influenced by the reference in *Nemean* 3.79 to the ode itself as a cup "of song [sent] in the Aeolian breathings of auloi." The pipes themselves are not called Aeolian here. As for fragment 180, only the fact of some sort of conjunction between something that is called Aeolian and Dorian

[24] Conway 1972, 3.

hymns (a Dorian setting?) can be termed reasonably clear. What the link may have been, we cannot tell.

A late classical commentator on *Olympian* 1 remarks: "And with reference to the Dorian *harmonia,* it is stated in the *Paeans* that the Dorian *melos* is [the?] most dignified."[25] If Pindar has been correctly reported, he was using language remarkably like that found in later statements about ethos. Plato, Aristotle, and lesser theoreticians of music during the Hellenistic and Graeco-Roman periods were to describe Dorian in similar terms. The words attributed to Pindar have no parallel, however, either in the epinician odes or in any of the other fragments, although considerable portions of twelve paeans have survived. Against this we can balance the fact that dignity marks his poetry beyond that of all others; Aeschylus is his only possible rival.

In his extant works, Pindar nowhere uses *Phrugios,* "Phrygian," or any epithet for "Ionian" or "Iastian"; neither do the prose paraphrases or other testimonia. These two important modes must therefore be left out of account. There is no escaping the evidence: Pindar only once named a mode and called it a *harmonia,* in his reference to Lydian in *Nemean* 4.45; and even this has been questioned, as not necessarily a technical reference to modality. (The mention of "some *harmonia*" in *Pythian* 8.68 certainly is not technical, but there we have a very different context.) Again in the Nemeans, as part of the first epode of *Nemean* 8, he uses *Ludios*—not with *harmonia,* to be sure, but in a brilliant image, unquestionably musical. "I come," he says, "bearing a Lydian headband intricately fashioned [= woven] with ringing sound," *Ludian mitran kanachada pepoikilmenan* (15). As Bury explains in his note on this line, the *mitra* "was a band of wool which formed the foundation of the crown of leaves," This crown was the *stephanos* (more accurately "wreath") with which a victor was crowned. The metaphor of a wreath of song (*Liederkranz*) recurs in a fragment: "I weave an intricate fillet [*poikilon andēma*]."[26]

The weaving of song, explicit here and barely concealed in the description of the *mitra,* is too familiar to require further examples. *Kanachada* (Attic *kanachēda*), an adverb, forms the centerpiece of the

---

[25] Frag. 56 Bowra, 67 Schroeder. West (1992b, 180 n. 65) gives the exclusive superlative without comment; we cannot be certain that this was the sense intended.

[26] Frag. 169 Bowra, 179 Schroeder. See Snyder 1981 on the "web" of song in Homer and the lyric poets (including the similarity between shuttle and *plēktron*).

gradually lengthening line. Used first by Hesiod to express the sound of river waters, it "refers to the sound of the instruments, especially flutes" (Bury, in his note on line 15). The basic noun, *kanacha* (Attic *kanachē*), denotes a clear, ringing sound. In *Nemean* 9.39, Pindar himself uses the plural with *aulos: kanachai aulōn* there differentiates the penetrating quality of the double-reed pipes from the "cries" (*boai*) of the phorminx. By the beginning of the seventh century, the author of the *Homeric Hymn to Pythian Apollo* had already used *kanachē* of phorminx strings made to sound by a plectrum (49).

We may conclude that the poet did not think it his business to provide direct information on such points. The phrase *Ludiai sun harmoniai* in *Nemean* 4.45 is the only exception—a disputed one; it does seem highly uncharacteristic. Pindar wrote the victory odes for small groups of aristocrats who either would have recognized the mode and meter or else (more likely) cared little about either. Music was so much a part of their ritual and social activities that they could not have been expected to stand back and view it with detached interest. By the same token, we must not look for detachment from Pindar, himself an aristocrat and a passionate advocate of ideals that already had fallen more and more out of practice. The one significant difference between him and the *aristoi* for whom he composed the epinicians is the fact of his being a lyric poet. A profound consciousness of this characterizes the texts throughout. His attitude toward his vocation and toward the vexed question of professionalism has received attention from scholars in this century, notably from Hermann Gundert and Herwig Maehler. The thought of composing for a fee clearly troubled him, though at times he accepted payment.[27] Professional musicians had been a part of Greek life for centuries, and auletes were beginning to gain a prominence such as kitharodes had long enjoyed. We know of no instance, however, in which they came from the nobility. For Pindar, this was the complicating factor.

Whatever his difficulties, he came to terms with them. All but one of the victory odes have a positive, vigorous tone. In all likelihood, this mood owes more than a little to a deeply held belief in the power of music; and Pindar often seems to be concentrating attention on

---

[27] Pindar's composing for a fee: Gundert 1935; Maehler 1963. *Isthmian* 2.8 has a celebrated reference to "soft-voiced [i.e., weak-voiced] songs with silvered faces."

instrumental music, specifically that of the seven-stringed kithara, the concert lyre still called *phorminx* by poets of the time. The double aulos is mentioned as well in his earliest known epinician, *Pythian* 10, and three times in the Olympians.[28] Each of these passages links the two very different kinds of instrument in a single, compound phrase.

It is the lyre nevertheless, that fires the poet's imagination. The sung words of his hymns have primacy, as we have seen. He appears almost to forget this when he writes the first four lines of *Pythian* 1: "Golden phorminx that Apollo and the violet-haired / Muses hold in common, / you are heard and heeded / by the [dancers'] steps, start of a celebrations' joyousness; / and the singers obey your signals to begin, / whenever you shape the opening notes of the preludes that lead the choruses, as your strings are set trembling."

This very inadequate rendering attempts only to take account of the musical aspects of the text. Such aspects are numerous and sometimes puzzling; they are likely to have several levels of meaning that cannot all be acknowledged. At the literal level, for example, the lyre is *chrusea* because inlaid with gold, as might be expected of a large, splendid concert instrument. So, in *Iliad* 9.187, the captured lyre played by Achilles has a silver-inlaid crossbar that the poet calls simply *argureos*, "made of silver." Neither he nor Pindar supposed his listeners to be idiots. At another level, however, the ode is addressed to a golden lyre for other reasons. The blaze of gold and of fire springs up again and again throughout Pindar's poetry, as every reader has seen. *Ariston men hudōr*, "Water is best," to be sure; but "gold, a blazing fire" comes next—*ho de chrusos aithomenon pur* completes the opening line of *Olympian* 1. Yet the main reason is still to seek, and we shall find it in the mention of Apollo that immediately follows *chrusea phorminx*. The god's bow and sword are golden, but especially his locks (*chrusokomas* five times, *chrusochaita* once); and in *Nemean* 5 he plays a seven-stringed phorminx with a plectrum of gold.[29] Here, inlay work is once again what a Greek would probably have seen with the mind's eye.

Identification of Apollo with the minor deity Helios came later

---

[28] *Pythian* 2 is the one ode without a strong, positive tone. Double aulos: *Pyth.* 10.39 (498 B.C.); *Ol.* 3.8 (476), 7.12 (464), 10.93–94 (for a victory gained in 476; written later).

[29] Golden bow, sword: *Ol.* 14.10; *Pyth.* 5.104. Golden plectrum: *Nem.* 5.24–25.

than the first half of the fifth century, but the symbological parallels are strong. "Helios signifies the sun in its astronomic aspect, just as Apollo symbolizes it in its spiritual aspect," according to J. E. Cirlot. Of Apollo he says elsewhere: "In mythology and alchemy, his spiritual and symbolic significance is identical with that of the sun. . . . The spreading golden hairs which crown the god's head have the same meaning as the bow and arrow (sunrays)."[30] So in *Pythian* 1.12, the long line that ends the first antistrophe of the poem, the "arrows" (*kēla*) of the golden lyre "charm [*thelgei*] even the gods" through the skill of Apollo and the Muses. Lattimore's "enchant" for *thelgei* gives the original meaning, but Pindar has gotten beyond the level at which music is credited with the force of magic. *Kēla* involves a play on words: *kēlein* is "to charm, beguile," often through music. Apollo and the Muses exercise this charm through their expertise as musicians, *amphi sophiai*. H. W. Smyth renders the phrase as "with the environment of poetic art."[31] Precisely: throughout the first two strophes, which rank among the most famed descriptions of music's power, the poet creates an environment, an ambience. *Sophia* is not "wisdom" (Lattimore) but the specific "skill" of lyre playing and singing, the "know-how" sense of the *soph-/saph-* root.[32] So, in *Nemean* 6.26–27, the poet himself speaks as archer: "I trust that . . . I may hit the mark, as one who shoots from a bow."

The repeated mention of Apollo and the Muses brings us back to line 1. Both he and they possess the skill of playing the instrument that clearly was central to the performance of a danced choral ode. Moreover, we note that Pindar is speaking to it and not to the Muses. In both of these respects, he typifies the lyric poets. Like his Aeolic predecessors, he addresses the kithara as if it were endowed with life

---

[30] Cirlot 1991, 143, 14. In a third passage (222), he notes the frequent association of mouth and fire as concepts in the Old Testament, and also the existence in legend of animals that breathe fire. "Jung," he observes, "explains these associations by synaesthesia and suggests that they are connected with Apollo, the sun-god who is depicted with a lyre as his characteristic attribute. The common link between the symbolisms of sounding, speaking, shining and burning finds a physiological parallel in the phenomenon known as 'coloured hearing' whereby some individuals experience sounds as colours." He goes on to claim a double aspect for the symbolism of fire, "creative (as in speech) and destructive (devouring)." Only the first of these appears in Pindar's images expressing the force of poetry and music.

[31] Smyth 1968, 372, sec. 1682a.

[32] *Sophia* as "skill": Maehler 1963, 63, 82.

and reason and possessed a personality fully capable of response. He calls it a *kteanon* or "possession," a variant of the much more common *ktēma* from the same root; but to do so is by no means to depersonalize it. "Of all possessions [*ktēmatōn*]," says Herodotus, "the most valuable is an intelligent and kindly friend." Aristotle speaks of a slave as a *ktēma ti empsuchon*, "a kind of possession that has a soul"; so might Pindar have described the kithara.[33]

These opening lines of *Pythian* 1, an ode dated to the year 470 B.C., offer a rare chance to see and hear the beginning of a choric performance early in the fifth century. The performers dance as well as sing, and their dancing is mentioned first. *Basis*, "going or movement," here stands for the steps of the dance, the choreography. More precisely, with the indirection typical of Pindar, *basis* represents the dancers. They are listening for the moment when they are to begin the pattern of steps that they have learned; or perhaps that sequence has already gotten under way, and they are now continuing to take their cues from the kithara player (*kitharistēs*).

Whatever their precise nature, the cues or *samata* (Attic *sēmata*) likewise govern the singing. The metrical pattern of this epinician is dactylo–epitrite: thus the first line, *Chrusea phorminx, Apollōnos kai ioplokamōn*, scans as

$$- \smile - - - \smile - - \smile - \smile \smile -.$$

To us, habituated as we are to the time divisions of modern Western music, this sequence could suggest the following:

$$\tfrac{7}{8}\ \flat\!\flat\ \flat\ \flat\flat\ |\ \flat\ \flat\ \flat\flat\ \flat\flat\ \tfrac{2}{4}\ \flat\flat\ \flat\ |\ \flat\flat\ \flat\ |\ \flat\ \updownarrow$$

But Greek lyric meters do not operate according to our conventions. They involve such basic combinations as the choriamb (- ˘ ˘ -), epitrite (- ˘ - -), and glyconic (x x - ˘ ˘ - ˘ -). These we find difficult, perhaps alien, although the polyrhythmic nature of contemporary music has compelled trained musicians to cope with similar complexities.

The pattern of long and short syllables in the opening line of *Pythian* 1 is only a single example out of many classified as dactylo-epitrite. Lines 2, 3, and 4 all differ from it, and also from each other; we must take into account this degree of complexity. There is also a

---

[33] *kteanon* (of the Muses and Apollo): *Pyth.* 1.2. *ktēma*: Hdt. 5.24.3; Arist. *Pol.* 1253b32.

fact plain beyond any reasonable doubt: the men who performed these odes, probably at short notice, were not trained musicians; at best, they were gifted amateurs. We see, accordingly, that their situation can hardly be equated with the intensive, month-long training of tragic choruses; and with reference to the difficulty of singing and dancing in the performance of epinicians, we can only conclude that both must have been fairly simple to execute. The requirements of the dance need not have included matching every syllable with a step.

Many favor the conjecture that movements of the body, especially the arms, formed an integral part of the choreography.[34] Unfortunately, almost nothing is known about the ways in which the Greeks used cheironomy (*cheironomia,* "gesturing" as a system), hand signals to indicate how music should be performed. It is found in many cultures, preceding written notational systems or coexisting with them. The cues (*samata*) that Pindar mentions in *Pythian* 1, speaking as if the lyre itself gave them, may well be cheironomic.[35]

It was possible to simplify dance steps, but this could not be done with the text. As singers—*aoidoi,* now no longer meaning "bards"— the chorus sang every syllable. No doubt both singing and dancing had formed a part of their lives since childhood, a much more accepted part than is the case with us. Normally, however, a dance was one of the two simple kinds, circular or in facing ranks, that Homer describes; Greek villagers still perform them.[36] We know of nothing

[34] Much evidence can be found in Egyptian art; Hans Hickmann (1956, 1958) has carefully assessed this. In an otherwise thorough article on cheironomy in the *New Grove Dictionary of Music and Musicians* (4:191–96), Edith Gerson-Kiwi makes only the barest mention of its existence among the Greeks. See now Ellen Hickmann and Lise Manniche in Riethmüller and Zaminer 1989, 1:40–41, 74; but Hans Hickmann's 1958 article remains fundamental. For many years the late Lionel Pearson sought to interpret Pindar's metrics so as to take into account the practical exigencies of musical performance: see, for example, his 1977 article. His last work, an edition of Aristoxenus' *Rhythmics* (1990), has been criticized as fundamentally flawed; but the introduction and commentary contain much that seems challenging.

[35] Perhaps the lyre did in fact give such "signals." The modern parallel would seem to be a violinist's or flutist's practice of moving the instrument in a slight flourish, to indicate the point at which a chamber group should begin playing or should cut off a note. This is suggestive for aulos playing, especially with reference to the aulete posted at the center of choric-orchestic action in dramatic performances.

[36] Baud-Bovy 1967, 3 n. 1. The rhythm of Homeric and of modern Greek dances: Georgiades 1958, 53–58.

else save the exercises in gesture and footwork designed to give young men the balance, agility, and rhythmic economy of motion that a warrior needs.

We must suppose, then, that the chorus of amateurs lacked the training necessary for any choreography that closely followed so subtle and intricately varied a meter as dactylo-epitrite. This would have been preeminently true of Pindar's epinicians, where dactylo-epitrite rhythms take on an unmatched complexity. The same lack must have characterized amateur singing. These impromptu choristers, whose friendship with the victor was undoubtedly the main criterion for chorus membership, had first learned children's songs and later some part of the vast sung repertoire of a nonliterate oral culture, then only beginning to change toward literacy. Of necessity, they joined at times in a hymn, perhaps a paean or processional. Their only customary singing, however, was done at drinking parties. It consisted of the patriotic or moralizing works called *skolia* (singular *skolion*), seldom longer than four lines. These had come down from one generation to the next; the same melody, sung to one's own lyre accompaniment, might serve for several different texts. Although a stock of generally known melodies existed, there is no reason to think that it was large.

The fact that gentleman amateurs got through the 50 or 100 (or more) lines of an epinician at all must be thought remarkable. Their feat brings up once more the question of whether the melody followed the ever-changing patterns of tonemic word accent or vice versa. Arguments for the former possibility were noted earlier. We have now looked at the chorus as a group of men with certain abilities and limitations, brought together temporarily in order to sing and dance an ode especially composed for the particular occasion. They have had to learn an entirely new text, but the melodic setting might involve well-known material such as the "horseman's nome."

Without doubt, these singers—who were dancing at the same time—would have had an easier task if the melody did not constantly change. Their duties would have been easier still if it was familiar or at least incorporated familiar elements. Pindar clearly indicated that he was setting *Olympian* 1 and *Isthmian* 1 to the horseman's nome. How and to what extent he did so remain conjectural, but there is no getting around the basic fact. For the earlier fifth century at least, that fact should settle the long dispute about pitch accent and melodic contour in the performance of strophic lyric poetry. The melody retained its recognizable shape, undoubtedly with modifications. Since the epodes differed metrically from their matching pairs of strophe and antistrophe, they probably received a different melodic treatment. One way or another, considerable latitude may be conceded. Nevertheless, the words could not have retained, distinct and entire, the array of pitch accents. Here too compromise was possible. Unlike either Classical or Modern Chinese, Classical Greek did not possess a large number of homophones, distinguishable only by pitch and context. Actually, vowels and diphthongs were differentiated far more precisely than in Koine, or for that matter than in Modern Greek.

The importance of context can hardly be overestimated. Classicists know that a passage of Hellenic poetry or prose is largely (if not wholly) intelligible even without printed or spoken accents. The defining force of context accounts for much of this intelligibility. Also, readers or listeners who have had a thorough training in Greek know where an accent should go, and which accent it should be. They are in this respect comparable with the fifth-century audience. Such knowledge exists partly in its own right, but it is contextual to the extent that pitch-accented syllables may modify the normal pitch of syllables immediately following.

Although we have gone far into the opening lines of *Pythian* 1, certain problems that they contain have not yet been explored: these concern preluding. *Ambolai,* a shortened form of *anabolai* (plural), are preludes on the lyre. *Anaballesthai,* "to play a prelude," occurs in Homer; it describes the moment when the bard draws in his listeners with the phorminx, signaling that the narrative is about to begin. Thus *anabolē* (singular) applied to musical performance refers to the use of an instrument without the voice.[37] *Proöimion,* by contrast, may denote either music or words. Accordingly, Pindar may be distinguishing here between *anabolai,* played only on the lyre, and *proöimia* (plural), in which the chorus have begun to sing the ode. Yet it is difficult to see how the first four lines of *Pythian* 1, for example, could be termed a prelude. Probably we ought instead to take *hagē-*

---

[37] By extension, *anabolē* came to be used with the meaning "dithyramb" by writers of Old Comedy. This change took place during Pindar's last years, or perhaps even earlier.

sichorōn . . . proöimiōn as a "defining" genitive, nearly synonymous with *ambolas,* on which it depends. Instrumental preluding, then, constitutes the introduction; the poet has aptly described it as leading the chorus, *hagēsichoros.*

Such an interpretation accords with the evident fact of the importance that the lyre has in this ode and in many others. Its presence and stature refute Gilbert Norwood's theory that an individual symbol dominates each of the odes; the role of the lyre goes far beyond that.[38] Whenever the musical symbolism of these poems takes on larger dimensions, it will be found to rest on a correspondence between two things: the ordered fitting together of musical sounds, and order in the universe (*kosmos*). The former not only symbolizes the latter but embodies it and actively fosters it. In this last respect, we must go beyond Cirlot's excellent description of the lyre as symbolizing "the harmonious union of the cosmic forces."[39]

Pindar never speaks slightingly of the aulos. It had a place in the performance of at least some of his odes, and one of them celebrates a victorious aulete. It could not, however, provide him with a cosmic symbol. Homer's Olympians know nothing of its existence: Apollo, the first kitharode, plays a phorminx. Legends concerning the "discovery" of the aulos give credit variously to one or more Phrygians— Olympus, Hyagnis, Marsyas—or to Athena, but never to Apollo. There was a well-known account, probably very ancient, of a contest in which Apollo's lyre and song vanquished the aulos music of the satyr Marsyas. For Pindar, the "golden" instrument that the golden-haired god shares with the dark-haired Muses was a natural choice, and the only choice. Even this, he concedes, cannot bring universal tranquillity: the sound of the Muses' song (*Pyth.* 1.13) instead brings terror to "whatsoever things are not beloved of Zeus." Nevertheless, the scheme of things entire that his reason and sensibilities grasp is marked by a predominating orderliness. This scheme represents cosmos, not chaos—always the view from the summit of Greek

---

[38] Norwood 1945.

[39] Cirlot 1991, 195. We need to go instead in the direction of another comment by Cirlot: "In India, the sound of Krishna's flute is the magical cause of the birth of the world. The pre-Hellenic maternal goddesses are depicted holding lyres, and with the same significance" (300). An ordered fitting together is always the generalized literal meaning of *harmonia,* even in masonry (Blümner 1969, 3:99, 139; 90 n. 5 on *harmottein* and *sunarmottein* used of fitting stones together).

thought. Although it has elements in common with Pythagorean theories of analogy, we have no evidence that the poetry actually reflects these theories, whereas one description of the afterworld strongly suggests the influence of Orphic beliefs.[40]

Lyric poets of the earlier fifth century show an interest in melody and even in mode (*harmonia*) such as has not previously been seen. In 422, Ion of Chios wrote a pair of elegiac couplets to the lyre, as the opening of a longer poem. They have survived in the *Introduction to Music* formerly attributed to Euclid, now rightly assigned to Cleonides. The attribution of these lines to Ion has been generally but not universally accepted (Denys Page rejects them). Their content and probable date serve, in any case, to suggest the changes that were taking place. A possible translation would read: "Eleven-stringed(?) lyre, keeping an ordered array of ten steps / [that lead] to the concordant crossroads of the *harmonia* ["of Harmonia" as a goddess?]: / formerly the Greeks all played you as seven-toned through four [notes], / raising a meager music [*mousan*—or *Mousan?*], / [whereas now] . . ."[41]

Text and meaning have been disputed for more than a century; the last extended study of the many problems involved appeared in 1961.[42] Its author concludes that Ion's lyre had eleven strings arranged in three tetrachords. Among these groups of four notes, one note was shared (here enclosed in parentheses): B C D (E) F G A B' C' D' E'. The three groups are thus B–(E), (E)–A, and B'–E'. Except for four notes, this tuning accommodates the scale sequences that Aristides Quintilianus gives as the *harmoniai* mentioned by Plato in

[40] Orphic influence: frag. 114 Bowra, 129 Schroeder.

[41] Ion of Chios frag. 3 Edmonds, 32 West, omitted in *PMG*.

[42] Levin 1961. In a shorter study, Comotti (1972) has tackled the problem anew; but he too takes *hendekachordos* to mean "having eleven strings," and his understanding of the text of the fragment is open to question. See now the reliable translation and notes by Barker (1984a, 273–74). Maas (1992, 76) suggests that the opening phrase, *hendekachorde lura,* could refer to a harp. This conclusion is reached by ignoring the *s'* ("you," acc.) in the third line and so mistranslating ("the Greeks all plucked the seven-toned," which has no meaning). Maas's renderings (79, 82–83) of Timotheus, Plato, and Theocritus—where *aiola* appears as "Aeolian"—are similarly afflicted; and see n. 28 to chap. 5. West (1992b), who declares repeatedly that an instrument of eleven strings is being described, translates *heptatonon* as "at seven pitches" (357) and makes the point that the "concordant crossroads" may refer to the choice of either a conjunct or a disjunct tetrachord (227).

the *Republic.* The four extra notes, quarter-tone increases in pitch, would have been inserted (according to this modern interpretation) above the boundary notes of the first and third tetrachords, namely, B, (E), B', and E'. Supposedly they were obtained by pressure on the string, exerted by a finger or by the plectrum.

The interpretation has been carefully worked out. It may seem correct as a means of accounting for the instrument that Ion has described, but important questions are left unanswered, and certain details of the attempted proof need to be examined. What Ion meant by his opening epithet, *hendekachordos* (eleven-stringed?), does not at once appear. *Chordē,* becoming *-chordos* as the second element of a compound, begins as "string"; but at some undetermined, early time it takes on the alternative meaning of "note." The resulting ambivalence plagues our attempts to interpret musical references by Greek writers. In the modern analysis outlined above, the possibility that *hendekachordos* means "producing eleven notes" on however many strings does not receive even passing mention. Eleven strings are assumed; what is taken to be the point at issue is whether their sequence was continuous or gapped, in a pentatonic scale. Sachs's arguments for pentatonic tuning are, in effect, matched against Winnington-Ingram's objections to them. The accordatura proposed for Ion's instrument is based on an acceptance of the hypothesis of a continuous sequence.

Like other bold conjectures that Sachs made about Greek music, his theory of gapped tuning has long been out of favor. The difficulties, however, will not go away. Throughout the fifth century and long after its close, vase painters show seven-stringed *lurai, kitharai,* and *barbitoi* with great frequency. Instruments of the lyre family appear very rarely with a larger number of strings. The practical difficulties of accommodating many strings on one of these instruments must also be taken into account. The extended fingers of the left hand, held upright or tilted slightly away from the body, cannot effectively damp strings set close together. If the complement exceeds seven by much, the lyre must have a yoke of such length that the arms that support it angle sharply outward.

In one vase painting from the Geometric period, such a lyre does appear, and similar instruments are found today in several regions of Africa. Almost without exception, however, Aegean art from Mycenaean times to the Hellenistic and Graeco-Roman periods shows a different type of lyre. It is U–shaped or horseshoe-shaped, and the sound chest varies more than the arms. These are either vertical—the sign of a very early stage—or bowed in a continuing curve that turns inward.

The parallels in Africa are, as they have been for centuries, the Ethiopian *krar* (or *kerar*) and *bagana*.[43] Sociologically, as well as in shape, relative size, and manner of performance, these may be compared with the *lura* and the *kithara,* respectively. Such instruments will not readily accommodate more than about a half dozen strings (the *bagana* may have ten, at the outside); and we have seen that Greek artists, with overwhelming consistency, show seven. Very possibly a virtuoso kitharist or kitharode might have fitted extra strings to his instrument, as expert guitarists sometimes do today. Such exceptional stratagems could have provided the basis, such as it was, for the pronouncements by late anthologizers that X added an eighth string, Y a ninth, and so on. Evidently their claims are meant to document a hypothesis: that instruments of the lyre family generally, indeed universally, took an increasing number of strings. This must be called solemn nonsense. The anthologizers knew less about Greek music than we do, which is little enough.

It is indeed possible that the elegiac couplets attributed to Ion describe a specialist's instrument, one with more than the normal complement of seven strings. (Yet vase painters never show such an instrument, even when a professional competition provides the context: see plates I, IV.) The parallel would then be with the aulos, which vase painters continued to represent in its everyday, uncomplicated form. Unless we accept such a solution for the problem of Ion's lyre, his lines must describe the production of four extra notes on the standard Hellenic lyre of seven strings. These notes could have been harmonics. The first harmonic, which is easily produced at midstring, sounds the higher octave; the second, more difficult to achieve, gives the fifth above that octave. Neither, of course, meets the requirements of Aristides' set of scales; for he gives them in the enharmonic, which involves quarter tones. Microtonal intervals call for the momentary alteration of string tension by pressure at one end, near the point

---

[43] See Paquette 1984, 250.

where the string is fastened. If Greek lyre players managed this, there is no agreement on how they could have done so. Otto Gombosi's theory, formed by analogy with a technique employed in playing the Japanese *koto,* involves wedging the plectrum between tailpiece and bridge. This procedure seems awkward and slow at best. It also would have ruled out any use of the highly popular enharmonic genus in solo kithara–playing, for which the fingers of both hands must have been required.

We have already come well into the fifth century. It is worth noting with regard to instruments that by midcentury their form, compass, and place in Greek life had become stabilized. Thus what had been achieved could, if need arose, serve as a point of departure.[44]

[44] It may prove helpful to consult Appendix A at this point.

{5}

Fifth-Century Music

Such diversity and such a rapid succession of meaningful events characterize the fifth-century musical scene that it could profitably be examined from a number of vantage points. Four aspects will form part of the discussion here: the musical components of dramatic performance, attitudes toward music in the works of major playwrights, the nature and supposed power of modal scale structures, and the differing concerns of musical amateurs and professionals or specialists. I focus mainly on musicians and what they played. Music theory will not receive detailed treatment.

With rare exceptions if any, performances of tragedy, comedy, and satyr play had no accompaniment except what one aulete provided. He played the usual double reed pipes familiar from countless vase paintings. There is no indication that his instrument had greater than normal capacities; all the evidence from art indicates otherwise. He himself possessed rare skills, obviously. For the wealthy Athenians who bore the expense of dramatic performances as *chorēgoi,* it was a point of pride to have the best available accompanist. Actually, this result could only be hoped for, since the order of choice was determined by lot.[1] The aulete probably had as much importance as the chorus trainer (*chorodidaskalos*) in determining whether a given drama received the kind of presentation that might win first prize.

We know very little about the training undergone by each chorus

---

[1] Pickard-Cambridge 1968, 76; on the likelihood that *chorēgoi* paid for auletes, 88.

for the performance of a sequence of plays. The choristers, amateurs all, were taken out of their ordinary routines for a month, with compensation for lost wages. They lived and trained together, under a regimen that must have been uncommonly demanding.[2] Throughout these weeks of intensive drill, the aulete of record may have been with them; if he was not, some musician must have substituted for him. It is conceivable that a kithara player had the task at times. The famous Pronomus Vase, which celebrates a virtuoso aulete, could be interpreted as showing the moment when the nameless *kitharistēs*—as little noticed as a rehearsal pianist today—hands over his duties to the master, Pronomus himself.

During the actual dramatic competition, responsibility and power lay entirely with the aulete. We cannot entirely dismiss the possibility that other instruments besides the aulos made some kind of appearance, but far too much has been made of this on the basis of not very much evidence. Then as now, stage lyres existed; two short fragments surviving from Sophocles' tragedy *Thamyras* prove this.[3] We must ask, however, whether the playwright would have done violence to the illusion created for a celebrated legend, known since Homer's time, by having the main actor perform set pieces to his own accompaniment. As for the lyres that occasionally figure in Aristophanic comedy, the situation and the text itself—notably the thumping onomatopoetic mockery of *tophlattothrat*—suggest that they were used as props.[4] Probably Euripides gave *tumpana* the same kind of role in the *Bacchae;* if they served as percussion—a supposition for which we have no evidence—the case would still have been very different from the use of a kithara or lyre. Vase paintings show that a *tumpanon* was struck with the hand in a number of ways; but it did not possess anything like the "vocabulary" of pitches and timbres that can be expressed by the single-ended *tabla* of northern Indian music,

---

[2] Plato (*Leg.* 665e7–8) speaks of the dieting and even fasting undertaken by choristers. On the civic pride that these men felt, see Ath. 628e–f.

[3] *Thamyris* is a common alternative spelling, now standard; the form known to Sophocles ended in *-as*.

[4] Pickard-Cambridge (1968, 165–66) comments judiciously on the *tophlattothrat* passage in the *Frogs* (1268, 1304) but grants the lyre too large a role. West (1992b, 67) interprets the Aristophanic Euripides here as "wishing to imitate a citharode without actually having a kithara to hand." See West (ibid. n. 86) for other words that represented the sound of a plectrum on lyre strings.

much less the fully melodic resources of stringed instruments.[5] The most generous allowances for exceptions cannot constitute a challenge to the supremacy of the aulos. It is worth repeating the point made earlier: the rule, invariable so far as we know, was that an aulete and no one else accompanied performances of tragedy, comedy, and satyr play.

We must next ask what the placing of this musician was and what were his movements, if any, within the theater area. Probability and common sense lend support to the tradition that he entered it along with the chorus and left it when they did. The difficulty lies rather in fixing his position between entry and exit; on this point Hellenic literature provides no evidence. Once more we must have recourse to probability and accept the considerable likelihood of the belief that performances at Athens during the Great Dionysia took place in the theater. If such was the case, only one formation and placing would have made sense: a ring of chorus members around the perimeter of the *orchēstra*. The *thumelē* or altar at its center would have been the aulete's vantage point. In the Hellenistic period, this was to serve as the concert platform for solo contestants in the two recognized types of musical competition, known as *thumelikoi agōnes*.[6]

The question of where the altar or altars were placed in a Greek theater has provoked more discussion than agreement. This was especially true during the half century preceding publication of three magisterial works by Arthur Pickard-Cambridge: *Dithyramb, Tragedy and Comedy* (1927), *The Theatre of Dionysus* (1946), and *The Dramatic Festivals of Athens* (1953).[7] By now, several hypotheses seem persuasive: first, that beginning in the fifth century or earlier, the *thumelē* of Dionysus was separate from the "stage altars" essential to so many plays; second, that it often consisted of steps and a flat, raised area; and finally, that its practical, nonritual function in the dramatic competition was to provide a central placing for the aulete. By the same token, it "may have formed a central point round which the chorus

[5] Paquette (1984, 206, 208–12) offers examples of the various techniques and comments on them.

[6] LSJ (s.v. *thumelē*) simply equates it with *orchēstra* in late usage. This fails to take account of the Hellenistic period.

[7] The first and third of these works have had notable and continuing influence, thanks to second editions; these were revised by John Gould and David M. Lewis and by T. B. L. Webster, respectively.

stood or moved in its dances," as Pickard-Cambridge says (making the point with more caution than may have been needed). "Probably the flute-player who accompanied the chorus," he adds, "stood on the step of this central altar."[8] The comments put forward here on auletes in drama are based on these assumptions.

Seen from above, the theater area and the surrounding arc of seats partially resemble the concentric rings of a target. The center of this pattern—the bull's-eye, so to speak—is the *thumelē*. It was also the absolute center of attention for any contest involving kitharodes, kitharists, aulodes, or auletes. In dithyrambic competitions, its importance was less but must still have been considerable, for much the same reason as in drama.

Performances of tragedies, comedies, and satyr plays were governed by conditions very different from those of the dithyramb. No longer was activity confined to the *orchēstra;* for much of the time, it was the actors who commanded a spectator's attention. Their ordinary spoken dialogue, in iambics, had no accompaniment; but they might shift to a different meter for any of three types of vocal delivery other than speaking. These were recitative, aria (lyric monody), and the interchange between actor and chorus known as the *kommos.*

Dramatic recitative apparently lay between speech and song; it may have resembled the stately *recitativo semplice* of early Italian opera.[9] During the Hellenic period, it had no name that has survived. The term *parakatalogē* occurs only twice, in late treatises. While it may have seen service as early as the fifth century, the double prefix suggests a later origin. The question of whether it had an accompaniment remains unsolved. The pseudo-Plutarchian *De musica* ascribes accompanied recitative to Archilochus, but nothing backs the claim; we have no reason to take it seriously.[10]

We cannot, however, rule out the possibility of aulos accompaniment for some instances of recited verse. Recitatives inserted in lyrics

---

[8] Pickard-Cambridge 1946, 132. This was also the view of the most eminent German scholars who had written on the Greek theater.

[9] See Pickard-Cambridge 1968, 156–67 (sec. C, "Delivery, Speech, Recitative, Song").

[10] *Parakatalogē:* ps.-Plut. *Mus.* 28, 1141a (as the invention of Archilochus); ps.-Arist. *Pr.* 19.6, 918a10. Since this last work goes under the name of Aristotle, one must keep in mind the fact that it incorporates theorizing from various periods, possibly as late as the sixth century A.D.

must have had this, one would think, to avoid the strangeness of having the aulete suddenly fall silent for a brief time. All three of the great fifth-century tragic poets use the trochee (- ˘) or anapest (˘ ˘ -) —the types of noniambic foot associated with recitative—for a number of purposes other than interjectory. In every one of these instances, the question of an accompaniment is relevant, and apparently unanswerable.

One point, at least, can be taken as established: the recitative of classical drama could not have required special instruments, the *iambukē* and *klepsiambos* mentioned by Athenaeus' more obscure sources.[11] Shifts between meters were too rapid to allow this, as Pickard-Cambridge notes. Furthermore, even if such a feat could somehow have been managed, the resulting one-man-band effect would surely have met with merciless treatment from the critical Athenian theatergoers. We come back, then, to postulating the use of the aulos and nothing else. That the aulos accompanied lyric monodies in drama cannot be doubted; and the aulete must have played during exchanges between actor and chorus as well, certainly during the formal *kommos* or "lament," and perhaps during broadly similar passages in which the actor had anapestic lines.[12] Whenever he did support any of the actors, what he played was particularly prominent.

The nature of this aulos accompaniment in the Hellenic period remains largely unknown. Pickard-Cambridge has stated the position usually taken: "That [Mixolydian and Dorian] were not exclusively used [in tragedy] is shown by Aristoxenus' own statement . . . that Sophocles had introduced the Phrygian mode . . . , and by a passage

---

[11] Athenaeus (636f) speaks of the *klepsiambos* as having more or less passed out of use. Pollux (4.59) classifies it and the *iambukē* as stringed instruments; he gives no other details. Several authors of recent works concerned with ancient Greek music (Barker, West, Maas, and Snyder) accept the conclusion that *iambukē* is a variant form of *sambukē*. Although the sambuca remains mysterious, with no certain representation in art, references by Plato, Aristotle, and others indicate that it was a stringed instrument. The *klepsiambos* is thus classified in Poll. 4.59 and in Ath. 636b–c; further references in West 1992b, 77, 132. Accordingly, it is all the more unlikely that either instrument could have provided any of the accompaniment for drama. Conceivably they were used, during and after the Graeco-Roman period, for the excerpts from tragedy that became so popular as concert pieces; Athenaeus compiled his vast anthology in the third century A.D.

[12] Here the iambic trimeters of dialogue could actually be delivered by the chorus, responding to the actor's lyrics.

in the Aristotelian *Problems* which justifies the use of the Hypodorian and Hypophrygian modes for the lyrics sung by the actors."[13] Unfortunately, the references cited for Pickard-Cambridge's claim come from late sources, and they fail to support several of the main conclusions drawn from them. One instance must suffice: with regard to Aristoxenus' claim for Sophocles preserved in the anonymous biography of the poet, the term used is *melopoiïa*. Usually this means "melodization"; it never served as a synonym for *harmonia*.

Such dubious testimonia provide no trustworthy foundation on which to build a hypothesis about fifth-century modality. The Attic dramatists mention *harmoniai,* as do the two great fourth-century philosophers, but do not assign any of them to drama. It should be remembered also that, by the time of Aristotle's death in 322, tragic composition had apparently become an insignificant enterprise, while the writers of comedy had dispensed with music altogether except as an irrelevant diversion. This was the background against which Aristoxenus, the earliest known commentator, made his pronouncements on the modes employed in drama.

No evidence, then, has come down from the Hellenic period; and a number of reasons make it unlikely that later figures were privy to information not available to us. The relevant inscriptions, such as the victor lists, included no reference to modality. Also, the entries in a dramatic competition were intended for that occasion and no other; the revival of "classic" tragedies was a late development. Until near the close of the fifth century, playwrights were responsible for the musical settings; and given the individual, "occasional" nature of competing in the dramatic festivals, we ought not to assume, in the absence of clear evidence, that a contestant was somehow obliged to use certain modes while avoiding others—an assumption often made by writers on Greek drama and Greek music.

As composer, the poet at Athens did nevertheless operate under certain constraints. These were the limitations of the aulos and also of choral singing, when this was combined with execution of the movements needed for a processional or for the dance. Such singing

[13] Pickard-Cambridge 1962, 258. See the anonymous *Vita Sophoclis* 23; ps.-Arist. *Pr.* 19.48.

was especially difficult, of course, when performers had to dance as well.[14] It would not have been either reasonable or productive to demand anything more than uncomplicated melodization and choreography from the amateurs who made up the chorus throughout the Hellenic period and, for a time, even beyond. It also seems reasonable that the same melody was retained from strophe to antistrophe.

"To the most interesting problem—the action of the chorus while delivering the strophe and antistrophe of the stasimon (and of the lyric portions of the parodos)—there is unfortunately no answer."[15] Pickard-Cambridge's frank admission states the fact of the matter, and Webster's *Greek Chorus* takes us no farther. In any attempt to bring the indistinct general picture into sharper focus, perhaps the only point that can help us remains the importance of the aulete. Once the presentation of a play had begun, he alone controlled its music—how, we do not know. Some use of gesture seems highly likely, however. The best-known modern parallel may be the concertmaster's use of his bow when there is no conductor. All such procedures exemplify cheironomy; our almost total ignorance of actual *cheironomia* gives much cause for regret.

From this general discussion of the music of the theater we turn now to the testimony offered by the playwrights themselves—Aeschylus, Sophocles, Euripides, Aristophanes, and others. In a fragment from a lost comedy, Aristophanes has Aeschylus (525–456 B.C.) boast: "I myself devised the dance figures for the chorus."[16] This assertion would seem to imply the existence, early in the fifth century, of specialists, men sought out for their skills by some dramatic poets—though not by Aeschylus. Concerning the nature of his choreography we know nothing.

A musical dimension is unmistakable in the seven extant tragedies of Aeschylus. The poet does not mention auloi or kitharas directly, as Euripides was to do. He pays attention chiefly to choral song, aria, and recitative, in that order of importance. The concept of *nomos,* broadly denoting any traditional melodic pattern, holds particular interest for him, almost always as a choral form. His uses of such

[14] Lucian *Salt.* 29–30; see Pintacuda 1978, 81–82.
[15] Pickard-Cambridge 1962, 251.
[16] Aristophanes frag. 677 Kock; cited in Ath. 21e–f.

genre words, like his way of referring to instruments by indirection, tend to have an ironical twist, even a paradoxical one.

From these kinds of indications within the text, with minor help from fragments of the lost plays, and with frequent recourse to conjecture, some have sought to construct a rationale of Aeschylus' attitudes toward music. Whether any such synthesis can meaningfully be termed a "philosophy of music" we need not attempt to decide. Certainly, the text cannot bring us nearer to an understanding of the way it was presented musically. To put the case in Plato's terms, knowledge must not be confused with opinion, much less with guesswork. This game, at which a few have tried their hand, really is a dangerous one. Two widely accepted beliefs about the nature and performance of Hellenic music will serve as examples: that rhythmization simply duplicated the metrical schemes, and that in "note-for-note accompaniment"—as we misleadingly render *proschorda krouein*—every note of the sung melody was matched on the kithara or aulos. If the accounts of instrumental technique put forward here are correct, neither presupposition will stand up to examination.

The anonymous *Life* of Sophocles (ca. 496–406 B.C.) pictures a strikingly handsome youth who, at sixteen, was already exceptional in his mastery of singing, lyre playing, and rhythmic bodily movement. Here is remarkable promise. How he fulfilled it as poet, the world knows; but none can say what he achieved as composer. The *Life* reveals nothing until the concluding section (23), which we mentioned earlier: "Aristoxenus says that he was the first of the poets from Athens to borrow the Phrygian manner of composition [*tēn Phrugian melopoiïan*] for his arias and to use an admixture of dithyrambic style." The first point tells us little, since the customary interpretation of *melopoiïa* as "mode" is wrong; and out of many possible meanings, the second may have any one or more. Both statements can be taken as suggesting the adoption of a more impassioned melodic and rhythmic idiom than Aeschylus had employed for solo lyrics.

Mention of the dithyramb may also apply to such monodies. If it concerns choral lyric instead (or as well), one outburst from a semichorus in the *Women of Trachis* comes to mind. Almost incoherent with emotion, they cry: "I am borne aloft [sc. in the dance, by joy], nor will I reject the aulos" (216–17). Now what had begun as a paean to Apollo, Artemis, and the Nymphs (205–15) abruptly changes for six lines (216–21) as the ecstatic women address the aulos directly: "O master [*turanne*] of my soul!"[17] For a few moments, they "*imagine themselves to be bacchanals*," as R. C. Jebb remarks in his note on line 220. "The music of the aulos," he adds, "suggests the spell of the *kissos*," the ivy sacred to Dionysus, symbol of his worship.[18]

The spell is quickly broken. Nevertheless, so long as its power lasts, this shift of mood effects a remarkable contrast. Even today, it can prove disconcerting. Since the change is not due to metrical contrast in any significant degree, it must have depended on two elements: one that has come down to us, the text, and another now wholly lost, the musical setting. To have some idea of the music used for this interjected passage would be exceptionally useful, since the passage seems to have connections with several prominent features of fifth-century music. The aulos was widely believed to have originated in Phrygia; the Phrygian *harmonia* itself had close associations with the dithyramb, as the appropriate modality; and throughout much of the century, dithyrambic style unquestionably influenced the style of other genres. The first and third of these points bear upon the innovations that Aristoxenus reportedly ascribed to Sophocles.

The texts of Sophocles' seven extant plays and the fragments of his many lost works seldom employ music as symbol. All but a very few of the references to music occur in choral or solo lyric, and it is in choruses that they have the greatest effectiveness. Every reader of the plays has seen how the mood of the chorus can shift from hopeful joy to grief, when their hopes are dashed. It is in one or the other of these contexts that music is mentioned most often; the irony of false happiness provides an especially striking setting.

By contrast, Euripides (ca. 485–406 B.C.), who produced tragedies at Athens during most of the latter half of the fifth century, refers frequently to music. The eighteen extant tragic texts, the extensive surviving portions of a satyr play, and some of the many fragments of lost tragedies (principally the *Antiope* and *Hypsipyle*) contain a wide

[17] Not a hyporcheme; see Pickard-Cambridge 1962, 256.

[18] Thus in the *Antigone* the chorus break into an excited song invoking Dionysus, whom they hail as *chorag' astrōn*, "chorus leader of the [choir of] stars" (1146).

range of references. Their diversity, which rules out any attempt at a brief summary, shows the poet's involvement with the active, rapidly changing musical scene.[19]

A penchant for innovation marks many of Euripides' attitudes: music constitutes only one example of his innovativeness, but it is a very clear example. We find new terms or new usages expressing basic concepts. When he deploys his references, Euripides at times seems not only an innovator but an opportunist into the bargain, concerned with immediate effect at the expense of a larger coherence. More often he adopts a strategy like that of Sophocles, but the exceptions stand out. Probably one reason for this is the impression of libretto writing that his lyrics can give. H. D. F. Kitto comments on the choruses of the "melodramatic" tragedies—for example, the *Orestes, Helen,* and *Iphigenia in Tauris*—as follows: "Some of these odes are quite as empty and nearly as silly as some of Mozart's libretti; if we had Euripides' music, and Greek ears to hear it with, would it all perhaps sound as marvellous as Mozart's operas?"[20] Unfortunately, we have neither. On the basis of the texts alone, we can only note the lyric rhythms employed and the references to music. Occasionally, the choice of meter coincides with what is mentioned in the text. This happens in a chorus of the *Helen* (1338–52) where cymbal, tympanum, and aulos all figure briefly. Kitto notes that the words and rhythm clearly are imitative here, "and therefore probably [the] music too."[21] As he points out, the ode itself exemplifies the poet's willingness to provide the audience with an irrelevant diversion.

At times, Euripides found the chorus to be a necessary evil, ill suited to his ways of shaping tragic form. Yet the god-maddened women of the *Bacchae* gave him a voice not matched for its power by any other chorus from Greek drama, save for the relentless Erinyes of Aeschylus' *Eumenides.* Like his predecessor, he drew upon an existing liturgy. "Both in form and in content," says E. R. Dodds on lines 64–169, "the ode seems to be fairly closely modelled on an actual cult hymn."[22]

---

[19] Details in the *New Grove Dictionary of Music and Musicians* 6:294–95, s.v. Euripides.

[20] Kitto 1950, 346 n. 2.

[21] Kitto 1950, 346 n. 1, on 1346–47; the reference is too limited.

[22] Dodds 1944, 69.

Three times, once just before the ode begins and twice during it (59–61, 120–34, 152–67), Dionysus and his followers speak of *tumpana,* hand-held drums. An entire antistrophe recounts an aetiological myth, intended to explain the origins and transmission of the *tumpanon.* The chorus describe it by a periphrasis, "this circle of stretched hide" (124). The pronominal adjective *tode* may have the implied meaning "[this] that I am holding"; and Dodds says that "the singers accompany their words with the wild eastern music of the kettledrum."[23] Only the first of the two relevant references, however, has to do with immediate performance. Even here, we cannot say whether the tympana served as anything more than props. If the chorus did play them, this drumming accentuated the rhythm of the aulete's melodic line. In the mythologizing of the second reference (126–29), the chorus speak of precisely this combination. Actual playing of the drum, however slight its role, would have been appropriate both here and in the epode that closes the long lyric sequence. Of course, the contention that Greek musicians did not normally play different instruments at one and the same moment applies to aulos and lyre: the tambourinelike *tumpanon* is not in question. Unlike the modern kettledrum and the northern Indian *tabla,* it had no melodic capacities. It served only to punctuate the rhythm and remained a distinctly foreign instrument associated with orgiastic, non-Greek cults.

Aristophanes' criticisms in the *Frogs* establish, beyond any reasonable doubt, the fact that Euripides would sometimes set a syllable to more than one note. This practice, common in Western music from very early times, struck fifth-century Athenian conservatives as being radical to a degree that we can scarcely comprehend. The same play contains a broader charge—that Euripidean lyric settings borrowed melodies usually a part of brothel scenes and drinking parties; the accusation cannot be confirmed. We also have comments by critics who lived during the Graeco-Roman period or later, but their testimony is unreliable. Thus Dionysius of Halicarnassus (first century B.C.) declares that Euripides ignored the pitch accents of certain words in a lyric monody from the *Orestes* (140–42).[24] Clearly, he had

---

[23] Dodds 1944, 69.
[24] Dion. Hal. *Comp.* 11.

access to a copy of at least some portion of the play, not a mere text but a score, which justified his remarks; yet that score could have borne little or no resemblance to the original melodic setting.

The same must be said of the few Euripidean lyric fragments with musical notation that have survived in papyri. One, from the same play to which Dionysius referred, has been known for a century. The oppressively large amount of learning and ingenuity expended on it has yielded few solid conclusions. Another, a few words from the *Iphigenia in Tauris,* came to light only recently. Already, however, the same kind of intensive assault is well under way, and already the same result can be foreseen.

In both cases, lack of success may be attributable mainly to the material itself, which offers little to musicologists beyond some variant use of notational signs. As it happens, the *Orestes* fragment does contain examples of setting more than one note to a syllable, the practice lampooned by Aristophanes, and also of the lack of correspondence between word accent and melody that Dionysius found in his notated text. Both fragments, however, suffer from the same discontinuity as the text. Anything written on papyrus is separated from the Hellenic period by decades at the very least, usually by centuries. Almost all of the surviving texts or fragments bear out this generalization; a copy of Timotheus' *Persians* may be the lone exception.[25]

The last great Hellenic dramatist is the comic poet Aristophanes (ca. 444–ca. 380 B.C.). His final work, the *Plutus,* belongs to the early fourth century and the greatly altered political climate at Athens. The ten earlier comedies are another matter. In them, he holds up a mirror to the passing scene—one that distorts reality yet leaves it recognizable. Like Plato, he looked fondly to the past and thought the present a perplexing, upsetting time; anything new was met with an almost instinctive distrust. Inevitably, the music of which he approved was that which dominated the system of education revered in his father's and grandfather's time, though (as he believed) neglected in his own. Freeborn youths could easily achieve a command of it. A *kitharistēs* taught them to sing brief examples of traditional poetry and also to

[25] Interval between the Hellenic period and that of the papyri: Kenyon 1932, 35; Kenyon gives the distribution of papyri by century.

play the *lura,* imparting that modest degree of skill needed for accompanying oneself. Their repertoire was no less modest: it consisted chiefly of the short poems they had learned, the *skolia.* They were expected to know how to perform one of these during the drinking and socializing that followed dinner. While it was very much a social accomplishment, this skill constituted a mark of culture as well. Comparisons have been made to the ability of an educated English gentleman, in the eighteenth and nineteenth centuries, to "cap" a line of Horace or Vergil.

Such was the literary and musical portion of *hē archaia paideia,* the "old-fashioned" schooling that Aristophanes praised in his early play the *Clouds.* He uses *archaia* in a wholly complimentary way, like a Roman's use of *priscus,* although some of his contemporaries gave it quite another sense. According to him, this training once had involved "keeping intact" the *harmoniai* handed down from earlier generations.[26] Some contrast must be intended with the modal deviations that had gained acceptance in his own day; the reference to "keeping intact" may include an oblique, punning reference to the "slack" (*chalarai*) modes. Another passage, from the *Knights* (989–91), shows for a moment what was involved in learning to play the *lura.* The chorus have a story about the demagogue Cleon that begins thus: "His schoolfellows say that time after time he would tune his lyre to the Dorian [*dōristi*] alone, and that he refused to learn any other." This reflects reality, the elementary training in *mousikē* at (or perhaps before) the middle of the fifth century. It tells us that schoolboys could not shift from one *harmonia* to another merely by sounding a different grouping of strings on the seven-stringed lyre; neither could they do so by somehow producing one or more additional notes from the set of open strings. For a change of mode, some or all of those strings had to be retuned; and at this point our scanty knowledge runs out. Dorian seems always to have been the basic mode throughout the fifth century, but others were taught. What these were, and what pattern of intervals figured in the tuning process, we cannot say; no Hellenic writer offers this information.

It might seem an arguable position that the playwright here was speaking of retuning in accordance with the interval shifts that consti-

---

[26] Ar. *Nub.* 961–71, esp. 968: *enteinamenous tēn harmonian, hēn hoi pateres paredōkan.*

tuted a change from one octave species to another. In this system, the intervals of Dorian were extended over a double octave, and the species (*eidē,* plural of *eidos*) were taken at various starting points, in echelon. The time at which octave species first appeared has not been established; a date toward the end of the fifth century seems probable. By midcentury or earlier, the system of octave species could not have gained acceptance among lyre teachers; they would have been the last to embrace musical innovations. The old-fashioned education won approval from Aristophanes precisely because of its conservatism. When the present passage on tuning differently for different *harmoniai* is taken together with the statement that under the old regime schoolboys preserved traditional modality, only one conclusion can be reached. Both accounts must presuppose modal tunings earlier than the system of species, tunings that embodied, or were associated with, a high degree of individuality.

Aristophanes concerned himself with lyre playing chiefly as an index of social attitudes. It had been the vital center of the traditional curriculum; now it was dismissed by sophisticates. They found it *archaia,* "old-fashioned" in a sense not at all complimentary. Literary aesthetes (Agathon), Sophists (Prodicus), philosophers (Socrates), and specialists in musical theory (Damon) all displayed this contemptuous attitude. So it seemed, at any rate, to a conservative such as Aristophanes. To his way of thinking, Socrates was destroying *mousikē,* the old culture that the *kitharistēs* passed on to schoolboys when they learned to sing time-honored lyrics to their own accompaniment. The words held an unquestioned supremacy, but the lyre was indispensable. The son of a stonemason, Socrates had not received this training as a boy; knowledge of the fact may have contributed to Aristophanes' hostility, if indeed it was real.

To categorize Aristophanes' feelings about Socrates is far from easy, but there can be no denying or explaining away Aristophanes' disapproval of the new trends in Athenian life. Among these, none can have been more widely perceived, or misperceived, than the innovations now called the New Music. The term, which originated in modern Germany, corresponds to no one Greek phrase. It embraces a considerable range of techniques, both in composition and in performance, and reflects many disparaging comments by Hellenic writers, especially by comic poets. These playwrights frequently described the music of their time with the term *neos,* "new" in a pejorative sense (like Latin *res novae* for "revolution"), or more often with *kainos,* "novel, newfangled."[27]

The comic poet Pherecrates, Aristophanes' older contemporary, gives us another fifth-century reaction to these changes. From a lost play (perhaps the *Chiron*) that Ingemar Düring dates to about 410, we have a speech by *Mousikē,* Mistress Musica herself. She appears onstage, personified as a woman wronged and physically abused, and proceeds to detail the outrages that four poet-composers have inflicted. They are leading proponents of the "New Music": she names Melanippides, Cinesias, Phrynis, and—the worst of all— Timotheus.[28] The following portions of the text are relevant:

(1) My troubles began with Melanippides, (2) the first who took and unstrung me (tuned me lower) (3) and made me a loose woman [literally "more slack" = lower in pitch?] with a dozen notes [or "strings," *chordai*]. (4–5) . . . (6) But Cinesias, that damned fellow from Attica— (7) what with composing disharmonious twists and turns (modulations) in his strophes, (8) he's ruined me. . . . (9–11) . . . (12) Phrynis, by slipping in his special kind of screwbolt? [*strobilon*] (13) and bending me and twisting me, destroyed me completely (14) while he kept up a dozen modes on five strings. (15–17) . . . (18) But that Timotheus . . . has really sunk me (19) and worn me out the worst way. . . . (20) He's made more trouble than the rest of them put together, (21) with his tunes that wriggle out of a straight course like ant tracks, (22) in disharmony, and notes pitched sinfully high (23) and shrill whistling sounds [*niglaroi*]. He crammed me as full (24) of wrigglers [*kampōn,* "cabbageworms"] as a head of cabbage . . . , (25) and if he happens on me when I'm out walking by myself [i.e., performing solo instrumental music], (26) he strips me and undoes me with his dozen notes [see above, on 3].

[27] In a series of definitive articles, Lukas Richter (1967, 1968) has treated and provided with a context the phenomena that constituted the "New Music."

[28] Although many readings have been disputed, the sense emerges clearly enough to illustrate conservative reaction. For the text, see ps.-Plut. *Mus.* 30, 1141d–1142a. The lines numbered 22 to 24 are added separately at the close of 1142a. Here they have been inserted before the last two lines. So Düring (1945), whose readings are followed in all important instances. In Maas 1992, 77–78, both text and translation contain numerous errors and omissions; see also n. 42 to chap. 4. Maas's brief comments are sound.

It is clear that Pherecrates combined technical musical meanings with sexual ones (no doubt underlined by the use of gesture) whenever possible. Innocent references, such as the one to cabbageworms, are the exception.[29] For the most part, the vulgar or obscene levels of meaning seem obvious; and they contribute nothing to an understanding of what may have been involved musically.

Two further points should be noted. First, Pherecrates was not aiming his play at an audience of specialists in music theory any more than Aristophanes was. Such specialization had barely begun to take on a recognized existence. Second, he relied, as did Aristophanes, on the audience's having some knowledge of music, both past and present: how it was performed, what its peculiarities were, which poet-composers enjoyed particular fame or particular notoriety, and a good bit besides.

With this much by way of caveat, we can attempt to make sense of Pherecrates' criticisms. First, he lists the four dithyrambic poets out of proper chronology, and he does so for a reason. Cinesias studied with Melanippides and Timotheus with Phrynis; Düring surely is correct in arguing for the teacher-pupil relationship as the important one here. He does not differentiate sufficiently among the four, however.[30] They do all appear in the dock as innovators who have ruined "the old simple music" with their devices, but the particulars of the individual indictments vary greatly.

Melanippides of Melos is the first to come before the bar (1–3). On Düring's interpretation, he introduced lower tunings, making music "more slack," or perhaps "quite slack." This reasonable conclusion does not take us very far. For example, Pherecrates fails to say whether the tunings made a new *harmonia* available. There is nothing particularly innovative or startling about mere emphasis on a lower tessitura, though Düring does not argue for anything more than this. Several of his incidental points bear repeating: *chordē* often means

---

[29] In line 24, *kampōn* may be taken as the genitive plural either (1) of *kampē* accented on the second syllable and meaning (among other things) "twist" or "turn" in music or (2) of *kampē* accented on the first syllable and meaning "cabbageworm" or the like. LSJ does not mention the latter interpretation of this passage.

[30] Düring 1945 is of great value: the teacher-pupil relationship, 180; lack of differentiation, 179, where he rightly observes that "in reality the same complaint is directed against all of them." Also valuable are the translation and notes in Barker 1984a, 236–38.

"note" rather than "string"; also, *dōdeka,* "twelve," may serve as a round number meaning "many," just as *pente,* "five," may stand for "a few"—though Düring rejects this interpretation for line 14. All three words figure importantly in the plaint of *Mousikē,* and two of them must be interpreted correctly if the reference to Melanippides is to yield a proper sense. In all likelihood, the poet presupposes the normal Hellenic kithara of seven strings. On them, Melanippides produced a multiplicity of notes. Some must have been produced in addition to those sounded by the open strings; otherwise, *dōdeka* would lack point. In line 3, *chordē* still needs to suggest "string" along with the primary denotative meaning (in context) "note," for the sake of the pervasive sexual punning.[31]

Melanippides made his influence felt in Athens from a considerable distance: throughout most of the period between 450 and 400 B.C., he was court musician to King Perdiccas of Macedonia. Presumably, Pherecrates is referring to the early part of Melanippides' career. He censures Melanippides for using lower tunings and for adding notes beyond the string notes. As material for the study of Greek music, the indictment is singularly cryptic; what follows may provide context.

Judgment is next passed on Cinesias (450–390 B.C.), a specimen of native talent. *Attikos* (6) seems to have been a good deal less complimentary than *Athēnaios,* "Athenian." For whatever reason, Cinesias endured an exceptional outpouring of ridicule and abuse from writers of comedy: here, Pherecrates describes him as *kataratos,* "accursed." None of the other three receives such harsh treatment, and what follows (7) hardly justifies it. We are told that within the strophes of his poems he composed *exarmonious kampas,* modulations alien to the *harmonia.* The adjective *ex(h)armonios,* which appears nowhere else, finds a partial echo in *ektrapelous,* "(going) out of a straight course (21)."[32] As for the accusation, if *kampai,* literally "twists or bends," refers here to modulations, then *exarmonious* simply defines what these must have been by their very nature. To go "outside" the *harmonia* was their function.

In Düring's view, that *harmonia* is Dorian considered as mode and

---

[31] Anderson 1966, 231 n. 53.

[32] The *h* sound—the rough breathing—is not usually indicated when it occurs within a Greek word, but there is evidence that at times it was pronounced.

diatonic considered as genus. He holds that *exarmonious* indicts the use of "chromatic tunes."[33] Thus what incensed Pherecrates would have been Cinesias' frequent resort to these two kinds of modulation. This was done not (or not only) between one strophe and another, as some have supposed, but between individual cola (*kōlon*, plural *kōla*). These were the metrical units, two to six feet in length, that made up a strophe. Such chromaticism was prominently associated with the "New Music," and it unsettled conservatives. For Pherecrates, Cinesias' twisting and turning of the melody brought utter confusion to his dithyrambs (8–10).

Phrynis of Mitylene is the next to be arraigned (12–14); he had left Lesbos for the larger opportunities of Athens around midcentury. In the revised version of the *Clouds,* dated to the period 418–416 B.C., Aristophanes criticizes the "bothersome bends" (*duskolokamptoi kampai*) that had now become popular in imitation of Phrynis (*kata Phrunin*) (971). These had made their way even into the old-fashioned education, and they must have done so much earlier, for he treats as a reality their occurrence in the way that schoolboys sometimes sang. For this transgression the schoolmaster (*kitharistēs*) regularly administered a beating, on the ground that the offender was "making away with a whole covey of Muses" (*Nub.* 972).

It might seem an odd way of speaking, but what was said three lines earlier provides the justification. There, Aristophanes sketches a scene from the dear dead past: in the good old days, well-behaved pupils would sing the good old songs such as "Pallas, dread sacker of cities." According to him, when they did so they "kept intact the *harmonia* that their (fore-) fathers handed down." Düring sees a reference to Dorian; this is possible, but not susceptible of proof. In any case, Aristophanes speaks of a single *harmonia,* sung as the previous generation or generations had sung it. No room for modulations here: none, at least, until Phrynis had introduced or popularized their use and others followed his example. The burden of the complaint voiced by *Mousikē* shows what underlies the attack on Phrynis in the *Clouds.* It also shows that LSJ's translation of *duskolokamptos kampē* as "an intricate flourish in singing" misses the mark.

Still, singing is Aristophanes' concern; the lyre accompaniment

---

[33] Düring 1945, 185.

goes unmentioned. For Pherecrates, writing perhaps a decade later, lyre playing is, on the contrary, the main concern, indeed almost the only one: in more than two dozen lines, *Mousikē* speaks just once of singing. Her attack on Phrynis is the most difficult and disputed part of the fragment. Disagreement starts with the text of line 14: is it *en pente chordais* (so Düring), literally "on five strings," or *en pentachordois*, "in pentachords"? The manuscripts are principally divided between the former and *en pentachordais*, which a number of editors have emended to *-ois*. The emendation is mistaken: fifth-century comic poets do not talk of pentachords, and the terms *pentachordos* (adjective) and *pentachordon* (noun) occur only in late writers, as technical jargon. *Pentachordais* must be a scribal error for *pente chordais*.

Why do five strings seem to be mentioned? Five-stringed lyres or kitharas appear in Greek art only on a few occasions. A succession of editors, unable to accept either *pente* or an anachronistic mention of pentachords, altered the number to seven or nine or eleven.[34] These are counsels of desperation, understandable in the face of so intractable a problem. The interpretation of *pente* as "a few" is tempting but lacks parallels. In the same line, however, *dōdeka* occurs—a round number, like *Dutzend, douzaine,* or *dozen* today. Aristophanes called a particularly supple and ingenious courtesan *dōdekamēchanos,* "the girl with the dozens of tricks" (*Ran.* 1327). In line 3 of the present fragment, the sexual double entendre proclaims itself. It may also be present, far less noticeably, in line 14; no one could have missed it in line 12: *idion strobilon embalōn tina,* "inserting a special screwbolt (?) of some kind."

Both lines might become clearer if the meaning of *strobilos* were known. It remains a mystery, although Düring and others have attempted to explain it as being a tuning device.[35] We are left with the name and scarcely anything else. Pherecrates does note its special nature with *idios,* and adds *tis.* As a description, the combination

[34] The alteration was effected "according to different theories of the development of the kithara," as Düring (1945, 190) rightly observes. He himself takes *pente* literally, with unhappy results, and postulates the use of a five-stringed instrument on which pentatonic scales were played.

[35] Düring 1945, 187. He elaborates a suggestion originally put forward by Schlesinger (1970, 145). It is now generally agreed that the mysterious cross-shaped object that figures (though never in use) in scenes of lyre playing is not a *strobilos*.

suggests that Phrynis had come up with something unusual, perhaps ridiculous. The actor who played *Mousike* could have produced from the tatters of his robe a stage prop, so that the reference would pass muster. One possible choice would have been an elongated top; this was an early meaning of *strobilos*. Later, the word came to have many other senses, including "rotating shaft." A sexual meaning is obviously intended for the present passage, possibly through the resemblance to an *olisbos,* a leather phallus.[36]

The criticisms that Pherecrates and Aristophanes level at the "New Music" apply to conditions during the last years of the fifth century B.C., around the year 410. From the lament of *Mousike,* we see that references to playing many *harmoniai* on a lyre apparently did not strike an Athenian audience as being out of the way, supposing that we have correctly read and interpreted Pherecrates' text. As for Aristophanes, when he speaks in the *Clouds* of the twists and turns imputed to Phrynis, he begins with comparable directness and uses the term *harmonia*. Also, his "multiplicity of Muses" (972: *pollas . . . Mousas*), though oblique, could be a substitute for "many modes" (*pollas harmonias*). "When Euripides, Pherecrates, Aristophanes or Plato spoke of *harmonia* in a general sense," says Düring, "they took it to denote a tune of a certain character, a *melōidia* or *agōgē tēs melōidias* with a certain characteristic sequence of notes."[37] Düring has provided an excellent basic definition of mode, one that may be valid for as late a period as the first half of the fifth century.

Mousike has saved the worst until last. The other offenders were arraigned in two or three lines apiece, relating to technical musical matters. If lines 22–24 are included, Timotheus of Miletus (ca.450–ca.390 B.C.) gets three or four times as much attention (18–26), an indication of his importance. He was, and he remains, by far the best-known practitioner of the "New Music," which he championed openly and loudly; his claim to be a defender of tradition has never convinced anyone. The present-day fame, or rather notoriety, of Timotheus comes from the fact that the text of his most celebrated composition has in part survived. This is the kitharodic nome (*nomos*)

---

[36] Paul Brandt (Hans Licht, pseud. 1974, 494–95) discusses *strobilos* with reference to sexual activity. According to him, it is "a nickname which needs no explanation." He seems unaware of the occurrence of the term either in Pherecrates or in the comic poet Plato (245 Kock).

[37] Düring 1945, 194.

known as the *Persians,* for solo voice with kithara; it dates from the period 419–416 B.C. The work brought him phenomenal success, after the failure of earlier attempts. We can hardly escape calling both its diction and its metrics extraordinarily bizarre, although the latter can be reduced to simple systems, as West has recently reminded us. The style strikes some readers as libretto writing, like certain lyrics of Euripides but far more extreme. At all events, the *Persians* exemplifies the kind of lyric nome that Pherecrates abominated. Thus *Mousikē* alleges that Timotheus' melodies do not keep on an even course but writhe about and go shockingly high.[38] Here metaphors mingle with phrases that relate, more or less technically, to music. The two levels of usage overlap at times; they are difficult to distinguish even when a distinction seems to have been intended.

Pherecrates' reference to the high notes as *huperbolaious* (22) has a surprisingly technical ring; in the theoreticians' treatises from Aristoxenus onward, this same adjective will designate the highest tetrachord of any scale. Here, in the fifth century, it occurs unexpectedly. The other reference to high notes is *niglarous,* in the next line (23). The noun *niglaros,* sometimes identified with a small Egyptian aulos, means "whistle" in Aristophanes' *Acharnians* (554), produced in 425 B.C. Fifteen years later, another comic poet would presumably have used it with the same meaning; but the application of Pherecrates' image is much less clear. Although both context and grammar link *niglarous* with *huperbolaious,* the author of the pseudo-Plutarchian *De musica* cites the text in two separate installments. He places the lines numbered 24–26 here after all the rest and wrongly attributes them to another poet. This mishandling has somewhat disturbed the text of line 24, so that we cannot be sure about the correlative of *niglarous.*[39]

In a fragment of a lost comedy, Eupolis, a well-known comic poet contemporary with Aristophanes and Pherecrates, uses the verb *niglareuein* to describe the technique of producing the second harmonic on a lyre string.[40] Sounded by touching the string lightly at midpoint, this harmonic makes available the next highest octave note. One

---

[38] Düring (1945, 196) identifies the genus as chromatic; this seems mere conjecture.

[39] For one thing, the connectives *te . . . kai* do not seem to be employed correctly. See also above, n. 28.

[40] Frag. 110, 1: 287 Kock; Düring 1945, 196. This use of the second harmonic had been introduced early in the fifth century, by Lysander of Sicyon: see Barker 1982, and now West 1992b, 69, 342.

could perhaps argue that the resulting tone quality somewhat resembles that of a whistle, but it cannot be called shrill. As any string player knows, the opposite holds true; yet the nature of the charges brought by *Mousikē* requires that *niglarous* should convey a sense of earsplitting shrillness. Pherecrates, then, uses this term in much the same way as Aristophanes. What he seeks to describe is not the melodious, almost ethereal sound of octave harmonics, but something quite different: the painful caterwauling of voices pushed beyond their upper limit.

We must reckon with a number of complicating factors, among them the familiar ambiguity of *chordē* (or *-chordos*) and uncertainty as to whether a number of compositions are dithyrambs or nomes; only in the case of Cinesias are the former mentioned, as Barker notes. Nevertheless, the direction of Pherecrates' attack appears clear enough, and the lines with which it closes (25–26) give the impression of a calculated rounding off. In line 26 *aneluse,* "undoes" matches *anēke,* "unstrung," in line 2. Melanippides had been the first to debauch *Mousikē;* Timotheus, last and worst, uses precisely the same means—a dozen notes (3, 26). As before, a hint of the meaning "strings" is necessary for the double entendre. By repeating *dōdeka chordais* and by once again using this phrase to close off the line, Pherecrates rather neatly establishes the limits of the monologue.

The one new point at the end is the picture of *Mousikē* being caught while walking alone, something that respectable Greek women did not risk. On the level of sexual innuendo it suggests, therefore, that she has become a prostitute. Where music is concerned, it must refer to preludes and interludes on the kithara. Pherecrates' point of course involves the aulos as well, and to an extent at least as great; but mentioning it would not have suited his comic strategy.

The plaint of *Mousikē* may be accounted feeble alongside any comparable passage from Aristophanes. It is valuable because it is the last text from the Hellenic period to deal more than briefly with the realities of musical performance. No Greek poet after Pherecrates will seek to tell us as much, and it is not necessarily his fault if we sometimes fail to understand what he says.

Passing reference has been made to theories of musical ethos. During the later decades of the fifth century, these found a uniquely eloquent and powerful champion in Damon of Athens. Critics have devoted a good deal of attention to him; at times they have exaggerated his place in the history of Greek music, although it is without question a prominent one. Only four brief statements come down to us as his own words; three of these have to do with musical ethos and its furtherance of moral behavior in society.

So far as we know, neither Damon nor anyone else before Aristotle's time used *ēthos* of music, with reference to those powers of ethical characterization and habituation that were ascribed to various modes and, less often, to rhythms. The same caution applies to the adjective *ēthikos*. The form *ēthea,* the uncontracted plural of *ēthos,* occurs several times in Homer, always to denote the accustomed haunts or lairs of animals. During the same early period Hesiod, in the long didactic poem that we call the *Works and Days,* uses the singular as well as the plural; the three occurrences all describe a human being, or the likeness of one in the person of Pandora. As the gods assemble her and grace her with dangerous charms, Zeus commands Hermes to place in her *kuneon te noon kai epiklopon ēthos,* "a shameless mind and a deceitful nature" (67).[41] Obeying, Hermes endows her with "lies and wheedling talk, and a deceitful nature" (68). The human of whom the poet uses *ēthos* is an imagined mate for a man who wishes to make the right choice in marriage. She should be sixteen; she must also be a virgin, so that her husband may "teach her good habits" (*ēthea kedna didaxēis*) (699). This last phrase recurs near the beginning of Hesiod's other long surviving poem, the *Theogony:* the Muses sing the *ēthea kedna* of the immortals (66–67).

Almost from the beginnings of Greek literature, then, *ēthos* could be used in any of three distinct ways. It might describe habitual human behavior, with the use of a metaphor of place; it was qualified by adjectives expressing moral evaluation and was closely associated with others (such as "shameless") of the same order; and it could be taught. Hesiod assumes this last point, as the Sophists and most other Greeks did two centuries later. It does not seem an exaggerated claim to say that the groundwork was laid early for speculations about musical ethos.

To be sure, there is a long way to go before we reach the theorizing

---

[41] Used metaphorically here, *kuneos* means literally "of or like a dog." *Epiklopos* is not a metaphor: it derives from *klōps,* "thief."

of a Damon, let alone that of the fourth-century philosophers. Though he is avowedly didactic, Hesiod never connects ethos with music. Neither Damon nor Plato gives the term a musical context, despite the strong connection that both make. Only in Aristotle does it appear, along with *ēthikos,* as a part of numerous allusions to the affective properties of mode. The pre-Damonian period offers few clues to what used to be called the theory of ethos; its origin is disputed, and the question probably will remain open. Opinion is divided between two possibilities—Greek beginnings as against foreign—when both may well have played a part. Those who propound a doctrine of native origins see Pythagorean influence everywhere, with little proof.[42]

From the fifth and fourth centuries we have the names of more than twenty Pythagorean philosophers, but almost no writings. One long fragment and three shorter ones survive from the treatises on mathematics and harmonics written by Archytas of Tarentum, who represents the Pythagorean tradition of the first half of the fourth century.[43] One of these excerpts deals in part with music:

> [In the case of auloi,] when the breath expelled from the mouth falls on the holes nearest the mouth, a higher note is given out because of the greater force, but when it falls on the holes further away, a lower note results. Clearly, swift motion produces a high-pitched sound, slow motion a low-pitched sound.
>
> Moreover, the "whirlers" [*rhombos,* an instrument whirled round on a string] . . . which are swung round at the Mysteries: if they are whirled gently, they give out a low note, if vigorously, a high note. So too with the reed [*ho kalamos*]: if one stops its lower end and blows, it gives out a low kind of note; but if one blows into the middle or some part of it [*hoposton meros*], it will sound high; for the same breath passes weakly through the long distance, powerfully through the lesser.

This passage is one of the earliest attempts by a Greek thinker to account for the varying ways in which sound is transmitted. Not

[42] Ancient speculation about rhythmic ethos comes almost entirely from late sources. We do have a very brief reference in Plato to Damonian theory on the subject (*Rep.* 400c1–3); it yields little that is not obvious. For a summary, see West 1992b, 157–59; Damon himself, 244.

[43] Freeman 1948, 79. The tradition that Archytas wrote a work on auloi is of doubtful validity.

surprisingly, the Greeks never got quite as far as a hypothesis of vibration frequencies. For our purposes, however, the passage proves interesting because of the musical examples Archytas has chosen. The instruments he mentions are auloi, rhombs or bull-roarers, and what he calls *ho kalamos,* "the reed."

His observation concerning the pitch of aulos finger holes could not be simpler. As for the bull-roarer, it was and is a noisemaker. Among adults, it has always been restricted to ritual use—in Greece, the secret rituals of the mystery religions.[44] Archytas' reference to "the reed" is another matter. It has been mistranslated in the German version given by Hermann Diels and Walther Kranz and also in the English one by Kathleen Freeman. The reason may be that the lexicons, LSJ at least, have not taken account of Archytas' usage. Like Latin *calamus,* the noun *kalamos* is basically "reed" but most often something made out of reed, for example, a pen or fishing pole or musician's pipe.

Normally, that pipe is in actual fact a pair of pipes with reed mouthpieces, the instrument that we call the aulos or double aulos. Archytas, however, cannot be speaking of this, since he has already done so. Though somewhat difficult, the Greek of his description admits of only one interpretation: it is that he had in mind the simple length of reed or cane that most often formed a part of the composite variety of syrinx. This instrument was regarded in late antiquity as having two forms, the *surinx monokalamos* and the *surinx polukalamos.* The former, a rarity, had finger holes; the latter did not, with a few unimportant exceptions. Throughout the Hellenic and Hellenistic periods, the syrinx was rectangular, again with a very small number of exceptions. Its pipes, therefore, had to be stopped in varying degrees so that the desired notes would sound. The stopping was done by plugging the bore with wax, and it is this method to which Archytas refers. For the makers of syrinxes, simple country types though they may have been, the process was not a random one; neither was it random as Archytas conceived of it. *Hopostos,* the adjective with

---

[44] The *rhombos* is mentioned at the end of a papyrus dated to about 30 B.C. that contains thirty lines from an Orphic liturgy; frag. 1B Diels-Kranz (hereafter D-K). For this occurrence, Freeman (1948, 7) translates it as "rattle," since here context clearly shows that it is one of the toys of the child Dionysus-Zagreus: it is listed along with a mirror and also knucklebones (*astragaloi*), prized by Greek boys.

which he qualifies *meros*, "part," can only denote a place in an ordered series.

Archytas' choices are unexpected. He ignores the quintessentially Hellenic instrument, Apollo's lyre, in favor of the bull-roarer. By the standards of lyre or aulos, the *rhombos* is not even a musical instrument: it is a child's toy or, like the sistrum, a noisemaker used in the secret rituals of the mystery cults. His further choice of the *kalamos* proves surprising from another point of view. For the final demonstration of his thesis, Archytas takes the simplest of all wind instruments. As a single, unelaborated pipe it was a country diversion; most often it constituted a mere component of the familiar herdsman's syrinx.

By the close of the fifth century, Greek literature had produced the last of its great works to come from the creative imagination. Aristophanes staged the extant version of his *Plutus* a dozen years later, in 388 B.C.; to the same or nearly the same time is ascribed the composition of Plato's *Republic*. This juxtaposition of works by authors both of whom were masters of Attic Greek shows how clearly the ascendancy had passed to prose.

Archytas' comments serve to underscore the fact that prose writers of the fourth century begin to give us some sense of the speculations about modality at the time. The first extant treatise on harmonic theory, by Aristotle's pupil Aristoxenus, comes from late in the century. After a long interval, other treatises were produced by theoreticians of the Alexandrian, Graeco-Roman, and Roman periods. To these must be added the large body of references to music that are contained in the *Deipnosophists* of Athenaeus, together with a very large number of entries in three lexicons, those of Pollux and Hesychius and also the huge Byzantine compilation known as the *Suda*.

This last work was compiled less than a century before William of Normandy led his forces across the Channel. The closeness in time between the two events may help to make clear how vast was the expanse of centuries over which scholars commented on the nature of Greek music. All too often their comments have been taken, and continue to be taken, as a credible and indeed authoritative body of knowledge. Since the nineteenth century there has been little critical examination of the authors' credentials or of the contributions made by early theorists. On the contrary: several influential studies must be termed uncritical.[45]

Nonetheless, from Hellenistic antiquity to the present day this material, gathering mass and force like an avalanche, has dominated many studies of Greek music. Since the 1920s, Winnington-Ingram had treated it with exemplary judiciousness; the general tendency, by contrast, has been to ransack it for terms with which to attempt a description of music played and sung during the classical period, from the pre-Hellenic centuries at least as far as the late fourth century. In varying degrees, the result characterizes almost every published treatment of the subject: the long history of Greek music is, so to speak, read backwards. This has had predictable consequences, one of them especially egregious: over the course of more than a century, various writers on the subject have identified the Hellenic *harmoniai* with the system of octave species (*eidē*), first described by Aristoxenus in the late fourth century. Several recent works show the error persisting.[46]

To ask what was the nature of fifth-century modality is to pose the most difficult question of all about a period that holds far too many difficulties. Of necessity, any answers will be controversial. On the basis of the evidence that we have been considering here, and of much else besides, a start can be made from the following assumption: during the course of that century, so filled with change of every kind, a shift occurred from the "old" *harmoniai* to octave species. Modes of the archaic and early to middle Hellenic periods were not interchangeable. At most, the probability is that they duplicated each other only to a limited degree, and that more characteristics than lie within our knowledge differentiated each of them. By contrast, oc-

---

[45] Three examples are the exaggerated importance given to Damon by Deiters (1870), the strong seconding opinions of Schäfke (1937), and the treatment of Damon as a veritable giant by Lasserre in the prefatory essay (almost a book in itself) to his 1954 edition of the pseudo-Plutarchian treatise *De musica*. The shortcomings of this edition have been set forth at length by Düring in his 1955 review, which few scholars of ancient Greek music seem to have read. Recent years have seen the publication of Barker's *Harmonic and Acoustic Theory* in the series *Greek Musical Writings*; the judiciousness of his translations and commentary contrasts with the excesses of these earlier works.

[46] Pintacuda 1978, 41 n. 32, 49; Michaelides 1978, 127; cf. 90 (*eidos* not connected with the seven *eidē* of the *dia pasōn*). The practice of reading music history backwards was, of course, to be found among the Hellenic Greeks themselves. For the case of Terpander, see West 1992b, 330.

tave species were segments of a single sequence of intervals, those of the Dorian *harmonia* taken over at some unknown point in its development. They contrasted markedly with the individual modes.

The shift between these two very different kinds of modality cannot have been sudden, nor can it have been complete at any one given moment. Such changes seldom, if ever, display the neatness dear to the hearts of many musicologists. Accordingly, we cannot say with certainty whether the few fifth-century references that bear closely on modality concern octave species or the individual forms that preceded them. Usually the possibility of making a distinction lessens because of the ambiguity that the texts themselves display. Sometimes the provenance or the date of an item of evidence has been called into question: so with Ion of Chios and Pratinas. Throughout the century, moreover, we find disappointingly few technical references, with scarcely any mention even of the note names. In view of all this, confident pronouncements about fifth-century music—and there is no lack of them in print—must be treated with more than a little skepticism.

During the fifth century, the only important instruments were the lyre and kithara, which underwent no fundamental change that can be seen in the vase paintings, and the aulos, which changed significantly. Some evidence does indicate an increase in the number of strings: we cannot explain away the story that the Spartan magistrates proposed to cut away extra strings from Timotheus' kithara.[47] Whether true or apocryphal, the story could not have come into being unless extra strings were a fact, at least in certain widely known instances. Yet hundreds of vase paintings demonstrate the rule: in every conceivable kind of situation, public or private, they show seven-stringed instruments. Extra strings were added by virtuosi; the process had nothing to do with everyday lyre playing.

The aulos must be looked at very differently. Even the most "primitive" flute with finger holes—an instrument as old as the Stone Age—admits of the use of cross-fingering (stopping two holes, with a third left open between them) and partial obturation (stopping only a portion of a hole). Such techniques will produce a variety of notes greater than could have been obtained on any normal lyre or

---

[47] Plut. *Instituta Laconica* 17; Edmonds 1967, 3:287.

kithara.[48] Leaving harmonics out of account, the range of an aulos is limited above all by its effective speaking length. Measurement of this length begins at varying points along the reed mouthpiece. Unfortunately, no mouthpiece has been found on any of the very small number of surviving aulos tubes preserved whole, or even accompanying the numerous fragments of body tubes. Nevertheless, many have sought to learn the secrets of these relics, by estimating the missing portion or again by fitting facsimiles with reed mouthpieces.

A less problematical approach has been taken recently by Bélis in an examination of the Louvre auloi, which have been dated to the end of the fourth century.[49] Through careful measurement of the distances between finger holes, she has demonstrated that the borings actually embody certain of the ratios specified by late theorists. Looking to the earlier period, it will be recalled that these finger holes, shown in a great many vase paintings, apparently numbered four (the Neolithic complement!) or five throughout the fifth century; but we do not have sufficient evidence to be sure that we know the whole story. At least some of the fourth-century innovations, such as auxiliary finger holes and rotating metal sleeves, may have made their first appearance decades before that century began.

Neither the literature of the time nor its art offers proof of ensemble playing in the strict sense, that of two or more instruments heard simultaneously. Of course, this is not to say that both kithara and aulos did not figure in the presentation of accompanied choral works. References in Pindar alone to the "mingled sound" of the two would disprove such a claim. Usually they were separate, however, and when both were included in a performance there is no evidence of their having been used at the same moment. We cannot be sure that this did not in fact occur at times, at the octave, for example, where differences in intonation would not have posed a problem, or at the keynote.

The development of music in Greece will be less difficult to understand if we take into account the separateness of strings and wood-

---

[48] Overblowing has been omitted from consideration here. Its use by auletes is very far from established fact. See Baines 1957, 201, and Schlesinger 1970, 52–56, on the separate possibility of raising finger hole pitches by a perfect fifth through shortening the vibrating length of the tongue of a single-reed mouthpiece.

[49] Bélis 1984a.

winds. Repeated modern attempts to set up a general theory of lyre tuning or notation or modality itself have been predicated on only one of the two main instruments. Their failure should warn us that kithara and aulos may have been more separate in performance than has generally been realized.[50]

During the fifth century, the amateur musician remains a recognizable figure. Only in its last decades does the traditional education lose ground to a significant degree; and it was not by any means entirely displaced, though the protests of Old Comedy writers may give this impression. It is plain, however, that their indignation had a basis in reality. Especially during the latter half of the century, the specialist increasingly invades and seeks to take over various areas of culture: prominent among them is *mousikē*. He has a variety of names, including *mousikos;* this term now begins to denote not a musician but an expert in the theoretical aspects of melody and rhythm. Eventually it was to be the epithet par excellence of Aristotle's brilliant pupil Aristoxenus; for the fifth century, Damon exemplifies it.

Another name given to the specialist is *philosophos,* reportedly coined by Pythagoras. The early pre-Socratics, products of the oral tradition, couched their thoughts in the form of aphorism or verse; they rarely touched on music. The first to do so were the Pythagoreans, in the second half of the century; but their order frowned on the expression of any views other than those of the Master. Socrates received no training in *mousikē* in boyhood; as a man, he proved to be its enemy.[51] Shortly before his death he declared, according to Plato, that he had always thought *philosophia* the chief and most important "music," *hē megistē mousikē.*[52] Few statements could have made clearer

---

[50] "The kind of tune suitable for the *kithara* is not appropriate for the *aulos,*" says Aristides Quintilianus (2.12, p. 77.26–27 W-I); translation by Barker (1989:479), who mentions also Pl. *Rep.* 399c–e and ps.-Plut. *Mus.* 29–30, 1141c. The central point in the strictures leveled by the Platonic Socrates is his claim that the "panharmonic" instruments—those that make available the whole range of *harmoniai*—are really imitations of the aulos (399d4–5). The author of the pseudo-Plutarchian *De musica* refers to the revolution in musical composition that Lasus achieved by taking the *poluphōnia* of the aulos as his guide.

[51] His father, a stonemason, was typical of a class that did not receive a training in *mousikē.*

[52] Diogenes Laërtius (1.12; echoed in 8.8), on the authority of Heraclides Ponticus, says that Pythagoras first used the term *philosophia* and called himself a *philosophos.* See Kirk and Raven 1971, 229, n. 3 to citation 278. The Platonic Socrates on *philosophia* and *mousikē: Phd.* 60e2–61b7; Anderson 1966, 252 n. 69; Havelock 1963, 284.

the error involved in choosing the term "music" to render *mousikē*. The Greek term designates here the oral training in poetry—sung to lyre accompaniment or recited without it—that had for so long been the means of transmitting the values and precepts of Greek culture.

Toward the end of the century, this oral basis was increasingly replaced by the use of written materials; Plato makes Socrates himself comment on this.[53] *Philosophia* had begun to supplant *mousikē* as the carrier of values and precepts. Moral excellence could no longer be conveyed by the all-encompassing term *aretē;* instead, Plato's earliest dialogues are to seek out the nature of individual virtues. With the *Republic,* Plato moves to deal with the role of poetry and music in forming or reinforcing or actually subverting two of these virtues, courage and prudence. For what would today be termed elementary and secondary schooling, Plato and Aristotle alike will regard music as having continuing importance. Ethical concerns with the system of *mousikē* had begun to take dim shape in the Pythagorean reverence for number; they emerged clearly in the teachings of Damon.

Finally, it is easy to forget that the everyday process of music making went on, scarcely affected by the innovations of virtuosi and philosophers' debates. A few auletes, most notably Pronomus, and an undetermined number of kitharodes became celebrities. Ordinary musicians continued in their traditional ways with little or no change, so far as can be determined. They held much the same status as before, since the temporary popularity of the aulos would have affected only performers of some prominence. Thus hired or slave auletes, wearing the customary long and elaborate robes, continued to provide ceremonial accompaniments for sacrifices and funerals. Such scenes looked much as they had on the Minoan-Mycenaean frescoes and the Hagia Triada sarcophagus. The piping was provided by men; the *aulētrides,* scantily clad young women, were paid to provide all-male gatherings of symposiasts with aulos music and with fellation.[54] Usually their earnings went to the pimp or procuress who had had them trained. Their accomplishments as musicians did not

---

[53] Copies of the works of Anaxagoras for sale in Athens: Pl. *Ap.* 26d10-e1.

[54] At times they were simply call girls. This is illustrated by a story that Diogenes Laërtius tells to show the self-control of the philosopher Zeno in sexual matters (7.13). Although girl lyre players do appear as a part of early symposium scenes, Greek art never shows a respectable woman playing the aulos. (A Muse may do so, however.)

have to be impressive; probably they played with less skill than many amateurs.

It is these amateurs who should be remembered along with the others whom we have mentioned, especially the countless freeborn women who in their private apartments played an impressive array of stringed (but not wind) instruments—the lyre, the barbitos, the so-called cradle kithara, several varieties of harp, and still other harplike instruments that cannot be identified with certainty. A hand-held drum, the *tumpanon,* provided the rhythmic emphasis that could never be obtained sufficiently on plucked strings.

Many of these day-to-day facts continued unchanged throughout the classical period. Such activities did not call attention to themselves; they went unrecorded except for the genre scenes of which potters, or rather patrons, were so fond. The recoverable history of Greek music in the fourth century is something quite different, for the evidence is supplied by philosophical treatises.

{6}

Plato and Aristotle

Plato reveals little concerning the world of the practicing musician. Unlike Socrates, he was an aristocrat; he claimed descent from Codrus, the last king of Athens, and from Solon as well. It was inevitable that he should have received a thorough training in *mousikē* and *gumnastikē*. Here again he differs from his teacher, a late learner. Like any aristocrat of his time, he thought expert musicianship to be *aneleutheron,* not befitting the freeborn man (*eleutheros*). The dialogues afforded a unique opportunity to display his bias; only in this respect, perhaps, was Plato unusual. Yet we may wonder whether another *aristos* would have carried the manner to such an extreme. He seems almost to take a perverse delight in pretending not to know what he must have known perfectly well; or he will claim only a vague recall of details concerning Damonian theory that would have been entirely familiar.

Besides the fact of social status, two further points may explain Plato's affectation of ignorance and his imperfect recollection. He was speaking through the persona of a stonemason's son, a man who had received no musical training except in old age. He could not, therefore, step out of character. The second point, far more controversial, is one that the Dutch scholar A. J. Janssens was beginning to develop in 1941. He suggested that Plato's statements constituted a rebuttal ("repliek") to those made by Damon. The projected studies never appeared, and in any case classicists do not care to be told that Plato sometimes differed with his celebrated predecessor (*expertus dico*).

Janssens' published articles are so little known, however, that his view deserves mention here. Had these publications been written in one of the major languages, they might have met a different fate.

It has been remarked that Plato avoids using technical musical terms. *Harmonikos* does appear for the first time in the *Phaedrus*, contrasted with *mousikos*, but it is an isolated instance. The same passage presents harmonicists as ridiculously proud of the ability to produce "the highest and lowest note [*chordēn*]."[1] It is because of his distaste for all forms of cant that Plato uses nontechnical language here. His choice of words does not come from ignorance of the relevant terms: in the *Republic* (443d6–7), he uses both *nētē* and *hupatē*, and *mesē* as well. He never gave *eidos* the special technical meaning "octave species"; neither did Aristotle. Thus, when Socrates declares in the *Republic* that the category of musical sounds includes "four *eidē*, from which all the *harmoniai* are formed" (400a1–6), at least we know what *eidos* does not mean. As for a positive interpretation, there has been much dispute. J. Adam ably summed it up at the beginning of the twentieth century; in a recent work, Barker continues the discussion with equally good judgment. Despite some difficulties, both favor D. B. Monro's thesis, quoted by Adam, that the *eidē* referred to here are "the four ratios which give the primary musical intervals—viz. the ratios 2:1, 3:2, 4:3, and 9:8, which give the octave, fifth, fourth and tone."[2]

With Plato, as with any figure from the close of the fifth century or the first half of the fourth, we must often make our way through a difficult and well-nigh impassable borderland between theory and practice. On many occasions it proves impossible to say with confidence whether the one or the other, or perhaps both, may be meant.

---

[1] *Phdr.* 268d8–e1. In *Philebus* 17c4–9, the same point is made and in almost the same terms (4:*baru kai oxu*). As Barker notes (1984a, 184 n. 3, sec. 162), the noun *harmonikos* is "Aristoxenus' word for his predecessors in the field of 'harmonic analysis'"; they studied *harmonikē* (*technē*), the science of the *harmonia*. The term was first used in this sense by his teacher, Aristotle (*Top.* 107a16).

[2] Adam 1938, on 400ab; see also Barker 1984a, 133 n. 35. Even Aristoxenus uses the term *eidos* throughout the *Harmonics* in one of two ways, either as having a broad, nontechnical sense or with reference to the three kinds of genus. Only in the last few lines of his treatise does he apply it to octave species, and even there the placing of intervals within the tetrachord according to genus is a powerful factor. The 9:8 ratio for the tone, however, goes outside the terms of the tetractys.

If Plato proves elusive, an added reason can be found in the *Philebus*. There he declares *mousikē* to be full of *empeiria*, trial and error, "since it tunes a concordant level [*to sumphōnon harmottousa*] not by measure but by experiment based on practice." This empiricism, Socrates goes on, is the special mark of "the whole art of aulos playing . . . , which goes hunting after the position [*to metron*] of each of the movable(?) notes [*hekastēs chordēs . . . pheromenēs*] by experimentation." The result proves to be "a considerable admixture of uncertainty, with little that is firmly established." Later in the dialogue, he gives a summary of these remarks: "*Mousikē*, as I was saying a little while ago, is full of experimenting and imitation."[3]

Socrates' phrase *hekastēs chordēs . . . pheromenēs* catches our attention. He is claiming that auletes hunt in a trial-and-error fashion; further, that they do so not for every note, *hekastē chordē*, but either (1) for every one that is *pheromenē* or (2) for every note while it is in this state. The qualifying term is the present middle-passive participle of *pherein*. One of the commonest Greek verbs, it means "bear, carry" in any of a multitude of possible senses. When it occurs in the pseudo-Aristotelian *Problems* (19.35a, 920a36-b3; *phora*, the cognate noun, also appears there) this participial form denotes the vibration of a string that has been set in rapid motion. It may have been for this reason that Benjamin Jowett here translated Plato's use of *pheromenēs* by "vibrating." But Plato does not have stringed instruments in mind; nor did Greek musical or acoustical theory ever quite succeed in conceptualizing our system of measurement according to vibrations per second.

Several possibilities remain. One nontechnical explanation might be that Socrates is carrying through his metaphor from hunting. On that hypothesis, *pheromenēs* would mean something like "on the wing." It has been placed between two strongly colored verbs: *stochazdesthai* originally meant "aim at," as a bowman does; *thēreu-*

---

[3] *Phlb.* 56a3–7; *empeiria*, understood here, has just been mentioned, 55e6. A summary is found at 62c1–2. Barker's careful discussion of text and meaning in 56a (1987) is indispensable for any examination of this passage. General agreement will be found between his arguments and those independently put forward here. He has briefly shown that neither "guesswork" nor "estimate" correctly renders *stochasmōi* in a4. It remains true that this noun and the verb *stochazdesthai* often do denote guessing in Hellenic writers, not least in Plato. A detailed study of the usages might be useful.

ousa, "hunting for," is a metaphor at a short remove from the literal sense. This circumstance might be thought to give support to the translation just proposed. Or again, Plato may instead have allowed a term that properly fits only *chordē* as "string" to remain—this despite the fact that the noun must bear the sense "note," its other common meaning. The metaphor of the hunt might still apply, though on another level.

A third possibility can be suggested: this passage may contain the earliest example of *pheromenos* in the technical musical sense that Aristoxenus and later writers repeatedly give it: "movable." The movable notes (*phthonggoi*) are the two within the tetrachord that shift position according to the genus, or variety of genus, that happens to be in use. As *pheromenoi,* they are distinguished from the *hestōtes,* the "standing" (i.e., fixed) notes at either limit of the tetrachord; these do not undergo change. The latter would appear to be what Socrates, earlier in the dialogue, had called "the limits of the intervals" (17d1). Throughout the *Philebus,* he shows a great deal of concern for measure (*to metron*), the art of measurement (*hē metrētikē* [*technē*]), and mensurability generally. Here the "measure" of the note—that is, its placing within a modal sequence—comes under consideration.

The boundary notes of the tetrachord could be determined precisely in any of a number of ways, for example, by overblowing or by altering the amount of the beating-reed mouthpiece that was covered by the player's lips. Socrates' words, therefore, do not apply well to the fixed notes, but they eminently suit the two notes located in varying positions between them. These sounded from two finger holes on the "archaic" aulos, which had a single row of openings and no apparatus. The instrument of Plato's time afforded a greater variety of choice, a fact that provoked his sharp displeasure; and to this variety we can add the fingering techniques used to modify pitch. In the passage under discussion, *pheromenēs* has no sure translation; but whether or not Plato intended the technical meaning "movable," his reference seems to apply best to the shifting inner notes of the tetrachord.

If Plato did (quite uncharacteristically) admit a technical usage into his style, this does not warrant assuming any established system of genera, with clear distinctions. The *pheromenoi*—the variable notes placed toward the lower portion of the tetrachord's compass—may have varied unsystematically during most, if not all, of the archaic and classical periods. Traces of this instability can perhaps be discerned in Plato's use of *pheromenēs* here; and arguably it appears in the persistent tradition that the early form of the enharmonic genus had undivided semitones instead of two dieses (quarter tones, approximately).

The empiricism that Plato here calls *stochasmos,* from the act of aiming an arrow, contrasts with the comfortable certainty afforded by measurement. Early in the fifth century, the aulos enjoyed general popularity for a few decades among freeborn Athenians. They knew nothing about it otherwise, save for what would have been obvious from hearing the instrument on many occasions. Specialists such as Damon were exceptions, and Plato at times betrays the fact of his association with some of these men. Yet it is also a fact, and one that a number of scholars have pointed out, that the musical "innovations" that Plato attacked were already a half century old.

One wonders, then, whether devices and techniques to expand the capacities of the aulos form his target here as well, and if so, whether they really are new. Rotating sleeves and lateral rows of additional finger holes are usually mentioned when such questions arise, since surviving specimens or sizable fragments of Graeco-Roman auloi display both features, along with speaker keys. Late writers connect the early development of this type of aulos with the brilliant Theban school, particularly the aulete Diodorus; and certainly Aristophanes recognizes the preeminence of Thebes as a center of aulos playing.

Again, in a discussion of parallel—not divergent—double pipes, Anthony Baines describes the process of "tuning the pipes just off unison so that their notes 'beat'. The tuning is done by pushing the reeds in or out, and it may take a considerable time; one folk-music explorer in the Balkans witnessed a man take over an hour tuning before he began his piece."[4] It is not possible here to pursue the possibility (only now beginning to gain attention) that the diverging pipes of the double aulos were tuned overall in an interval relationship not precisely a unison. Baines's comment leads, however, to the thought that getting just the right extrusion of its two reed mouth-

---

[4] Baines 1957, 196. Barker (1987, 106) speaks of auletes tuning in advance "by adjusting the length of reed protruding from the bore"; as he acknowledges, this was by no means a prominent part of their activities.

pieces cannot have been a quick or easy matter. So far as anyone knows, the process was accomplished by trial and error. It had to be done with precision, or every note would simply have seemed out of tune. The sight of an aulete experimenting with his reeds could have sufficed to make Plato level the criticisms voiced in the *Philebus*.

This conjecture does not depend on the presence of keywork and similar apparatus; the uncomplicated double aulos shown on vase paintings will illustrate the point involved. On the other hand, it deals with a kind of unison, one that was to be classified as an example of *homophōnia* rather than *sumphōnia*. The question thus arises of what Plato would have understood by *to sumphōnon* in this passage of the *Philebus*. There is no easy answer; technical usage seems still to have been far from achieving a fixed state. Even late theorists differ somewhat regarding the division between *homophōnos* and *sumphōnos* intervals. Accordingly, we ought not to rule out the possibility that, for Plato, a near unison was a "symphonic" tone relationship.

Whether Socrates or someone else is the speaker, Plato's part in a new attitude toward *mousikē* (which occasionally verges on the meaning "music" even in the dialogues) becomes manifest through his reliance on the phrase *rhuthmoi kai harmoniai*. By using it, he gives rhythms equal stature with modal structures and separates them from the original complex of meanings originally bound up with *harmonia*. The terms *rhuthmos* and *harmonia* occur in many of the dialogues. They are perhaps best known because of the special attention that they receive in the *Republic*. At times the singular of each is found; this may have a generalized meaning.[5] When a discussion of music provides the context, the two terms tend to be closely joined plurals, *rhuthmoi kai harmoniai*. For Plato, they represent principally the horizontal and the vertical dimensions of melody. *Rhuthmos* applies also to the performance of a text, for which Plato sometimes uses the specific term *metron,* and to a dancer's movements. The analysis of rhythm does not long antedate Plato's own time; definitions first appear later.[6] Nevertheless, when he came to maturity studies in music theory

[5] Barker (1984a, 163–68, app. A to chap. 10, "Plato") discusses in detail the concept of *harmonia* as found in the dialogues.

[6] A treatise on *rhuthmoi* and *harmoniai* is ascribed to Democritus (68B15c D-K), who was born probably a generation earlier than Plato. On the related point (made below) that Greek writers before Plato did not have this double scheme but used single terms,

had already become a part of the intellectual milieu at Athens. Damon was a famous name; a supposed attempt to recollect his doctrines concerning the rhythms leads Socrates to venture upon the only references to this subject in the dialogues that could be thought at all technical.

Evidently Plato takes *rhuthmoi kai harmoniai* to be what we might call the ordinate and abscissa of music. They make possible the plotting of the way any musical utterance is expressed, whether vocal, instrumental, gestural, or any combination. Earlier Greek writers did not possess this schema; they use single terms such as *aoidē* (*ōidē*), *melos,* or *nomos*. Speaking of "rhythms and modes" betokens a new, analytic phase: the history of Greek music has now advanced farther than we tend to realize. In other cultures, for example, those of India and the Arabic-speaking countries, the course of modal development strongly suggests that both *harmonia* and *nomos* originally denoted a melodic–rhythmic complex recognized as distinguishing the music making of a particular community or group.

Actually, to speak only of melody and rhythm will not suffice if we are attempting to visualize an unknown (or barely known) early period. The prehistory of mode involves dimensions and circumstances that most would now place to one side, as extramusical. Only occasionally does it become evident that certain of these factors have retained their validity in non-Western music: thus we have the well-known association between a particular *rag* and a time of day.[7] So far as thinking about music is concerned, Plato has adopted a sophisticated conception. Rhythm now becomes a separate province instead of what it once was, a characteristic of mode. The new division into two elements suits a time when a standardized scale system was increasingly accepted as normal.

Whether Plato assumes such a system is a question that continues to be debated. The lack of any generally accepted answer can be attributed largely to Plato's reluctance to name and describe *harmoniai;* exceptions are easily tallied. In the short, early dialogue on courage

---

Barker aptly suggests that Pindar may foreshadow such a scheme when he speaks of devising a sparkling new *tropos* for fitting the voice to a Dorian sandal (i.e., meter; the hidden reference may be to the *kroupezdai*) (*Ol.* 3.4–5).

[7] Alan Lomax and his associates (1968) have made clear the presence and importance of these factors in the musical cultures of nonliterate peoples today.

that bears his name, the soldier Laches probably speaks for the average educated Athenian of the time. He maintains that the finest *harmonia* is not that achieved on a lyre, through training acquired during childhood. Rather, one who truly merits the designation *mousikos* (here a wholly ethical term) has harmonized word and deed, making them concordant (*sumphōnon*) "in Dorian and not Iastian—and not in Phrygian or Lydian either, I take it, but in the only truly Hellenic *harmonia*." According to Laches, the man himself and the words that he speaks display a mutual appropriateness and harmoniousness (*harmottonta*).[8]

This homily is unusual, perhaps unique, in shifting the adverbs *dōristi, iasti, phrugisti,* and *ludisti* entirely away from a musical context. With one possible but highly suspect exception in the *Epistles,* Plato never does so, although he employs the underlying equation on countless occasions. Here he makes Laches choose Iastian as the opposite of Dorian, evidently because it formed an obvious contrast that would at once come to mind. Phrygian and Lydian are added as an afterthought, perhaps with a hint of hesitation. Distinct from Dorian, they do not contrast with it but instead are grouped together with it, in a triad accepted as basic throughout the classical period. Laches' words have a special value: they reflect the thinking of freeborn Athenians, men who had undergone a schooling in *mousikē* but took no special interest in music during later life. It is noteworthy that, for Laches, music theorists do not deserve to be called *mousikoi;* he makes no bones about taking an antitheoretical stance.

Elsewhere, Plato names and characterizes modes only in a short passage from the *Republic* (398e10–399a4). Socrates asks Glaucon, as one knowledgeable about music (*mousikos* has its technical sense here), to identify them; but the descriptions are his own from the outset. We learn the following: Mixolydian, Syntonolydian, and some others of that sort are mournful, literally "dirgelike" (*thrēnōideis,* "threnodic," from *thrēnos,* "dirge"). They prove useless even for women who wish to be thought respectable, not to mention men. Some varieties of Iastian and Lydian "are called slack [*chalarai*]" and are associated with drunkenness, conviviality (at the *sumposion*), softness, and idleness. They must be thought wholly unprofitable for

---

[8] *Lach.* 188d2–8; cf. 193d11–e2; Anderson 1966, 240 n. 18.

warlike young men such as the Guardians (*phulakes*). As Glaucon says, this would seem to leave only Dorian and Phrygian. Like Laches, he and Socrates omit all mention of Aeolian (*aiolisti*). One explanation has been that it could even then be equated with Dorian, as was the case later, and thus might be considered a variety of "the only truly Hellenic *harmonia*."

Certain features of this interchange remain to be brought out. First, Socrates sets its direction when he reminds Glaucon of their earlier conclusion: sung texts have no need of mourning (*thrēnoi*) and lamentation being added. "Which, then," he goes on, "are the mournful *harmoniai?*" The same approach prepares the way for Glaucon's naming of other modes; this involves mentioning Chalaro-Iastian and Chalaro-Lydian, the only instance of anything like a description that is not made by Socrates. Untrained in *mousikē,* he speaks as an ordinary Athenian, with a far more down-to-earth approach than Laches shows. His field of reference is the day-to-day experience of a freeborn man. Accordingly, he shows no great concern with music. He sees it in terms of the common occasions of public life—the wake, the *sumposion*. Mourning is a fact of life and of death: what modes are heard when it takes place? The same question arises about the symposium, the chief opportunity for music making. All too clearly, there will be no cakes and ale for the Guardians.

The approach that Plato has Socrates choose here seems nevertheless to be entirely natural. Save for the actual names of the modes, we encounter no technicalities. *Chalaros,* "slack," must of course be mentioned; many believe that it formed an integral part of two of these names. Here, however, we are skirting a disputed area. What proves unsettling is the way in which Plato deliberately takes advantage of the ambiguity of *chalaros*. Its well-established musical meaning comes from string tuning, but like the English translation it may equally well refer to morals. We have seen that, long before Plato, Pherecrates placed the same double entendre (or a very similar one) in the complaint of a much put-upon *Mousikē*. From a poet-composer of Old Comedy, such byplay was to be expected; when Plato employs it as a part of serious argument, the maneuver appears disingenuous at best.

Such considerations apart, mentioning *chalaros* does bring in the factor of pitch, which turns up persistently in connection with the *harmoniai*. To begin with, we know that absolute pitch in our sense had no meaning for Greek musicians; relative pitch did. Though many details remain uncertain, it does appear that within *harmoniai* the center of gravity varied significantly. In effect, this shift made some of them high and others low, within the baritone vocal compass that always set real limits for much of Greek music. Pitch also entered into the relationships between one *harmonia* and another. This fact had practical importance: modulation (*metabolē*) was practiced in some compositional genres from the middle of the sixth century onward, if the late traditions about Lasus can be believed.

For Plato, pitch may be a noteworthy element. The possibility must at least be held open, because of the scale sequences (perhaps Damonian) that Aristides Quintilianus, five or more centuries later, presented as the *harmoniai* discussed in the *Republic*. Although they are remarkable in themselves, what guarantees our careful study is Aristides' extremely explicit declaration—recently misinterpreted— that they are the modes Plato had in mind when he gave directions concerning which ones should or should not be countenanced for the music of his ideal city-state.[9] The conventional signs used for notation are provided by Aristides in both the vocal and the distinctly different instrumental series. All of them originated, at a date that is still being debated, as letters of the alphabet or as forms apparently related to these letters. The six scales are here transposed and represented as sequences that cover portions of a gamut from B to e'. Tetrachords are set off by brackets; italics denote a pitch raised by a quarter tone. Thus rendered, Aristides' scales appear as follows:[10]

[9] T. J. Mathiesen, a recent (1983) translator of Aristides, has denied that this is what he is saying here, but errs both in the commentary and in the actual translation. The words *toutōn dē kai ho theios Platōn . . . mnēmoneuei* (1.9, p. 19.2–3 W-I) emphasize *toutōn*, "these," in no fewer than three ways: by placing it first in the sentence, by underscoring its importance with *dē*, "just (these)," and finally by supplying a second underscoring through the addition of *kai* to *dē*. Denniston (1934, 208–9, 307) makes the usage clear beyond any doubt. "It is just precisely these [modes], " says Aristides, "that Plato mentions in the *Republic*." Much later (3.1 p. 96.27 W-I), he uses the very same construction with regard to four successive numbers: *hōn dē kai ho theios Platōn en Timaiōi mnēmoneuei*, "It is just precisely these that the divine Plato mentions in the *Timaeus*." (Mathiesen has "call to mind" in both passages.) Aristides commits many sins against grammar, but often he does try for a pure Attic style. In these two almost identical instances, he succeeds. He could hardly have phrased his statements more emphatically, one would think, or more plainly. On Mathiesen's translation generally, see Barker's long review (1984b) of his edition.

[10] The diagram is from Anderson 1966, 18; it follows Winnington-Ingram 1968, 22.

	B	*B*	c	*c*	d	*d*	e	*e*	f	g	a	b	*b*	c'	*c'*	d'	*d'*	e'	*e'*
Lydian							e		f	—	a	[b	b	c'————————				e']	e'
Dorian						d	[e	e	f	—	a]	[b	b	c'————————e']					
Phrygian						d	[e	e	f	—	[a]	b	b	c'		d']			
Ionian	[B	B	c————				[e]			----g	a]								
Mixolydian	[B	B	c		d		e]	e	f			————b	(?)						
Syntonolydian	[B	B	c————e]							g									

Aristides omits to say where he found these *harmoniai,* or under what circumstances. They may have come to his attention while he was looking through a commentary on the *Republic:* this recurring conjecture cannot be either confirmed or refuted. Even if we could prove it true, the main questions about these scales would remain unanswered. Thus far, no theory has seemed more credible than that proposed by F. Bellermann in 1847, revived in 1922 by E. Clements, and modified in 1936 by Winnington-Ingram. According to their view, the scales may have been abstracted, as sequences, from specific melodies (Winnington-Ingram aptly suggests the term "styles" instead) that employed only the notes that Aristides includes. All of them are given in enharmonic, a choice consonant with an early date.

The gapped nature of several of these scales argues for their genuineness, though we lack the context that would enable us to say what sort of genuineness. Presumably, a forger would not have allowed such troubling irregularities; nor would he have been likely to put together such a sequence as this Lydian, which has a quarter-tone interval at both extremes. We have seen a similar difficulty with the schematization of the *tonoi.*

Neither Aristides' Lydian nor the offending *tonos* can be taken seriously as a part of musical practice. By contrast, several kinds of evidence witness to the reality and importance of gapped modes. The Aristoxenians had divided scale systems into continuous and "transilient" (*huperbata*)—that is, gapped. Aristides himself takes this characteristic even farther back, to the late fifth century. The *harmoniai* handed down by Damon's followers, he claims, show the "movable" notes within the tetrachord occurring with varied frequency, or actually omitted altogether. For him, this happens because of ethical considerations; it exemplifies the compositional skill known as *petteia,* "selection," which he calls the most valuable part of composition.

Elsewhere he declares that *harmoniai* "did not always include all of the notes"; and it is reasonable to suppose that when he speaks of *petteia,* he has in mind the six Damonian scales identified with those of the *Republic*.[11] Finally, the place of gapped scales in Greek music is assured by the nature of finger–hole spacing on surviving auloi and on some of those shown by vase painters. To this, many would add (more controversially) a vast body of comparative evidence from reed pipes in use today throughout the world.

The question remains, Do Aristides' scales in fact match the *harmoniai* described by Socrates and Glaucon? Recently Barker has concluded that they do. He states the case for his belief in thoughtful and (to this reader) convincing detail; this is a rarely useful contribution to the explanation of a difficult topic. A few years earlier, West had taken Aristides' Ionian, B *B* c e g a, to be the probable embodiment of the four-note scale on the phorminx played by Homer's bards: B c͡ e͡ a.[12] In his equivalent note values, this would be e f͡ a͡ d'. The note names represent the string names *hupatē, lichanos, mesē,* and *neatē* (*nētē*); these are respectively "highest," "forefinger," "middle," and "lowest" ("string," *chordē*) as the tilted lyre was held. Within the tetrachord e——a, the lowest interval, e–f, is the undivided tetrachord assigned to the old enharmonic scale. Late classical writers claimed to know of this form; and so far as we can tell, the tradition that had come down to them is likely to have been based on fact.

Certainly Barker and West have reason to regard Aristides' scales as a valuable window on antiquity, perhaps even (as West maintains) "the means to break into a lost world." A few words of caution must be added. Obviously, these sequences are too much the components of a homogeneous pattern to be identified with *harmoniai* of the early or even of the middle Hellenic period, much less with those of prior times. What Aristides has recorded typifies, it would seem, a stage intermediate between two very different kinds of scale. First came modes that did not duplicate each other to any significant extent. Eventually they were succeeded by the echeloned, closely interrelated scale structures of octave species and *tonoi.* The standardization evident in these six scales vexes any attempt to view them without the

[11] "Movable" notes in the Damonian *harmoniai* and *petteia:* Aristid. Quint. 2.14, pp. 80.25–81.6 W–I; incomplete *harmoniai:* 1.9, p. 18.9 W–I.

[12] Barker 1984a, 163–68; West 1981, 121.

preconceptions of the Aristoxenian system. Yet there is no solid reason to deny that they may originally have come from the decade 390–380 B.C., when Plato wrote the *Republic*. As we noted, he makes the action of his dialogue take place a generation earlier than the time of composition; the year 421 has plausibly been suggested.[13]

This introduces a complicating factor. So does the point trenchantly made by L. Laloy, M. I. Henderson, and not a few others: where music is concerned, Plato shows himself to be well behind the times, viewing with alarm supposed innovations that actually were old hat. Conceivably, then, he has Socrates assign praise or blame to *harmoniai* on the basis of preconceptions that go back beyond 421 B.C. (when Aristophanes was mocking various "enemies" of *mousikē*, not least Socrates), to a time nearer midcentury. The argument may be thought extreme; yet one could accept it as an unlikely possibility and still recognize in Aristides' scales an early attempt at the standardization that resulted, probably around the years 470–450 B.C., in an established common pattern of intervals constituting the octave species. They are an unusually intriguing and valuable gift, as welcome as it is unexpected, from the last major writer on musical theory.

West reasonably argues that for the beginnings of Hellenic modality we do better to consider Aristides' scales than to rest content with the elaborately developed patterns of the theorists. Yet we must heed Winnington-Ingram's words of caution: "In the first place, it is not certain that the tradition has reached us through Aristides uncontaminated, nor do we know for certain what exact stages of development they represent or how far we can postulate corresponding diatonic and chromatic forms; secondly, it is a hazardous matter to draw inferences about modality from bare lists of notes. They tell us the kind of thing the old [*harmoniai*] were, but are hardly conclusive for the modality of any particular one."[14]

Conceivably, the scales offered by Aristides as "Platonic" and extremely ancient may be altered forms of the ones that Plato had heard. Whatever the measure of validity we may grant them, they show how radically the forms of music had changed even by Plato's time. Such "bare lists of notes" accord with the new, limited definition of *harmo-*

---

[13] West (1981) does not deal with this question of the "dramatic date." He does place Aristides' *harmoniai* around the year 420, very close to the usual dating.

[14] Winnington-Ingram 1968, 23–24. See West 1981, 118; 1992b, 174–75.

nia that Plato employs. They give little idea of the complex of traits that had marked the *harmonia,* from the archaic period through much of the fifth century; nor do they afford any sense of how a performer may have brought the notes to life.

Once, however, Plato does seem to come to our aid with regard to performance, when he lays down a series of rules for conducting a lesson in lyre playing. For a proper understanding of this much-disputed passage from the *Laws* (812d1–e6), we need to be aware of its context. The chief speaker, identified only as the "Athenian Stranger," has been explaining to Cleinias, a Cretan, the duties of the *grammatistēs,* who taught reading and writing to boys when they were between the ages of ten and thirteen. After the thirteenth year, they were to take lessons on the lyre for a period of three years (809e7–810a2).[15] Digressing for a time, the Stranger returns to the problem of what is to be admitted into the curriculum for reading and memorization (812b6–7). He decrees literary censorship and then comes back to the main point at issue. In his view, lyre teachers too must follow rules. He suggests that if they recall the earlier recommendations concerning the sexagenarian "singers" (*ōidoi*) of Dionysus, the result will be to assign the lyre teachers "what is fit and proper for their teaching, and also for the whole process of educating [*paideusis*] as it concerns such matters" (668c4–671a1; cf. 667e6–668c3, on *mousikē*). Since Cleinias does not in fact recall this advice, the Stranger obliges with a summary (812b9–c7).

We now see (he goes on) that the lyre teachers, no less than the aged choristers who are to exercise cultural censorship, must be especially quick to perceive whatever has to do with the rhythms and structures (*sustaseis*) of the *harmoniai.* Such quickness will enable them to determine the "rightness" (*orthotēs*) of a setting—that is, whether the poet-composer has assigned it the right mode and rhythm (670b4).[16] Moreover, he will not necessarily know whether his composition is

---

[15] According to Hippocrates (*Coän Prognoses* 1, p. 321 Kühn), a boy's voice changed in the fourteenth year.

[16] This shows how completely centered on the text Plato's conception of sung poetry was. It is not by coincidence that his well-known condemnation of instrumental music without words, on grounds of meaning and worth alike, occurs only a few lines earlier (669e2–4). On the confusion in the main statement of the three criteria (669a7–b3), see Anderson 1966, 105.

good as mimesis, apart from the question of its being right—though Plato fails to distinguish consistently between the two criteria. Like the aged "singers" of Dionysus, the lyre teachers do possess this knowledge. As a consequence, they will be empowered, and indeed required, to select for their young pupils compositions that will represent (*mimeisthai*) something of value. The word *homoiōma*, "likeness," which we occasionally find in the earlier dialogues, makes its first appearance in the *Laws* when the Stranger summarizes his earlier instructions. Lyre teachers are to choose from "likenesses of the good," here the good soul moved by emotion, "and again of the opposite sort." The latter they will reject; with the former, they will "en-chant the souls of the young."[17] Using the compositions thus sanctioned for performance, they will invite each student to pursue moral excellence (*aretē*): this he is to accomplish by following their precepts through the chosen examples of correct and edifying mimesis.

After Cleinias has assented to the accuracy of this summary, his companion specifies the limits that must be observed in teaching the lyre. "Well then [*toinun*]," says the Stranger (812b5), echoing the phrasing that he had used earlier when he referred to the teachers, "it is to reach these goals that the notes of the lyre must be employed with distinctness as the main consideration, by teacher and pupil alike rendering [literally "giving back"] the sounds of the instrument in unison with those of the melody."[18] Having stated what method should be followed, he now makes clear what should be avoided; the construction shifts somewhat with the change of topic.

To achieve the desired result, then, one must play only the notes of the original melody. This result (he continues) is not to be attained "by providing different notes [*heterophōnian*] and ornamentation on the lyre, when the composer of the melody sets forth one tune and the strings play another—for example, venturing to furnish wide inter-

---

[17] En-chant: *epāidein*, from *epi* and *aeidein*, Attic *āidein*. The noun *epaoidē* (Attic *epōidē*), "incantation," occurs from Homer onward.

[18] Commentators exaggerate the difficulty of 812d1–4. These lines have been wrongly burdened with punctuation in the Oxford text. Actually, they form a seamless whole. It must be realized, moreover, that *apodidontas* in d3 echoes the immediately preceding *sunakolouthountas* in c7. Both are circumstantial participles expressing means. As Smyth notes (1968, 458, sec. 2063), this construction often employs the present tense.

vals with narrow ones [instead], or a slow tempo with quickness, or low pitch with high, whether(?) at the octave or the fourth or fifth—and likewise in the case of the rhythms, by setting any and every kind of ornate variation to the notes of the lyre."[19] That sort of thing, he concludes, makes no contribution to the working knowledge of music and literature that the young are supposed to acquire in three years.

Nothing else in Plato, or in the entire range of Hellenic literature, comes so close to revealing the relationship between melody and lyre accompaniment. Here, of course, given the context of *mousikē* as a schoolboy's education, "melody" refers primarily to what is sung. Thus the Athenian Stranger is dealing also with the accompaniment of song by stringed instruments, which means only the lyre and kithara, together with their variant forms. Instruments with many strings had no part in public life or place in the *sumposion*. This passage and Socrates' criticism of instruments and modes in the *Republic* are the only examples in the dialogues of an attempt to deal more than briefly with what may have been the facts of Greek musical life. The last phrase has seemed to call for qualification here on several accounts, chief among them Plato's tendency to be much behind the times in musical matters. His preoccupation with what should be, rather than what is, also influences him powerfully.

Despite these and other hindrances to understanding *Laws* 812d–e, the passage suggests tacit conclusions, corollaries of its didactic and polemic text. They concern only a part of Greek musical life, and they extend neither to the social life of the middle- or upper-class Athenian nor to the period of his maturity. What they do concern is important—namely, the instruction in lyre playing that was considered indispensable to education, not merely at Athens but throughout the Greek city-states. Moreover, they cover the period of learning that came after reading and writing had been mastered, a process that lasted approximately from the fourteenth year through the sixteenth.

---

[19] As before (see the preceding note), the structure—weakening now—is held together by circumstantial participles expressing means. Here they are *parechomenous* (e1) and *prosarmottontas* (e2); and once again both are in the present tense. *Parechesthai* has the connotation of making a personal contribution. For *prosarmottein* as "to set (rhythms)," see *Leg.* 669c6 and LSJ s.v. I.2; for other observations on the structure, see Görgemanns and Neubecker 1966, esp. 161 and 163.

Under the traditional system, it was then that a boy experienced the passage into his culture.

Widespread literacy had been achieved late, probably not much before 430 B.C. By the time Plato wrote the *Laws,* more than three-quarters of a century afterward, literacy was a long-established reality, one that even utopian speculation could hardly fail to take into account. The content of Greek culture—*paideia* in the more extended sense—nevertheless consisted of poetry.[20] Its prime sources, the epics of Homer, were learned through recitation, without musical accompaniment. From an early period, the same had been true of elegiac verse. The other poetic materials, however, demanded reasonable competence in playing the *lura,* as the late designation *lurikos* (lyric) so clearly shows. In this process of transmission the larger, heavier kithara had no part; ordinary citizens were not expected or permitted to advance beyond a modest ability to accompany themselves on the lyre. This was the amateur's instrument; kithara playing was left to professionals.[21]

From Homer onward, the verb *kitharizdein* described the playing of any instrument belonging to the lyre family. It should not be thought puzzling, therefore, that a schoolmaster—who taught only the *lura*—always bore the designation of *kitharistēs:* his function was that of imparting the skill known as *kitharizdein,* here applying to the lyre proper. For the parallel term *luristēs* no evidence can be found until the

[20] For an understanding of the division of Hellenic culture into oral and written stages, the work of E. A. Havelock (especially 1963) is vital; that of his continuator, Bruno Gentili (1979), also has great significance. Havelock, however, does not adequately recognize the existence and the importance of a transitional period in Athens, argued by Thomas (1989), unfortunately without discussing music. The references have been diligently assembled by Lentz 1989; he follows Havelock closely and uncritically.

[21] On an Attic red-figure amphora from the late sixth century (Louvre G 1), a youth of slight build holds a kithara that almost dwarfs him. He stands on a podium, normally a clear sign that a musical competition is under way. But here we have instead a burlesque of such a contest, as Wegner (1963, 66) points out. Study of this unusual vase painting will do much to suggest the differences between amateur and professional, freeborn (*eleutheros*) and kitharode. The latter, beefy and alien-looking, remains an outsider. Throughout history, the individual musician has been an ambivalent figure, respected but feared and often shunned. See Simmel 1967 on the stranger and Erlmann 1983 on the status of professional musicians among the Fulani, a tribe of North Cameroon.

end of the first century A.D., when Pliny the Younger used it in a letter (9.17.3). Similarly, *lurizein* (with shifted pronunciation) and *lurōidos* prove to be late and rare. The contrast with *kitharōidos,* literally "singer to the kithara," is particularly striking. Thus *kitharistēs* as "schoolmaster" accords with the pattern of Hellenic usage.

It might at first seem that better grounds for surprise could be found in Plato's acceptance of outsiders—foreigners, as it were—to act as music teachers. We have seen what heavy responsibilities, moral as well as professional, he lays upon them. Yet for centuries mainland Greece (Sparta, then Corinth, and later Athens, as the center of musical activity shifted successively northward) had welcomed, and even summoned, the talents of virtuosi from Ionia or its nearby islands. To these same outsiders was ascribed by later chroniclers the "establishing" (*katastasis,* a term never used in the dialogues) of music along new lines, and a tone of evident approval marks such accounts. Plato himself looked repeatedly to Sparta, Egypt, and Crete for significant precedents, musical and otherwise. The present instance, then, conforms entirely to personal and national practice.

Given this background, we come back to the question of whether these rules governing instruction in playing the lyre reveal anything about fourth-century procedure. A long history of disagreement over their nature, ably summarized by H. Görgemanns and A. J. Neubecker (1966), suggests that any answer will have to be put forward with a good deal of caution. Taken as a whole, Plato's comments in *Laws* 812 constitute a reaction against what he considers to be examples of license: that much can hardly be denied. Once past this point, however, uncertainties loom. Efforts have been made to assemble, from the negative corollaries of these remarks in the *Laws,* a method for teaching and learning the lyre in fourth-century Athens. More wisely, H. I. Marrou presents Plato's recommendations as the thinking of one individual, with the salutary reminder that actual divisions into stages and categories were not fixed.[22]

Such an attitude is needed if we seek to grasp the relation of *Laws* 812 to reality. Plato represents a literate Athens that had passed beyond the oral stage of culture. Memorization, recitation, and singing to one's own lyre accompaniment had ceased to hold an essential,

---

[22] Marrou 1964, 490–92.

unchallenged place. To speak the plain truth, they no longer had any importance at all. On this matter at least, he chose not to face the facts. An aristocrat by birth and instinctively a conservative, he found it natural to take his models for *mousikē,* and for *paideia* generally, from severely repressive regimes of the past. Commentators who remark upon the fact of Plato's being behind the times in what concerned music seemingly fail to realize that, for him, this position was inevitable and quite probably deliberate. Reverence constrained him; he cannot be made into a chronicler of the curriculum that was actually followed during his time. His own school days were more than a half century earlier than 360 B.C., the first likely date for initial work on the *Laws.* He had studied singing and lyre playing at a time when widespread literacy had prevailed for scarcely more than a decade. These were the very years when Aristophanes was fondly recalling "the old-fashioned schooling" and accusing Socrates himself of casting *mousikē* into the discard.

When, therefore, Plato took up the question of a lyre teacher's responsibilities, change had long been the rule among professional musicians. The *poiētēs* as living composer had largely replaced the mythical or long-dead figures to whom melodies were often ascribed. As he labored to construct the changeless perfection of a city-state embodying "good order" (*eunomia*), Plato did face reality to some extent: he insisted that the melody be reproduced just as the composer had fashioned it. If a negative corollary lies underneath the surface here, it may be the conclusion that when teachers gave instruction, they did not always take pains to play just what had been passed on to them.

Yet such carelessness would not have been surprising. Unless they had acquired prestige independently, from compositions brought before the public, the *kitharistai* received no recognition from society; and there seem to have been only a handful of celebrated poet-composers at any given time. The ordinary, unknown lyre teacher can have had little reason to feel the professional and moral imperatives urged in the *Laws;* still less would he have had cause to act upon them. For the planning of Plato's city-state, however, it is essential that every such teacher adhere without deviation to the materials of the curriculum, once they have been certified as being properly composed and edifying. We noted that *parechomenous,* "(venturing to) provide" (812e1), refers to a contribution made on one's own part. As usual, Plato establishes his point with absolute precision: such individualism cannot be tolerated, and therefore he expressly bans it.

Everything in his list of rules reinforces that ban. Possibly the nature of particular points reflects what he, along with other conservatives, found to be excesses on the part of such composers as Timotheus, who unquestionably called attention to themselves. The attacks by Pherecrates and Aristophanes in Old Comedy reveal a similar attitude. With regard to the passage from the *Laws,* however, what matters for the writer, almost to the exclusion of everything else, is the principle that undergirds both of his large-scale plans for an ideal polis. This is the belief that the citizens of a well-ordered community must speak and sing and "do the same thing," *ta auta prattein.* Without exception, they are to "fulfill their own proper function," *ta heautou prattein,* and nothing else. *Ta auta* and *ta heautou,* "the same thing" and "the thing that is one's own": these are the cornerstones of Plato's state. His concern that they be well and truly laid may at times require attention to real or perceived shortcomings of music as actually performed; but we must not expect any great measure of enlightenment from such digressions.

Characteristically, he fights shy of jargon. If need be, he will invent a term of his own. Such seems to be the case with *manotēs,* used in this much-discussed passage from the *Laws* to denote a "wide spacing" of intervals. He says what he means; all the same, he has his eye elsewhere.

To continue, it is well known that Plato scorned as wrong headed, even comical, what he took to be misdirected theory. A notable example is the search for ever more finely shaded microtones: it amused him to see specialists spending their time on this. The nature of his reaction necessarily casts some doubt on the soundness of the assumption, so long and so widely held, that during the Hellenic period an enharmonic scale sequence with two successive quarter tones at the lower end of each tetrachord dominated Greek musical practice. If the late but continuing tradition of an original form of enharmonic with undivided semitone (for example, E F A rather than the quarter tone E *E* F A) has a foundation in reality, we may conjecture that this simpler form would have had Plato's approval. It would assuredly have been a great deal easier for amateur singers and lyre players, a category that included thousands of schoolboys.

Instruction in *mousikē* had a renewed and increased importance for the aged Plato. In the *Laws,* he lays down rules to assure its effectiveness and correctness as a general discipline. This contrasts with the training in lyre playing and in the singing of poetry that he had proposed a generation earlier, in the *Republic:* there, it had been designed for the Guardians (*phulakes*) alone. This is one instance of the greater reasonableness with which he treated several aspects of musical performance, once he had come—with the onset of old age—to envision the city-state of the *Laws.* Yet it was a vision, not a commentary on reality. Rough correspondences do exist with the old-fashioned education that Aristophanes had extolled; it could hardly have been otherwise. Evidently other borrowings were made as well: the city of *eunomia,* "good order," is a Cretan city; the austere precedents of Sparta and Egypt can likewise be seen. Always at the front of Plato's mind, nevertheless, is a conception of society as it could be, not as it was. Western philosophy has been called a series of footnotes to his thought; the same claim could never be made for musicology, at least outside the sphere of theory. Within that sphere, his achievements may not have received their due. Nevertheless, it remains true that the greatest representative of the age of philosophers has little to impart concerning the actual music of that age and those who, in childhood and maturity, performed it or listened to it. Understandably, his concerns lay elsewhere.

Plato's last work, the *Laws,* ends with the philosopher describing his theoretical statecraft as the stuff of dreams (969b6: *oneiratos hōs*). It exists only conceptually, "in words" (a3: *tois logois*) or "in reasoned discourse" (b6: *tōi logōi;* so *Rep.* 592a11). We come back to the cryptic assertion by Socrates, at the close of the *Republic* (592b2), that perhaps a model of it is established *en ouranōi,* "in the heavens," a phrase never satisfactorily explained. The translation suggested by the poet Thomas Gray, "in the idea of the divinity"—that is, in the realm where the Forms dwell—represents a position that some critics have taken; it may be right.

Only in that transcendental realm is Plato's thought truly at home; attempting to take him as a guide to the world of real music can bring little profit. The *harmoniai* that he heard in daily life engaged his attention—how seldom, and how briefly!—for no other reason than their supposed power to shape people's ethical natures. His consciousness was attuned rather to the invisible and (for mortal ears) inaudible cosmic *harmoniai* whose ratios undergird the universe in the *Timaeus,* and in the *Republic*'s myth of Er constitute the unearthly song of the Sirens. These, and not the mere creations of mortals, were what mattered to him.

Still less confidently can we look to Plato's great pupil. Not many would challenge Dante's famous description of Aristotle as "the master of them that know." This knowledge is seldom applied to music in any of the fifty treatises that make up the Aristotelian corpus; and the question of whether a *De musica* (*Peri mousikēs*) has been lost remains unanswered and thus far unanswerable. At the close of the *Metaphysics,* however, Aristotle states in passing that the aulos produces twenty-four notes (1093b3–4).[23] Whatever he had in mind, it can hardly have been an archaic system of individual *harmoniai*. His words do not fit the old modality.

The system that they do presuppose makes no clear appearance anywhere in his works. One passage (*Pol.* 1276b8–9), however, comes close: "We say that a *harmonia* [consisting] of the same sounds(?) [*phthonggōn,* which may be either "sounds" or "notes"] is different if it is Dorian in one instance and Phrygian in another." The context, once again essential for understanding the text, deals with changes in the constitution of a polis. These, it is claimed, make the state a different one, even though the same persons continue to make up its citizen body (as *politai*). Then: "So also with any other association [*koinōnia*] or composite [*sunthesis*]: we say that it is different if the form [*eidos*] of the composite differs: for instance, . . ." Here follows the statement about music. The same pattern of conditional structure is repeated, together with several of the essential words.

It should be clear, therefore, that *harmonia* does not mean "tune"

---

[23] Aristotle's pupil Aristoxenus, as Barker suggested in a letter concerning an earlier draft of this book, provides an explanation for this surprisingly wide range when he assigns a gamut of more than three octaves to the aulos (*Harm.* 20.32–21.5). What makes this possible is the "drawing up" or "drawing down" (or the "opening" and "closing") of the *surinx,* variously interpreted as "(reed) mouthpiece" or "speaker hole."

here, as the Loeb translator, Henry Rackham, supposed. To render it by "scale" (Jowett) is to miss the point; simply transliterating it (Schlesinger) begs the question. Context, so often ignored, shows *sunthesis* to be the controlling concept. Almost without doubt, it underlies Cicero's attempt to describe mode (*harmonia*) as recognizable from the intervals, "the varying arrangement [*varia compositio*] of which . . . produces a number of modes."[24] The elements that constitute *compositio* are precisely those of *sunthesis;* presumably the Greek term was in Cicero's mind when he used its Latin parallel. His effort to describe the *harmonia* underscores for us what had already been established through the arguments of the *Politics:* Aristotle was referring to pitches that, although they were relative, did not change. Their *sunthesis* might change, with the result that the "fitting together" (the literal sense of *harmonia*) thus effected could be recognized as Dorian or Phrygian; but the sounds or notes were, as Aristotle says, the same.

There can be only one reasonable conclusion: like Cicero three centuries later, Aristotle was describing a schema of interrelated scale sequences. Interrelationship was possible because they all used the same spacing of intervals; differentiation was accomplished by echeloning, and by the variation in the center of gravity thus produced. Aristotle says nothing further to identify the fourth-century form of this schema. Neither does he reveal anything about the nature of individual modes, beyond the kinds of ethos attributed to them. For these attributions, moreover, he avowedly relies on the opinions of specialists. Probably they perpetuated Damonian theory; as we know from Philodemus, this was still striking sparks as late as Cicero's day. But Aristotle does not choose to identify them, and so identification now can only be conjectural. His comments regarding the proper role of music in education and leisure hold considerable interest as philosophy; with the real work of Greek music and Greek musicians they have little connection. By the same token, his comments on the actual state of music go only a short way beyond what his teacher had said.[25]

During and after the Hellenistic period, which is held to have be-

---

[24] Cic. *Tusc.* 1.18.41.

[25] There is a profound difference between my estimate of Aristotle's comments on music and that given by Lord 1982. Barbera (1983) suggests that my assessment (see, for example, Anderson 1966, 111–46, esp. 145–46) acts as a counterbalance to Lord's.

gun following the death of Aristotle in 322 B.C., actual music making was less and less the province of amateurs. The professionals who took it over were known as *technitai Dionusou* or *Dionusiakoi technitai,* "artists of Dionysus." Their presence came to be so common and so much taken for granted that the mere phrase *hoi technitai,* with only the definite article, sufficed to identify them. They began as theater troupes, actors and musicians who staged complete concerts (for we can now begin to use that word) and performances of drama. Besides actors, chorus, and aulete, their number included such other personnel as the *didaskalos,* or chorus trainer, who remained behind the scenes.

They were far from being mere strolling players. "The artists of Dionysus," says S. Michaelides, "in their heyday, were treated as privileged persons; protected and favoured by kings and tyrants, they were acquitted of military service, enjoyed personal inviolability and were often entrusted with diplomatic missions. Their flourishing coincides with the decadence of the classical art. . . . The 'modern' spirit as regards music prevailing in the 3rd cent. B.C. and onward had as the main object of musical education the formation of skilled artists, technically well-equipped, conscious of their 'metier' and their social-professional rights."[26] We have reason to doubt whether such was really the principal aim of lessons in voice, kithara playing, and theory. It was assuredly one aim, nevertheless, and a well-known inscription from Teos describes a distinctly more technical curriculum than fifth-century schoolboys ever encountered.[27]

In the third century, Teos, an Ionian city, was the center of the various guilds, *koina* or *sunodoi,* into which the artists of Dionysus had organized their membership. As Michaelides says, these guildsmen were now "artists of all sorts: kitharists, auletes, aulodes, singers, composers . . . , actors, even poets."[28] They served Dionysus, and so their duties included his liturgy as well as the festivals celebrated under his sponsorship; at their head was a priest (*hiereus*) of

<hr/>

[26] Michaelides 1978, 322.

[27] *IG II.* 3088; *SIG³,* 578; for a brief account, see Marrou 1964, 193–94. It is difficult to gauge the extent to which the establishment at Teos was a "choir school," but this extent was probably greater than is acknowledged in the first section of the article on music education in the *New Grove Dictionary of Music and Musicians* (6:1–4).

[28] Michaelides 1978, 323.

the god. Once Rome had achieved dominion over the Mediterranean, they were known to speakers of Latin as *Dionysiaci artifices*. Theirs were the rules of stage etiquette that Nero strove so sedulously to observe. For several centuries they enjoyed great power; we possess more than a dozen inscriptions that detail their organization and privileges.[29]

The guildsmen of Dionysus brought to musical performance professionalism on a broad scale, and they altered the teaching of music by introducing a comprehensive curriculum. For the late Hellenic critic, even the liberties of dithyrambic composers signaled a loss, a grievous change for the worse. The technical demands imposed by a Cinesias or a Timotheus, with their "New Music," merely foreshadow the situation that was to bring the *technitai* into being. Throughout much of the Hellenistic and Graeco-Roman periods, these artists reflected the same shift away from the citizen body and toward the individual—a city man, but no longer a member of the polis—that appears so unmistakably in poetry, philosophy, and art. By reviving the famous old tragedies and keeping up the old rites, they celebrated the past. Through their embodiment of a new approach to music in practice as well as in theory, they were bringers of the future. With them, the history of ancient Greek music comes to a close.

[29] Nero and stage etiquette: Suet. *Ner.* 24.1; *The New Grove Dictionary of Music and Musicians* 13:112. See Pickard-Cambridge 1968, 306–21, app. A to chap. 7, "Inscriptions Relating to the Artists of Dionysus."

Appendix A

Fifth-Century Instrumental Resources

The following survey includes most, but not all, of the musical instruments that formed a part of the fifth-century scene; others are discussed in the text or the notes. For more extensive coverage, the index may be consulted. The fullness of detail that characterizes the relevant articles in the *Dictionnaire des antiquités grecques et romaines,* especially those by Reinach, has never been equaled, though some later treatments in *Die Musik in Geschichte und Gegenwart* repay attention. General works on ancient Greek music have not usually devoted sufficient attention to instruments: the outstanding exception is the most recent of such studies, West's *Ancient Greek Music* (1992b). Barker's two volumes (1984a and 1989), particularly the first, contain much helpful commentary on instruments. Wegner 1963, Paquette 1984, and Maas and Snyder 1989 provide a comprehensive range of illustrations. The material accompanying Paniagua's lp recording *Musique de la Grèce antique* (see the discography), which has serious faults as a presentation of the surviving fragments, does offer a detailed listing of instruments, with photographs.

I. Stringed instruments (Chordophones, in Mahillon's system of classification as revised by Sachs and Hornbostel; for a detailed scheme of the development of the lyre, see fig. 19).

A. Lyre proper (*lura, chelus;* see fig. 20a; pls. II, VII).

1. Size: about 1 by 2 1/2 feet.

2. Materials: wood and hide, in the classical period; sound chest originally the carapace of a mountain tortoise, arms (*pēcheis*) origi-

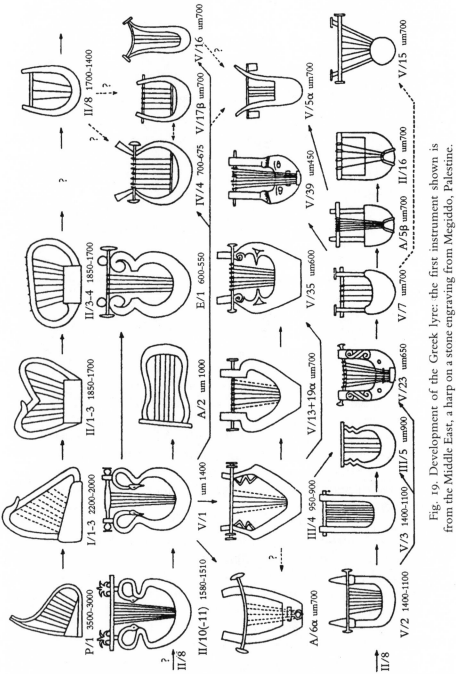

Fig. 19. Development of the Greek lyre: the first instrument shown is from the Middle East, a harp on a stone engraving from Megiddo, Palestine. (Reprinted from Aign 1963, 380; Megiddo harp: see Aign 1963, 118, fig. 75.)

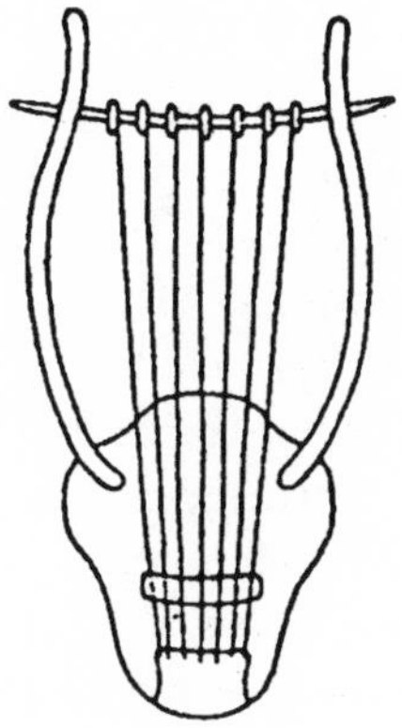

a. Lyre

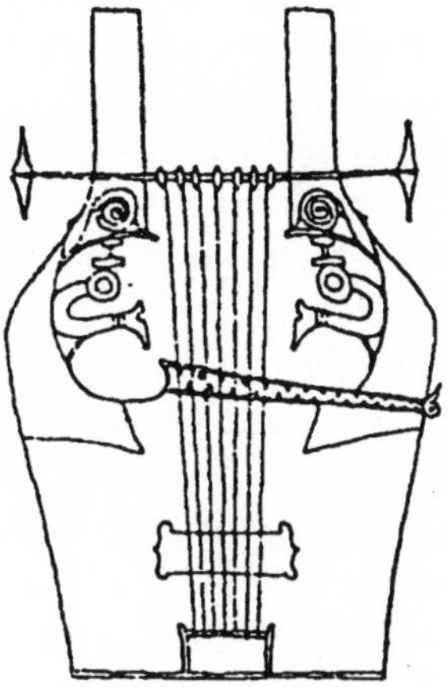

b. Kithara

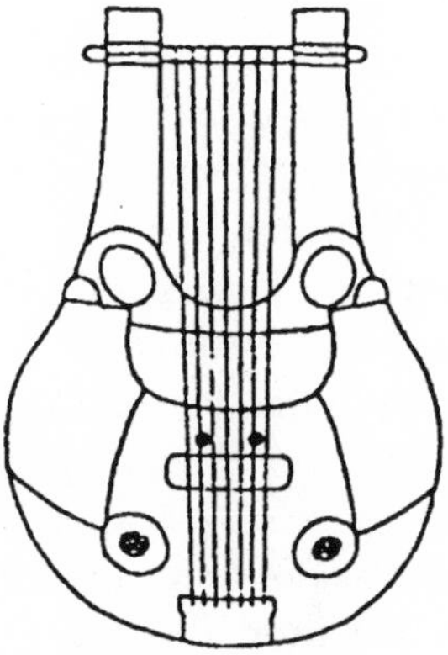

c. Cradle Kithara

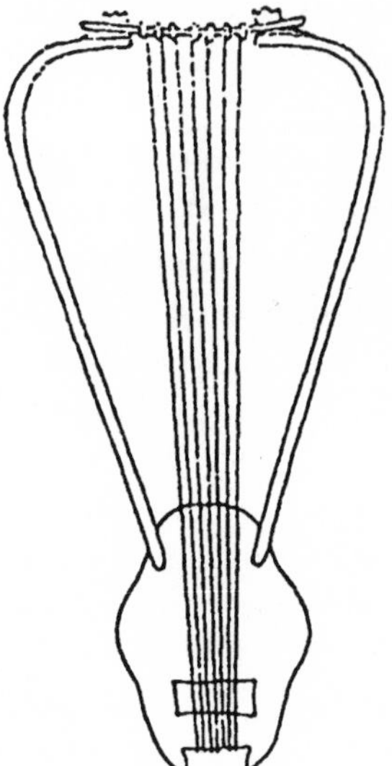

d. Barbitos

Fig. 20. Various stringed instruments: *a*, lyre; *b*, kithara; *c*, cradle kithara; *d*, barbitos; the kithara is closely modeled after the exceptional instrument shown on a red-figure amphora (see pl. IV); the other instruments are generalized representations. (Reprinted by permission of the publishers from *Ethos and Education in Greek Music* by Warren Anderson, Cambridge, Mass.: Harvard University Press, Copyright © 1966 by the President and Fellows of Harvard College.)

nally animal horns (*kerata*) and sometimes so today in Africa (the two stages: Blümner 1969, 2: 376, 389–90).

3. Construction: moderately convex arms of solid wood, fastened to a circular sound chest, with a crosspiece called a yoke (*zdugon*) joining their upper ends (untenable theory proposed by Roberts 1974, 79; 1979, 63–75, 67; corrected by Lawergren 1982a, 165–66). String holder (*chordotonion* or *chordotonos;* both terms post-Hellenic) at bottom of sound chest, bridge (*magas*) a few inches above it. A yoke wrapping (*kollops;* see pl. III) appears for each string, clearly distinguished from it (*Od.* 21.406–9), often with a wooden peg inserted in the wound string; no parallel with modern pegs (see the *New Grove Dictionary of Music and Musicians* 2:482, on the Burmese bowed harp).

4. Strings: gut (the strict meaning of *chordē*), a sheep's intestine and thus originally cylindrical, or sinew (Homeric *neurē* or *neuron*), a tendon, a cord or band of closely packed fibers attached to a muscle. A gut lyre string had to be composite; so also, very probably, one made from sinew. Cf. *Il.* 4.122: *neura* [plural] *boeia,* "a bowstring of bull's sinew"; from Homer onward, sinew for bows, gut for lyres. String making: Roberts 1974, 89–91; no detailed account since Bachmann 1975, 140–53, first published in 1925. Composite violin strings: excellent short treatment in Gill 1984, 37–43. Possible types of composite lyre strings: (1) interwoven strands, (2) lengths tied end to end, or (3) a combination. Ancient evidence favors (1), leaves (2) unexplained: Homeric *eustrephēs* (*neostrephēs* once), "well (newly) twisted"; *strephein* is clearly "intertwine" in the *Homeric Hymn to Hermes* (early sixth century?); this verb is used interchangeably with *plekein* throughout Greek literature to describe braiding or plaiting, whether literal or figurative. Thus variations in string diameter may have occurred from earliest times; vase painters could not show them.

5. Tuning: mechanism seems primitive, but modern counterparts (see fig. 21) prove astonishingly precise (Lawergren 1982a, 166, on a Gambian *kora* player retuning to within 1/200 of a semitone, as checked by strobe tuner; *The New Grove Dictionary of Music and Musicians* 7: 535–36, s.v. Gora [D. K. Rycroft]). Scale systems as patterns of tuning: scarcely any evidence until the fourth century (Pl. *Phlb.* 17c11–d3, on boundary notes); then much detail on a two-octave sequence (Aristox. *Harm.*); finally a set of gapped scales, presented by Aristides Quintilianus as those discussed in Plato's *Republic.* The stan-

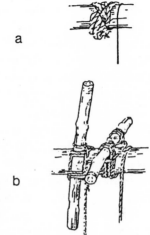

Fig. 21. Two tuning mechanisms used on lyres in Africa today. (Reprinted by permission of the publisher, from Wegner 1984, 104.)

dard seven strings of the Hellenic lyre sufficed even for the double octave of Aristoxenus, except for a single note. Additions to the gamut through the use of harmonics are a possibility, but most harmonics are faint, and they exclude microtones. No clear evidence that a string produced more than its fundamental note and perhaps the second harmonic. Tuning of the early lyre probably not uniform; the variants embodied modal individuality. The early heptachord: traditionally a stepwise sequence such as B C D E F G A. Vase paintings offer almost no evidence that another instrument figured in the process of tuning; but an aulos or pitch pipe (*tonarion*) may have been used. (See below, C.3.e.)

6. Accessories: *telamōn,* a strap of leather to steady the left arm; used only occasionally. Vastly more important is the plectrum (*plēktron*), first shown on a seventh-century Melian amphora (Athens, National Museum 911; Wegner 1963, 42, fig. 19; for a portion of this vase painting see above, fig. 13). References to use of the plectrum: *Hymn. Hom. Herm.* 53; Hdt. 1.155.4: *kitharizdein te kai psallein;* Pl. *Lysis* 209b7: *krouein tōi plektrōi* (contrasted with *psallein*). It was long, rectangular, and quite thick, made of hard wood or ivory; its tip extended for about an inch beyond thumb and fingertips, functioning as an extension of the hand (see pls. I, III). This could be hooked, but more often it had the shape of a knob or a heart: see Phaklaris 1977, 230–31, with fig. 11, a detail from the Pelion krater; cf. his fig. 12 for a

strikingly similar plectrum from modern Greece. At times the tip was oblong, at right angles to the shaft: Aristides Quintilianus (2.25, p. 130.11–12 W-I; Barker 1989, 531) speaks of the plectrum as shaped like the letter tau and goes on to note that wise men call Apollo the plectrum of the universe. Parallel from modern Ethiopia: a lyre player shown on a postage stamp holds just such a plectrum, grasping it in the manner described here; many representations in Attic vase painting. More significant is the fact that Greeks today hold it in the same way as their Hellenic ancestors (hand position in Phaklaris). Of necessity, the stroke was made toward the body, not away from it, with a progression from high to low. The cosmic parallel is the westward movement of the sun (Apollo as sun-god).

7. Performance capacities: with a plectrum, no note-for-note performance of any but the slowest melodies. Little fullness of sound or carrying power; a role confined to preludes, interludes, and solo work (a rarity). Playing with the fingers alone (*psallein*) was thought old-fashioned in Plato's time (Moutsopoulos 1959, 181–82). Hypothesis of left-hand plucking: no corroboration from the vase paintings, which almost always show the left hand. In all but a few cases, thumb and fingers are straight (see pls. I, IV); they cannot be plucking. The description of a lyre player by Philostratus (*Imag.* 6) proves this; Michaelides (1978, 191–92) completely misinterprets it. Neither will the Latin phrases *intus canere* and *foris canere* support the hypothesis of left-hand plucking, acoustically a disadvantageous procedure in any case; they prove nothing. The true function of the left hand: to damp in advance the strings not meant to sound; so among present-day Nubian tribesmen—and the working principle of the Autoharp today.

B. Kithara (*kithara*; *kithara* is not found in Homer's poetry; *kitharizdein* (verb) and *kitharistus* (noun) occur there, referring to the act of playing; *kitharin* in *Il.* 13.731 is an interpolation; *phorminx,* the term for its simpler predecessor in Homer and various early poets, survives into the fifth century, most notably in Pindar; see fig. 20*b;* pl. IV).

1. Size: much larger, heavier, and more massive than the lyre proper, and much more nearly square in outline; it often projects above the player's head (see pls. I, IV).

2. Materials: made entirely of wood, with inlay work of gold, silver, ivory, or other substances. Such phrases as *chrusea phorminx,* "golden lyre," can mislead.

3. Construction: square-bottomed, seen from the front (the view afforded by vase painters, almost without exception); a convex underbody, with triangular bottom and spined rear profile (convexity: Schneider 1946, 166; Cirlot 1991, 48)—a fact discovered only recently by classicists. Large, hollow arms greatly extended the area of resonance, amplifying the string sound to an unknown extent (in the violin, this sympathetic vibration produces an enormous increase). No separate sound chest: the whole of the kithara's interior constituted one.

4. Strings: under far greater tension than those of the lyre and undoubtedly thicker, but normally the same seven in number.

5. Tuning: not known to differ from that of the lyre, though the kithara's massive structure would have allowed strings having the same approximate length and diameter as those of a lyre to be tuned higher.

6. Accessories: a stronger supporting strap (*telamōn*) than for the lyre; also a cloth band that anchored the left wrist (see pls. I, III, IV). A plectrum was needed to bring out the instrument except in the rare instances of *psilē kitharisis,* solo playing at a competition.

7. Performance capacities: assured a role in public life to which the lyre could not attain. Goddesses might play the kithara; mortal women did not (Wegner 1949, 36–37), though maenads are shown with it on black-figure vases. "Kitharode," *kitharōidos,* was one of Apollo's most revered epithets. Kithara players all appear to be free men, socially above most auletes. Their costume, ceremonious and distinctive, sets them apart (see pls. I, IV).

C. Related instruments (among these, only the so-called cradle kithara and the barbitos have importance and an established identity).

1. Cradle kithara (see fig. 20*c;* pls. II*b,* VII): named *Wiegenkithara* by German scholars (apparently first in Wegner 1949, 31). Actually an oversized lyre; vase painters show it played by girls or women.

2. Barbitos (*barbitos; barbiton* a late form; an alternative name, *barmos,* in Alcaeus frag. 70.3 Campbell, 12.70.4 Page; see fig. 20*d*): discovery ascribed to Terpander by Pindar (frag. 110a Bowra, 125 Schroeder, Snell) and to Anacreon by Neanthes of Cyzicus (*Annals,* in Ath. 175e; Maas and Snyder [1989, 224 n. 121] give the reference as 637b). Supposedly associated with Sappho, but she uses only the terms *lura, chelus,* and *chelunna.* The Silenus followers of Dionysus are often shown with it; the Muses played it, as did mortal women in

everyday life. Its music was often a feature of symposia. It had long, delicate arms, and so—except for the harp—the greatest "speaking" string length of any instrument played by the Greeks. The result: lower pitches than on a lyre or kithara, apparently an octave or more below them; the reason remains a puzzle.

3. Magadis (*magadis*), pektis (*pēktis*), skindapsos (*skindapsos*), and trigonon (*trigōnon* or *trigōnos*), and sambuca (*sambukē*): the first two were part of the world of private music making by girls or women; the rest probably belonged to it as well; this may account for our lack of information about them.

a) Alcman and Anacreon use the term *magadis;* Anacreon may refer to it as having twenty strings (the text is corrupt). Sophocles (frag. 238 Pearson) clearly speaks of it as a musical instrument; we cannot be sure that anyone else does. The consensus now is that it was a kind of harp. According to later sources, it sounded in octaves and had twenty strings, a most unlikely number for the age of Alcman. In the pseudo-Aristotelian *Problems* (19.19, 918b40; 19.39, 921a12), the verb *magadizein* does mean "to sing in octaves." Aristoxenus (*Fr. hist.* 66) says it was played without a plectrum; he identifies it with the pektis. The claim in LSJ that *magadis* denotes a wind instrument in the fifth-century tragic poet Ion of Chios (frags. 22, 23 Nauck, Snell, *Tragicorum Graecorum Fragmenta*[2] 736; cited in Ath. 634f, c) has no foundation (see Barker 1984a, 294 n.170). Typical of late writers, Athenaeus (634c) does not know what it was, "whether a kind of aulos or a kind of kithara."

Recent scholarship shows disagreement continuing; the differences, however, are now more radical. Comotti (1983) argues for a harp with two registers of ten strings, tuned an octave apart. Against this view is Barker's contention (foreshadowed in 1984a, 297 n.187 and 300 n.26) that *magadis* denotes the performance technique of playing in octaves, not an instrument.

b) Sappho (frag. 156 Campbell, Lobel-Page; also, in line 11 of frag. 22 Campbell the incomplete form . . . *ktin,* for *pēktin,* must represent the first recorded mention of the pektis. Plato (*Rep.* 399c10–d1) condemns this instrument for making available too many notes, which means that it had more than seven strings—the assumption that it was a harp is safe for the Hellenic and Hellenistic periods. Graeco-Roman writers, however, sometimes refer to it as if it resembled the syrinx.

So Aristid. Quint. 2.5, p. 58.14 W-I; Barker 1989, 462 and n.24. West (1992b, 71) sums up the evidence from Hellenic sources: the pektis "was a plucked chordophone with many strings, characterized by the playing of octave concords, or the echoing of the melody at octave intervals, and strongly associated with the Lydians."

c) Even less is known about the skindapsos, not mentioned until about the middle of the fourth century; references in West 1992b, 60 n.56. The few details that supposedly describe it are either vague or incredible (for example, that it had four strings).

d) The name of the trigonon (originally *trigonos*) shows that it is a harp, probably the type with a spindle-shaped sound box. Plato (*Rep.* 399c10–d1) condemns it along with the pektis; this justifies the same conclusion. Aristotle (*Pol.* 1341a40) mentions it, along with the sambuca, as being among the instruments that fell into disfavor; no other significant references.

e) Some later writers seek to identify the sambuca with the *lurophoinix,* an obscure type of lyre, or with the magadis. Fortunately, we have a wall painting—late, but possibly from a Hellenistic original—that shows a sambuca being used together with a lyre (Landels 1966, 76–77; Maas and Snyder [1989, 184] add little), perhaps being tuned to it. Like the trigonon, it belongs to the harp family. Its boatlike frame seems to have been unique in antiquity; musical cultures of the present-day Orient provide several parallels, most notably the Burmese bowed harp. Its strings may have had the octave relationships attributed to the magadis. *Sambukistriai,* women who played the sambuca professionally, no doubt were often prostitutes, but all we can say with certainty is that the sambuca, as a variety of harp, was a woman's instrument.

II. Wind instruments (Aerophones)

A. Aulos (*aulos,* plural *auloi;* see fig. 22; pls. III, V, VI, VII).

1. Size: Hellenic auloi less than two feet.

2. Materials: double-reed pipes, made of wood, cane, bone, ivory, or metal (but not precious metal), separately or in combination; the tone was not affected.

3. Construction: each tube (*bombux;* see Michaelides 1978, 52–53) was cylindrical, less often oval, and almost always had a cylindrical bore. A kind of bell, curving upward from the left-hand pipe, marked the so-called Phrygian aulos, a deviant type though well known—it is

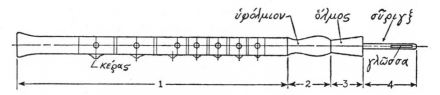

Fig. 22. Essential features of the double-reed pipe or aulos, shown here on a Graeco-Roman monaulos reconstructed from fragments found at Meroë in Egypt and dated to about 15 B.C. (Reprinted, by permission of the publisher, from Bodley 1946, 224.)

shown on the Hagia Triada sarcophagus. Figure 22 (from Bodley 1946, 224) shows a reconstruction of a monaulos (played with both hands) from fragments found at Meroë in Egypt and dated to about 15 B.C.

The length of this instrument is estimated to be a little less than 2 feet, longer than Hellenic auloi, which also had fewer finger holes and no rotary sleeves but basically resembled it. The terms given here in Greek are *holmos,* the socket into which the reed was fitted; *hupholmion,* the "bulb" fitted beneath (*hupo*) the socket (see pl. VII); *surinx,* the reed mouthpiece with a slender tongue (*glōssa* or *glōtta; glōttis* in late writers) cut out of its length; and *keras,* a small knob for easier handling of the pierced rotary sleeve fitted over each finger hole (one band is off center).

The actual fragments discovered at Meroë come from at least nine instruments. They represent a number of different types and show how an early, simple form with only three finger holes came eventually to quadruple its original compass. From the period around 500 B.C. we have two pipes—the Elgin auloi, in the British Museum—and major portions of a third—the Brauron aulos, discovered in 1961. The former are not a matched pair; the latter consists of (possibly) two-thirds of a single tube. Bélis (1984a) does not prove her claim, accepted by West (1992b, 100, but see n.84), that two Hellenistic aulos tubes in the Louvre collection are the two parts of a double aulos. All three specimens sound at least six notes. Two double reeds have been preserved separately (Baines 1957, 193, fig. 41; see pl. III); we do not have a single example of the fragile beating reed, shown above in fig. 22.

4. Unison playing: normally, Greek vase painters portray a pair of

matched pipes; the piper's fingers rest on the same portion of each, apparently performing the same tasks (see pls. IIa, V, VI). This raises the question of unison playing vis-à-vis heterophony. Polyphony need not be considered, despite the claims of Sanden 1957. Heterophony originates, as *heterophōnia,* in a passage of Plato's *Laws* (812d1–e6; careful discussion by Görgemanns and Neubecker 1966). Plato speaks of the dangers of playing on the lyre anything other than a doubling of the vocal melodic line; but this must have been selective; see Anderson 1966, 96–97, 251 n.65; Maas and Snyder (1989, 169) hold a not dissimilar view (see Maas and Snyder 241 n.25, on my comments). Plato is laying down rules for elementary education, in which the aulos never had a part; yet it was chiefly blamed for the real or supposed decay of musical standards.

A simple and unvarying unison, therefore, cannot be supposed. This would also mean ignoring the scattered references indicating that fourths or fifths occasionally were used. Neither can the use of a drone be dismissed. Nevertheless, the position taken here is that unison playing, though less than strict, was the usual practice.

The great advantage of unison aulos playing is its power to reinforce the sound and to make it "more vibrant, interesting and self-supporting" (Baines 1957, 194, of such playing on early reed instruments in general). This hypothesis goes far toward explaining Socrates' reference in the *Crito* (54d2–5) to the imagined voice of Athens's laws as resembling aulos music. For the affective force of the Hellenic aulos, comparison should be made to the shawm played today by French and Spanish Catalans: Baines (1957, 113) calls its sound "unbelievably exciting" and "fierce and penetrating." Ahrens (1976) attempts to show that the music of the launeddas and of several similar Middle Eastern woodwinds mirrors certain aspects of aulos melodies. Baud-Bovy (1983) is more convincing in his comparable treatment of Eastern European folk tunes.

5. Support devices: the skilled *aulētēs* might wear a leather muzzle, the *phorbeia* (see pl. VI), strapped around mouth and cheeks to preserve his embouchure. When conditions of performance were less demanding, lip pressure against the *holmos* would have sufficed, and auloi played without the *phorbeia* appear frequently in vase paintings. Normally they were angled downward, to a limit of about 45 degrees. Whenever possible, the little finger supported the pipe; the

thumb gave added support. Performers used the pads of the middle joints of their fingers to cover the holes (see pl. V).

6. Interval measurement: the music played by these double reed pipes lies very largely, but not entirely, beyond our knowing. A certain amount of conjecture is possible, and it has been undertaken by Landels (1963, 119) in his study of the Brauron aulos. With a bassoon reed, spacings between finger holes yield the following sequence of intervals in terms of cents (1/100 of an equally tempered semitone): 231, 267, 151, 165, 182. Neither pitch nor modality can be determined, but the intervals are identical with five of those in Schlesinger's basic modal series. For example, she gives the Phrygian *harmonia* on an aulos with six equidistant finger holes as 151, 165, 182, 204, 231, 267 (1970, 42, fig. 22). But the Brauron aulos has no interval of 204 cents, the major second that regularly forms the "tone of disjunction" between tetrachords. Moreover, its ascending order constitutes a very different arrangement: 182, 165, 151, 267, 231. Schlesinger's Phrygian ought not to embody a sequence radically different from that of an aulos that is older than the Persian Wars. Possibly an explanation may be sought in the fact that the Brauron aulos is jointed. Fragments of jointed auloi were found at Meroë in 1914 (Schlesinger 1970, 78–79; Bodley 1946 does not refer to them); it was conjectured that the sections might have been fitted together in a different order at different times (Southgate 1915, 14). Something similar may have occurred when the Brauron aulos was placed in the tomb: in this case, the upper section of one instrument could have been wrongly fitted to the lower section of another.

All of this is complicated by the fact that in a later article (1968), Landels gives tentative figures for a newly discovered aulos having five finger holes, which he dates not earlier than the fourth century: 156, 140, 202, 236. The two instruments prove to have not a single interval in common. During any such inquiry, one must remember that the notes actually sounded by a piper remained subject to a number of modifying influences. Late writers, classical and postclassical, were of course ready to produce the *harmoniai* of the "really oldest" Greeks, or to describe the scale that Terpander devised for accompanying libation melodies.

During and after the late decades of the fifth century, artists continued to show auloi with no more than five finger holes. Often they had only three or four, despite the many indications that technical refinements had been introduced into the craft of aulos making. It seems probable that vase painters were merely being faithful to the facts of ordinary life, where the "unimproved" aulos maintained its dominance. The new models, with their auxiliary finger holes and varied apparatus, would thus have been concert instruments, never intended for the ordinary piper. In much the same way, Boehm during the middle 1830s introduced a revolutionary keywork system for the transverse flute; yet during the remainder of the century, ordinary players—Gerard Manley Hopkins was one—continued to use instruments scarcely more developed than the Meroë auloi described by Bodley (Bate 1969, 112 and pl. 6, I).

7. Ensemble playing: a related point concerns the lyre. While it had increased to seven strings by Terpander's time, the aulos underwent no comparable extension. This disparity might well trouble anyone who contends that the two instruments sounded at the same moment and therefore needed to be matched. The near silence of the Greeks on the subject of ensemble playing should have suggested caution.

It is true that Pindar always mentions lyres and auloi together (the exception, *Olympian* 5.21, has therefore been thought suspect); also that vase painters often show them being played together. Here the evidence has been misread: Pindar never claims simultaneity. As for the vase painter, he was a resident alien, with no experience of the lyre-centered system of elementary schooling; he had an extremely limited working surface; and he was subject to a patron's wish for a visible inventory of household possessions.

This does not mean that the Greeks had no ensemble playing whatsoever. Certain occasions could call for both lyres and auloi; and there is no reason to doubt that the two sometimes sounded in unison. Nevertheless, we may suppose that such instances were exceptional. The fifth-century aulos would have overpowered the kithara, not to mention the smaller and weaker *lura;* it must usually have alternated with them, rather than competing.

B. Other forms of the aulos (the term itself is generic, as is noted in Becker 1966, 21; both the monaulos and the plagiaulos had minor roles).

1. Monaulos (*monaulos*): before the fourth-century writers of Middle Comedy at Athens, only Sophocles (frag. 241 Pearson) mentions

the monaulos, associating it with the lyre and, less closely, with the pektis. Like the pektis, it was regarded as foreign except for a pastoral version called the *aulos titurinos,* a native instrument of the Dorian Greeks who had settled in southern Italy. (Compare Vergil's prominent use of Tityrus in the *Eclogues* as a shepherd's name, and once even as a generic term for "shepherd," 8.55.) Despite the counterarguments of Reinach (in the *Dictionnaire des antiquités grecques et romaines* 5:313, s.v. Monaule; see Barker 1984a, 259 n.3, 264 n.20), we may conclude that, in some instances at least, it was the *surinx monokalamos,* or "single-reed syrinx."

The monaulos became common during the Hellenistic period. It appeared on a variety of occasions, sometimes as a part of funeral ceremonies. These normally called for the *epikēdeios aulos,* which provided dirges (see Matt. 9:18–25, on Jairus' daughter); Plutarch (*Quaest. conv.* 3.8.2, 657a) speaks of its power to rouse grief and cause tears. Fragments of monauloi, dating to about 15 B.C., were found at Meroë in 1921 (Bodley 1946, 230–33; fig. 22).

2. Plagiaulos (*plagiaulos,* sometimes called *plagios aulos* and perhaps also *plagiomagadis;* called *tibia obliqua* by the Romans): no evidence links the plagiaulos with Hellenic music; even a supposed reference to it in Theocritus (20.29) comes from a poem produced by a later writer. Eventually, in the second century A.D., it appears as part of the liturgy of Serapis, and it may originally have been part of Egyptian ritual (so *RE* 20 (1950) 1998, s.v. Plagiaulos [E. Bernert]). During the many intervening centuries, however, it never achieved a respected place in community life. The chief reason for this neglect probably was the fact that it belonged to the class of instrument (usually a flute of some kind rather than an aulos) prized for diversion and companionship by shepherds or farmers, but looked down upon by townspeople.

3. Syrinx or panpipe(s) (*surinx;* see pl. IIa). Played by a stylized Cycladic piper, a figurine from Keros dated to the period 2700–2500 B.C. (Thimme 1977, 302, 496–97; Haas 1985, 36–44). A pair of cowherds divert themselves with it in the *Iliad* (18.526); it appears next in two Homeric *Hymns,* those to Hermes (4.511) and to Pan (19.14–19, 24). Throughout the classical period, it continues to be associated with Pan himself and also with his kindred wood spirits, the Sileni and satyrs. It comes finally to be trivialized into a mere accessory for

the little winged *Erōtes* shown in countless Graeco-Roman statuettes and earrings.

The rectangular form of the syrinx played by the Keros piper was retained throughout the archaic period and also the classical; individual pipes varied in number between four and nine or ten, the average being six. This instrument followed its own course of development, related only minimally to that of the lyre or aulos. The chief and almost the sole musical instrument of the countryside, it had no importance for town life.

III. Percussion instruments (Membranophones and idiophones; the similarity in the forms is evident).

A. Hand-held drum (*tumpanon,* plural *tumpana*).

1. Size: seldom more than 2 feet in diameter.

2. Materials and construction: hide stretched over a wooden hoop.

3. Performance and use: beaten with the right hand (varying techniques; cf. the *tabla* in northern Indian music). Played only by women; no drumstick was used. Sometimes it merely provided diversion (Wegner 1949, 65, too limiting); most often, it figured in the ecstatic rites of deities from Asia Minor—Dionysus (along with his fifth-century epiphany, Sabazius, whose worship underlies Euripides' *Bacchae;* see *Bacch.* 120–34 and Dodds 1944 on *Bacch.* 78–79, 126–29), Rhea, Cybele. Like the aulos, it was considered exotic, an import from Phrygia.

B. Cymbal (*kumbalon,* usually as plural *kumbala*).

1. Size: votive or funerary examples vary in diameter from about 3 inches to 6 inches

2. Materials: made of bronze, as it is today

3. Performance and use: played only by women, like the drum, but more strictly limited to cult use. As part of the worship of Cybele, it became a symbolic chalice (*The New Grove Dictionary of Music and Musicians* 5:111, s.v. Cybele). This may explain St. Paul's scornful reference to a "tinkling cymbal" (1 Cor. 13:1: *kumbalon alalazon*), where the inadequate rendering "tinkling" conceals a possible relationship with Cybele's cult.

C. Clappers (*krotala,* only in plural as a musical term).

1. Size: larger than castanets.

2. Performance and use: like castanets, these often accompanied the dance but were held differently from castanets; most like the percus-

186 • *Appendix A*

sionist's slapstick. First in the *Homeric Hymn* 14.3 ("To the Mother of the Gods"), as part of a liturgy. This liturgical function continued, extended especially to the worship of Dionysus. Also highly secular uses, at drinking parties; there, exceptionally, young men rather than a hetaera might play them. Clappers accompanied such low dances as the kordax. On the *kroupezdai,* see Bélis 1988.

Plates

Plate I. Attic red-figure amphora, attributed to the Brygos Painter, ca. 480 B.C. Side A: Kitharode. Note the performer's massive neck. The outspread fingers of his left hand are damping strings not meant to sound, or about to do so. Here the function of the *plēktron* as an extension of the right hand is particularly clear. No vase painting better shows the elaborate costume worn by a kitharode. (John Michael Rodocanachi Fund, 26.61. Courtesy, Museum of Fine Arts, Boston.)

Plate II (*a* and *b*). Attic white ground pyxis, presumably from Eretria, 460–450 B.C. Side A: Poet (Hesiod?) and six Muses. The instruments (not all are visible here) are lyre, panpipes, auloi, and cradle kithara, the latter shown twice. A sixth

Muse apparently has no instrument. (H. L. Pierce Fund, 98.887. Courtesy, Museum of Fine Arts, Boston.)

Plate III. Attic red-figure bell krater, attributed to the painter Polion, ca. 420 B.C. Probably a scene from a satyr play. The instruments held by the three satyrs are unusually early examples of the so-called Thamyris kithara. All three satyrs are shown in different moments of the process of performance, and the performer on the left has the fingers of his left hand placed differently from those of his companions. Accordingly, unison playing cannot be represented. Artistic license, however, has an uncertain role. The wreathed aulete holds in either hand one of the two pipes of a double aulos; the short, stubby nature of the reeds appears very clearly. (The Metropolitan Museum of Art, Fletcher Fund, 1925. [25.78.66]. All rights reserved, The Metropolitan Museum of Art.)

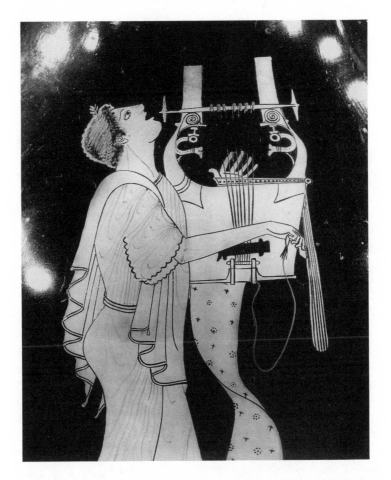

Plate IV. Attic red–figure amphora, said to be from Nola, attributed to the Berlin Painter, early fifth century B.C. Detail: Kitharode. As in the Attic red-figure amphora attributed to the Brygos Painter (pl. I), the singer has an unusually massive neck. By contrast, his arms and the fingers of his right hand are slim and elegant. His prominent buttocks, moreover, have an almost feminine gracefulness of line. All in all, this young performer deviates markedly from the physical ideals set forth for the youth of Athens by Aristophanes, who speaks of the same period from which the amphora comes. Although it would seem that kitharodes were treated with honor, the vase painters show them as alien physically. The instrument, with all of its accessories and ornaments, appears with splendid clarity; this kithara has come to be taken as the rendering par excellence of the Greek concert lyre. (The Metropolitan Museum of Art, Fletcher Fund, 1956. [56.171.38]. All rights reserved, The Metropolitan Museum of Art.)

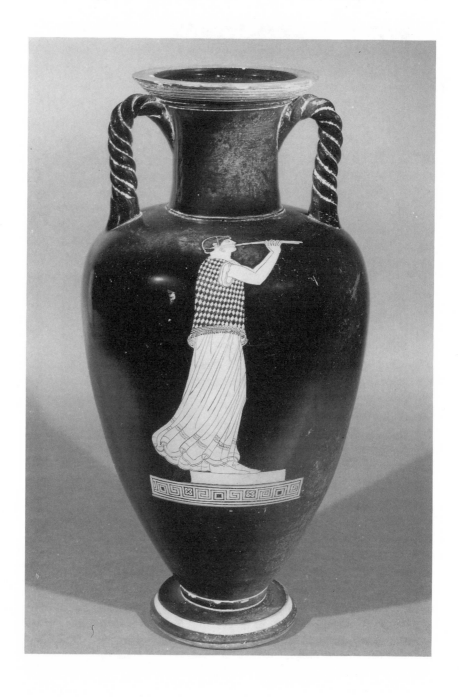

Plate VI. Attic red–figure hydria, by the Agrigento Master, ca. 460 B.C., from Kameiros, on Rhodes. Instruction in aulos playing. A bearded teacher (*kitharistēs*) plays a barbitos in unison (at the octave, presumably), or more probably in alternation, with a pupil who is playing an aulos. Most of a small lyre is visible, held by a youth who seems to have a plectrum, correctly grasped, in his right hand. Behind him, another youth holds up aulos pipes; on the wall by his head hangs a *subēnē,* a carrying case for the disassembled pipes. (British Museum E 171, reproduced by Courtesy of the Trustees of the British Museum.)

Plate V. (facing) Attic red–figure amphora, by the Cleophrades Painter, ca. 480 B.C. Aulete wearing a *phorbeia* or "halter." The podium (*bēma*) on which the performer stands shows that he is competing in a musical *agōn*. The musculature of his neck is even more developed than that of the kitharodes (pls. I, IV). In this, he resembles a professional football player, except that the demands of his art have resulted in a reverse taper, the greatest diameter being just beneath the jaw line. His thumbs support the two pipes while the other fingers cover the sound holes, not with the fingertips but with the pads of the middle joint. Looking very closely, we would see that his cheeks are puffed and his lips pursed, in the thin line now familiar from oboe playing. (British Museum E 270, reproduced by Courtesy of the Trustees of the British Museum.)

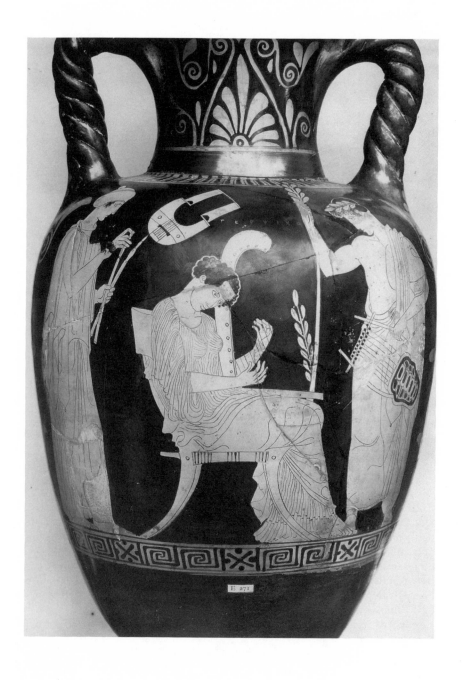

Plate VII. Attic red-figure amphora, attributed to the Peleus Painter, ca. 440
B.C. The names of the three figures appear on the vase: Melusa, Terpsichore, and
Musaeus. The two women are Muses; the name Melusa figures among a number
of noncanonical names for Muses, a reminder that the canon is late and artificial.
Melusa holds a pair of aulos pipes. She is not fixing in place a new reed, as some
have thought, but instead is fitting one of the bulbs that were set between the
barrel of the pipe and the reed. Terpsichore plays an arched harp, as upper-class
Greek women often did in the privacy of their own quarters. A foreign instrument, it never gained further recognition and had no part in public music making. At best a half-legendary figure, Musaeus was associated with Orpheus and
thought to be a very early poet. Here he holds a tortoiseshell lyre, known by the
name for the tortoise itself, *chelus*. The sound chest is clearly meant to be an actual
carapace, as in the story of the infant Hermes' invention of the first lyre (*Homeric
Hymn to Hermes*). The present instrument has eight strings, as do thirteen others
shown on vase paintings between 525 and 400 B.C. Such instances may be due to
carelessness, the usual explanation. In the background, a cradle kithara can be
seen. (British Museum E 271, reproduced by Courtesy of the Trustees of the
British Museum.)

Appendix B

Scale Systems and Notation

To sum up the history of Greek scale systems in a few sentences is easy; to go farther is very difficult. Thus one may say that up to the fifth century, *harmoniai* were individual, not interchangeable to any significant extent. At some point (probably late) in that century, so crowded with change of every kind, there emerged a sequence of tetrachords, fourths with two added notes in the lower portion of the interval; they were based on the old Dorian *harmonia*. The added notes varied, and the nature of that variance determined the genus, whether diatonic (semitone, tone, tone: for example, EFGA) or chromatic (semitone, semitone, tone plus semitone: EFF#A) or enharmonic (E, E plus quarter tone, E plus semitone, ditone), and beyond this the subtype of the genus. Under the new, fifth-century arrangement, one *harmonia* differed basically from another in structure only in that it began at a different place in the master sequence. Shifts between *harmoniai* had become readily possible; this procedure we have encountered as *metabolē,* "modulation."

Although the difficulty of going farther lessens somewhat with each successive period of Greek musical history, it is never less than formidable. The Minoan and Mycenaean cultures had lyres or lyrelike instruments with three strings, which suggests a limited compass. Yet the "Singer" of Pylos (ca. 1300 B.C.) has a five-stringed concert instrument, and the aulos finger positions shown on the Hagia Triada sarcophagus resemble those depicted on fifth-century vases, where lyres and kitharas have seven strings in the overwhelming majority of instances.

The evident fact that the Homeric phorminx was four-stringed may indicate an octave span, perhaps e–e', divided into the outer notes of two tetrachords and thus consisting of a pair of fourths such as e–a and b–e'. Again, the four strings may have represented an actual sequence rather than a framework: for example, a b c' e'. West (1981) has argued for this possibility and for these pitches, which center around what we know as middle C. Although they seem high for a baritone voice, such a predecessor of the later tetrachords may conceivably provide the answer to the riddle of Homer's music.

Looking ahead to the seventh century, we find a landmark event that can be dated to the first or second quarter of that century: the appearance of a seven-stringed lyre on a potsherd from Old Smyrna. Attica confirms this advance; five strings are shown around 700 B.C., but seven are found by midcentury and then later, in the *Homeric Hymn to Hermes* (590 B.C. or earlier?). Because it falls one note short of being an octave, the new, expanded sequence will accommodate two tetrachords only if the top note of the lower doubles as the bottom note of the higher. Such tetrachords, being in conjunction (*sunaphē*) were known as "conjunct" accordingly; a combination of two tetrachords was termed a "system" (*sustēma*). The arrangement of a conjunct system by tone (T) and semitone (S) was S T T S T T ; an example of the notes between which these intervals were set might be E F G A B♭ C D (diatonic genus), A being the so-called tone of conjunction common to both tetrachords. Comparably, a disjunct system was S T T T S T T, E F G A B C D E, the whole-tone interval between A and B being the tone of disjunction (*tonos diazeuktikos*).

These tetrachords, taken in the three genera, form the constituent elements of the Lesser, Greater, and Immutable systems (*sustēma teleion elasson, sustēma teleion meizon, sustēma ametabolon*), first set forth by Aristoxenus and his successors. The Immutable System is better called Unmodulating, for reasons that will become evident. Three tetrachords, taken conjunctly with an "added" note (*proslambanomenos,* sc. *phthonggos*) at the bottom, constituted the Lesser Perfect System. In the following diagram we must introduce the note names encountered first in the musical theorists (the traditional spellings are retained here):

Lesser Perfect System (genus: diatonic)

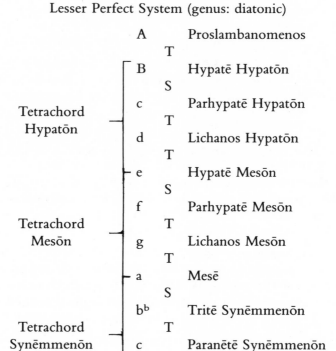

	A	Proslambanomenos
	T	
	B	Hypatē Hypatōn
	S	
	c	Parhypatē Hypatōn
Tetrachord Hypatōn	T	
	d	Lichanos Hypatōn
	T	
	e	Hypatē Mesōn
	S	
	f	Parhypatē Mesōn
Tetrachord Mesōn	T	
	g	Lichanos Mesōn
	T	
	a	Mesē
	S	
	b♭	Tritē Synēmmenōn
Tetrachord Synēmmenōn	T	
	c	Paranētē Synēmmenōn
	T	
	d	Nētē Synēmmenōn

Mesē, "middle," and *tritē,* "third," we noted earlier. *Hypatē* and *par(h)upatē* are "lowest" and "next-to-lowest"; *lichanos* is literally "forefinger" (the "licking" finger); *paranētē* and *nētē* are "next-to-highest" and "highest." Since *hupatos* is normally "highest" and *neatos* (contracted form *nētos*) is "lowest," there may seem to be confusion here; but we must remember the tilted position of the lyre—except for *proslambanomenos,* these are all names of lyre notes, adjectives modifying an unexpressed *chordē,* "string." Of the tetrachords, the third has notes that are "conjunct," *sunēmmena.*

The Greater Perfect System consists of the first two tetrachords given above plus the following two, placed immediately above *mesē* (a), with the tone of disjunction (a–b) intervening:

```
              ┌─    T
              │   b       Paramesē
              │         S
              │   c'      Tritē Diezeugmenōn
  Tetrachord  │         T
  Diezeugmenōn├─  d'      Paranētē Diezeugmenōn
              │         T
              │ ┌ e'      Nētē Diezeugmenōn
              │         S
              │   f'      Tritē Hyperbolaiōn
  Tetrachord  │         T
  Hyperbolaiōn┤   g'      Paranētē Hyperbolaiōn
              │         T
              └─  a'      Nētē
```

The notes of the first of these tetrachords are *diezeugmena,* "disjunct"; those of the second are *huperbolaia,* "added." It will be noted that this system contains two pairs of conjunct tetrachords, separated by the tone between a and b. They are, as it were, substituted for the *sunēmmena,* the highest tetrachord of the Lesser Perfect System. When the latter (Synēmmenōn) is added to them (as an alternative for Diezeugmenōn), the result is the Immutable—better termed Unmodulating—System. Since this contained both b and b♭, the modulation was built in; theorists pretended that *metabolē* was not really taking place.

We have referred earlier to *eidē,* octave species, without yet having the advantage of a formal frame within which to set them. That frame is the Greater Perfect System. The seven species of the octave (*eidē tou dia pasōn*) that it contained were differentiated according to the point at which their interval sequences began: Mixolydian, B–b; Lydian, c–c'; Phrygian, d–d'; Dorian, e–e'; Hypolydian, f–f'; Hypophrygian, g–g'; Hypodorian, a–a'. (For their naming, and for the role of pitch, see Winnington-Ingram's comment, below.) It must now be evident that they represented a profound change from the old *harmoniai.*

There remains one further complication, the existence of pitch scales, or *tonoi* (sometimes also called *tropoi*). It was possible to reproduce a portion of the Immutable System without changing the sequence of intervals within a given scale. Each scale had its pitch level, and it is here that the Greek scale systems came closest to our notion of absolute pitch. Aristoxenus enumerated thirteen *tonoi;* later theorists added two more at the upper end. It will suffice to give only seven of these, with the beginning note of each: Hypodorian, F; Hypophrygian, G; Hypolydian, A; Dorian, B♭; Phrygian, c; Lydian, d; Hyperdorian (or Mixolydian), e♭. They are cited because the same names make up the list of octave species; yet in terms of high and low the order is reversed. Although this may seem at first sight to be a paradox, there is, as Winnington-Ingram says, a simple explanation: "The *tonos* had the name of that species whose characteristic series of intervals it brought within a central range of pitch, i.e. the central octave of the Dorian *tonos*. It is reasonable to assume . . . that the original purpose of the *tonoi* was to bring the species within this range, and that the species received their names, not as segments of the [Greater Perfect System], but as different series of intervals within the same range" (1980, 665–66).

The system of *tonoi* first appears in the *Harmonics* of Aristoxenus, who was born at some time between 375 and 360 B.C.; its previous history remains unknown. In varying degrees, the same lack of knowledge characterizes our dealings with *harmoniai* and scale systems generally during the Hellenic period. Isolated exceptions exist— for example, the handful of references in Pindar and Aristophanes; and the sequences that Aristides Quintilianus presents as the *harmoniai* discussed in the *Republic* may well be what he claims. There is little else, however. Vase paintings cannot help here, and there continues to be more disagreement than consensus about scales embodied in the very few surviving auloi, though the direction of current research is promising. Riethmüller goes too far when he protests that "lists of scales provided with ascending and descending circles of fifths, and with modern notation and altered pitches" cannot have served any practical musical purpose. "The more complex and subtle they are," he concludes, "the stronger becomes the impression that what we are dealing with here is a kind of paper creation" (in Riethmüller and Zaminer 1989, 301). Yet it is difficult not to sympathize with his impatience. As a sustained (and impressive) attempt to bring together and make sense out of the whole range of evidence from pre-Hellenic to Graeco-Roman times, West's efforts in his recent handbook (1992b) stand alone.

We have almost no trace of any system of Greek musical notation that can be securely dated as early as the fifth century. One exception, and it may well be the only one, is the sol-fa trumpet call setting preserved on a vase painting (Bélis 1984b). Theoreticians of the Graeco-Roman period have left hints of systems that must have been far more comprehensive; these seem to have resembled the symbols recorded by Alypius, which provide our only means of attempting to understand the melodies of Greek antiquity.

Alypius is thought to have lived during the fourth century A.D., or not much earlier. It would have been a miracle if he had succeeded in preserving the musical practices of the Hellenic period, six or seven centuries before his time. Indeed, the arguments that we have advanced concerning oral culture and cheironomy can only lead to the conclusion that doing so would have been impossible. Yet in many instances the surviving musical fragments date from periods not widely separated in time from the age of Alypius. Moreover, the great majority of the symbols that they employ correspond, with a reasonable degree of precision, to the ones given in his tables.

These tables comprise two separate systems; Alypius distinguishes them as instrumental and vocal. Still in general use, his distinction is broadly correct but oversimplified. Controversy continues to surround the whole subject; we will not attempt here to convey the nature and extent of the ongoing debate among such scholars as Machabey, Duchesne-Guillemin, Marrou, and Pöhlmann. Some idea of it, together with much helpful information on the whole subject, may be gained from Chailley's chapter 7, "La Notation" (1979, 120–39). Also useful are the discussion by Isobel Henderson (her last contribution to the study of Greek music; completed by Wulstan and appearing in Sternfeld 1973, 1:42–48) and the brief remarks by Comotti (1989, 99–102). For a summary and careful discussion of previous scholarship, see now West 1992b, 254–76 (chap. 9, "Notation and Pitch").

Of the two Alypian systems, which occupy three octaves and a whole tone, the instrumental is thought to have come first. Recent scholarship has confirmed Westphal's contention in 1867 that its forms originated in an archaic Greek script, and has fixed the locale as very probably Argos; see Černý 1990 and West 1992a, 36–41. Its symbols are a mixture of Greek letters and archaic signs, presented in three rotated positions: normal, turned at right angles, or reversed. The altered forms represent a raising of the basic note, first by one quarter tone and then by two. We might naturally suppose that the distinction served originally to express interval sequences within the chromatic (1/2, 1/2, 2 tones) and enharmonic (1/4, 1/4, 2 1/2) tetrachords; yet Alypius does not differentiate between the two genera in any *tonos* except Lydian. This is by no means the only problem that his arrangement presents.

The Ionic alphabet became established officially at Athens in 403/402 B.C.; it had been in use there since about the beginning of the Peloponnesian War, a generation earlier. At some later time, not known to us, it also supplied most of the symbols for the vocal notation. These appear largely in their normal form; ten have right-angled or reversed forms as well. We find a half dozen instances of archaic forms: for example, koppa, and signs of unknown or disputed origin. Taking F as basic note, in accordance with Bellermann's generally accepted convention, the three octaves range from f″ downward to F, with g″ as the added whole tone. (For more than a century, the consensus has been that this is too high by about a minor third; thus the basic note would have been approximately a D.)

Though absolute pitch in the modern sense of that term seems never to have existed among the Greeks, the appearance during the fifth century of an extended scale system with basically interchangeable intervals made inevitable the acceptance of a convention that called for more or less fixed pitch. The end result was a complex centered on the octave that lies most comfortably for a baritone voice, the most common type in any musical culture. On this process of development, and especially on the emergence and purpose of the Immutable System, see above. The central octave, conventionally f′–f, is represented in the three genera by normal letters of the Ionic alphabet. The next higher octave, f″–f′, repeats that sequence with *ottava* marks (for example B′, as against B, for f″ in the chromatic genus) through O′ (for b′); it goes on to designate a′ and g′ mainly by reversed forms of letters taken from the last part of the alphabet.

Exclusive use of reversed or right-angled letters or of signs character-izes only the seven lowest notes, e–F, which can seldom have been required for notating melodies. As Samoïloff (1924) demonstrated, the Dorian pitch key (*tonos*) has the central place in this entire portion of the Alypian scheme; it is the two tetrachords of Dorian that the sequence of the Ionic alphabet represents.

The Alypian notation is presented in figure 23 as it appears in the table given by Henderson.

Alypius' tables can present only the vertical dimension of notation, namely, pitch. Rhythm, the horizontal dimension, was indicated by means of various nonalphabetical signs, not always wholly clear. Normally, they appeared on the suprascript level as the symbols for scale steps but were far less involved with them than is the case with our present-day system.

Pöhlmann (1970, 141, Appendix II) regards ten principles as now firmly established. His formulation of them, with added comment, follows:

    1. "Short syllables are not designated." Underlying this is the well-known fact that the melodization of ancient Greek poetry, considered as rhythm, normally reproduced the metrical pattern of long and short syllables found in the words of the text. Any departure from the rule had to be signaled. The short syllable must represent the *prōtos chronos* of theory, the basic time unit. Pöhlmann, together with a clear major-ity of other modern editors, sets it as an eighth note.

Fig. 23. The vocal and instrumental notations of Alypius. (Reprinted, by permission of Oxford University Press, from *The New Oxford History of Music* [New York: Oxford University Press, 1957], 1: 358, ex. 309.)

2. "A long mark over the note or alongside it designates a time-length of two units . . . in the case of single notes but also groups of notes."

3. "Signs for time-lengths of 3, 4, or 5 units are ⌐ ⌐⌐ ⌐⌐⌐." The long mark was termed *makra dichronos*, literally "a long of two time-units (or, in metrics, of two short syllables)." Of the three signs recorded in Bellermann's *Anonymus* 1.83 as representing a lengthening of three, four, or five such units, only the first can be found in a notated text, namely, the Song of Seikilos.

4. "The stigma (*stigmē*, 'point') stands on the arsis and may be repeated when necessary." The question of the meaning of *arsis* here has received much attention; Winnington-Ingram (Eitrem, Amundsen, and Winnington-Ingram 1955, 77–79) discusses it with his usual thoroughness. Particularly rewarding is his conjecture that the combination of macron and stigma (⌐ . .), as we find it repeated in the Berlin Paean, represents "the earliest form of rhythmical notation," first developed for "simple repetitive metres" (79 n.3). Pöhlmann, however, insists that the stigma was nothing other than a unit for beating time ("*Taktiereinheit*"), and warns against applying the modern concepts of "rising" and "falling" (1970, 141 n.3). On *arsis* as upbeat, see now West 1992b, 133–34, 268.

5. "The hyphen [a curved line underneath two notes] connects notes that pertain to the same syllable or, in the case of instrumental music, to the same rhythmic unit." We may readily grant, with Comotti 1989, 103, that this sign should indicate a close link between two or three notes placed on the same syllable. There is a clear similarity between the present use of the *huphen* (originally *huph' hen*, "in one"; so even in Plutarch) and that set forth by Greek grammarians, which does not differ essentially from the way we use the hyphen today.

But a question arises: What was the nature of the close link postulated by Comotti? Winnington-Ingram (Eitrem, Amundsen, and Winnington-Ingram 1955, 76) begins by asking whether it was melodic or rhythmic. He finds that accepting either alternative involves difficulties, yet seems to think only the second worth arguing. The evidence may be insufficient; besides, we cannot "assume that the hyphen necessarily had the same function in every piece." It is absent both from the *Orestes* papyrus and from the two Delphic hymns; and only these compositions double long vowels when one syllable is set to two notes. "May the duplication of vowels and the hyphen," he asks (77 n.2), "have been two different means employed to indicate the same phenomenon?" On such a hypothesis, the simpler of the two devices, the hyphen, survived; the more complicated appeared only in the early stages of rhythmic notation.

6. "The colon . . . seems to replace the hyphen in certain instances." This sign appears in the Berlin papyrus and in the Christian hymn from Oxyrhynchus. While its modern form as a mark of punctuation has not changed, understanding its ancient function in rhythmization or (less probably) in melodization involves an unusually large number of problems.

From Winnington-Ingram's extremely detailed study of colon usage in the papyri (Eitrem, Amundsen, and Winnington-Ingram 1955, 85–87), two points emerge with special force. One is the conjecture "that the function of the colon was to clarify the grouping of notes and that it could be used *ad libitum* whenever the writer felt that some clarification was required" (85), Later (87 n.1), he adds an observation much like Pöhlmann's but advanced with greater caution: "It does seem possible . . . that the absence of a hyphen was one of the reasons . . . for employing the clarificatory colon." Yet at once he goes beyond Pöhlmann: "There is a further implication—that the omission of the hyphen in certain cases was deliberate, from which it follows that its function was not exclusively rhythmical." The whole question must be called unusually complicated, almost intractable.

7. "For groups of three notes on one syllable, colon and hyphen are used together." (See above, comments on the sixth principle)

8. "The leimma [*leimma*] stands alongside notes; it may be combined with long marks and with the hyphen and stigma. A rounded form is attested as well as the pointed one. It occurs commonly in catalexis. Context must indicate whether it should be rendered as a pause or as a lengthening of the preceding syllable." Once again, many difficulties present themselves. Comotti (1989, 104) and Winnington-Ingram (Eitrem, Amundsen, and Winnington-Ingram 1955, 82) illustrate the kind of catalexis involved in Pöhlmann's statement; a line ending of two longs replaces (alternates with) one composed of long-short-long, so that a short syllable has been omitted. Comotti, however, shows no awareness of the careful attention that Winnington-Ingram (82–84) has given to the problem here—namely, the question of whether the time

value of the omitted syllable was "given to a note belonging to the preceding or to the following syllable" (82).

Mesomedes' *Hymn to the Sun* and *Hymn to Nemesis* contain sixteen instances of the catalectic ending with two longs. Only six of these have the leimma, always preceding the note to which the second long syllable is set. When each of these two concluding syllables has only a single note, the leimma appears over the second in five instances but is omitted in six. This can hardly be accidental. As Winnington-Ingram suggests, "Some distinction must have been intended": it is that the time value of the omitted syllable is given to the penultimate note when the leimma does not appear, to the final note when it does. The former case, he believes, represents normal rhythmization, while the latter must be "an alternative variety . . . , possibly a Hellenistic innovation, for the notation of which the aid of the leimma was invoked" (83). He convincingly rejects the claim that such normal handling of the meter "represents catalexis in the full sense of the word, the final syllable being followed by a pause (not noted)" (82 n.2). All three scholars emphasize the importance of studying each individual use of the leimma.

9. "The *melismos* and *kompismos* [resembling a lower-case *f* (with several variations) in normal and reversed forms, respectively] are performance markings with related significance, occurring between the same notes [repeated]." This requires qualification. The two terms denote kinds of repetitive action: *-ismos* always denoted a process of some kind. The symbols that indicate the use of one of these two types of process in rhythmizing are the *f* sign for *kompismos* and (according to one source) a plus sign for *melismos*. The first of these indicated repetition in instrumental music. It occurs in Berlin papyrus 6870; Pöhlmann (1970, 99) has closely discussed its use there. The second process had to do with repetition in vocal music. Like diastole, the two form a category separate from that of the other terms with which we have been concerned here.

10. "A diastole (**?**) or horizontal colon (**••**) may separate text and instrumental interludes." The second of these signs would appear to be an early form that fell into disuse. By contrast, the diastole appears twice in the *Orestes* fragment, twice in an excerpt from a comedy or satyr play, and once in a scrap of notated text with tragic vocabulary; the item and line numbers in Pöhlmann (1970) are 21.5, 6, 23.3, 7, and 27.4. In the last of these instances, the sign is followed at once by a

large capital gamma, not suprascript; this is part of the instrumental notation. The occurrence perfectly illustrates Pöhlmann's formulation. (The second definition of diastole given by Michaelides 1978, 78, is incorrect.)

Appendix C

Musical Examples

We possess more than forty papyri or inscriptions containing Greek musical notation; the majority are settings of liturgical or dramatic texts. By permission of the publisher, Verlag Hans Carl, portions of this material are reproduced here from the standard edition, Egert Pöhlmann's *Denkmäler altgriechischer Musik* (Nuremberg, 1970). The Leiden fragment was discovered after the publication of Pöhlmann's work. We have nothing from the Hellenic period. Much wishful thinking has taken place, especially with regard to the *Orestes* fragment, but nothing justifies it. Whether or not notation was a late discovery by the Greeks, the examples that have survived certainly are late. The Leiden fragment has been dated to the first half of the third century B.C.; nothing else comes from a time earlier than the end of that century. More than a little interest has centered on the relationship between the pitch contours of text and setting. The examples illustrate it briefly but clearly: the early ones, which are strophic, show no concern with achieving an equivalence between the two; later, nonstrophic, examples show the opposite.

The Leiden Fragment

Leiden Inv. 510, a papyrus fragment, was discovered in 1973 among the holdings of the Rijksuniversiteit. The handwriting dates it to the first half of the third century B.C., which makes it the oldest fragment of Greek music known to have survived. The contents are two excerpts from Euripides' tragedy *Iphigenia in Aulis,* lines 1500–1509 followed by lines 789–92; the first of these excerpts is given without musical notation. The following conjectural reconstruction of the text of lines 783–92 is based on that proposed by Thomas J. Mathiesen (1981), but several time values have been altered to correct false quantities:

The second excerpt forms part of a choral lyric, as the stasimon or "stationary song" (the meaning remains in dispute) that follows strophe and antistrophe. For this, the papyrus has a unique, mixed notation: instrumental as well as vocal signs appear above the text. Comotti (1977, 73) gives the gist of the passage: "The women of Aulis . . . sing of the arrival of the Achaeans . . . [:] 'Let the anxiety of expecting a servile fate, [one] that will afflict the women of Lydia and the wives of the Phrygians, remain far from us and our grandchildren.' . . . They wonder, intent on the loom, which of their enemies will make them slaves, when the country falls in ruin."

Text and Translation

The Greek words or syllables that have musical notation are boldface. Precise indications of accentuation are provided for the notated portions.

783 [*mḗ*]**te emoi**
784 **mḗte emoîs** [*i teknon teknois*
785 *elpis hade pote elthoi*],
786 *hoian hai* **polúchrusoi**
787 **Ludaì** *kai Phrugōn alochoi*

788   *stēsousi para histois*
789   *mutheusai* **táde es allélas.**
790   **tís ára me euplokamou komas**
791   *rhuma dakruoen* **t[a-à]s** (or **t[anusa]s**)
792   **gâs patrías olo**[*menas apolotiei; . . .*]

(The line divisions above are the standard ones, found in the Oxford Classical Text edition. The Leiden papyrus arranges the text differently, with divisions before 786 *hoian,* 789 **táde,** and 791 *t*[a-à]*s*.)

783   Never to me,
784   nor yet to my children's children,
785   may any foreboding come
786   such as that of the wealthy
787   Lydian women and the wives of the Phrygians.
788   At their weaving
789   they will say
790   to one another: "Who, then, will shear off
791   the lovely tresses of my hair, wet with tears,
792   now that my homeland is destroyed? . . ."

Pitch Key and Melodic Form

The basic *tonos* (pitch key) is Hyperaeolian; Hyperphrygian is used as well, in a modulation. Though these are among the highest *tonoi* (only Hyperlydian is higher), the melody lies remarkably low. Usually it goes no higher than f♯' (Mesē), and in three instances it plunges from e' almost to the bottom of the pitch key; in all, there are seven instances of g♯ (Hypatē Hypatōn, literally "lowest of the low [notes]"). The final steep descent of a sixth provides a setting for *patrias olomenas,* "now that my homeland is destroyed"; the mimesis of the fall to ruin can hardly be accidental. The e' g♯ sequence, in the same rhythm, has already served to characterize "the wealthy Lydian women"; the echo here may suggest the poignance of the contrast that the chorus now foresee. One notices also the similar melodizations for [*mē*]*te emoi mēte* and *tade es allēlas,* and the fact that the fixed notes of the tetrachord have unusual prominence.

Accent and Pitch

As given in the Leiden papyrus, the meter of Euripides' text has had at least three differing interpretations; no consensus has yet been reached. Although Mathiesen does correct some errors made by predecessors, his own scansion contains false quantities (784 *tek-*, twice, and *dak-*, 786 *-an*, 787 *Lu-*, 790 final *a*), and he assigns four syllables to *patrias* in line 792.

Some of the disagreement and confusion has been due to the new readings (real or apparent) of Euripides' text that the papyrus has given us. Thus the notated portion begins with *mēte emoi mēte emoisi [teknon teknois]*, whereas the received text has *mēt' emoi / mēt' emoisi*, – ◡ ◡ – | – ◡ ◡ – | ◡ as against – ◡ – | – ◡ – ◡. Though the Leiden papyrus has no elision, "even where the elision is not expressed," says Smyth, "it seems to have occurred in speaking" (1968, 23, sec. 70a). If it occurred in singing as well, the second *mēte e-*, with b and f♯ for the second and third syllables, may have involved a portamento, the voice gliding from the lower note to the higher.

There is no firm relationship between accent and pitch. Both *patrias* and *poluchrusoi* violate the "rule" for melodizing any word, that the accented syllable should be set higher, or at any rate not lower, than the others; in the case of *poluchrusoi*, the violation could hardly be more extreme. The two identical notes for *t[a-a]s*, a peculiar reduction of feminine genitive singular *tas* (long alpha, with circumflex accent), the definite article, do not represent the downward movement expected in the setting of a circumflexed syllable. Moreover, *emoi* on e' followed by *mēte* on d' b contravenes the principle that a final syllable bearing a grave accent should not have a higher note than the accented syllable of the following word.

Performance

The excerpt appears to be intended for performance by the guildsmen of Dionysus, either by a soloist or by a small group of secondary actors, the *sunagōnistai tragikoi* (see Pickard-Cambridge 1968, 310 for a list of four such musicians on a papyrus of 240 B.C., the approximate date of Leiden Inv. 510). Although a baritone range represented the norm throughout the classical period, the ranks of such professional companies must at times have included one or more singers who had what would now be called a first tenor range. The three occurrences of b♭ could have been sung falsetto; until 1830 or later, operatic tenors made use of this expedient for the upper register. It is highly probable that, as those who have worked with the problem now believe, these third-century fragments come from a professional's anthology of suitable dramatic arias.

Authenticity and Importance

The possibility that we have here a portion of the original setting of Euripides' tragedy (produced posthumously, about 405 B.C.) must be called remote. Apart from all the historical arguments, the melodization hardly consorts well with Aristophanes' criticisms of Euripides as a composer for the stage; and the three downward leaps of a sixth, so unlike anything in the *Orestes* fragment, seem bizarre in comparison with other tragic fragments generally. Yet it remains possible, though improbable, that the setting originated during the fourth century; and the fragment must in any case be termed an important discovery. The use of instrumental as well as vocal notational signs for the voice part remains unique—evidence, seemingly, of a period when the distinctions of the double system had not yet become firmly established. This feature strengthens the already convincing claim of Leiden Inv. 510 to be regarded as the earliest annotated text that we possess.

The Orestes Fragment

This fragment contains text and notation, instrumental as well as vocal, for lines 338–44 of Euripides' *Orestes* (408 B.C.). The papyrus, Vienna G 2315, dates from about 200 B.C.

Meter

The meter is dochmiac (x - - ᵛ -), with a number of the many variations that it regularly exhibits. Thus ᵛ ᵛ may occur for each of the syllables, long or short. Its rhythmic ethos is marked; the authors of a standard handbook on Greek and Latin metrics have commented on this point: "The staccato rhythm of dochmiacs makes them suitable for the expression of violent emotions, especially fear and despair. Here then we have one lyric meter which . . . can be associated with a particular mood or sentiment. . . . The dochmiac is the only lyric meter of which it can be said that it is calculated to evoke a specific emotional response" (Halporn, Ostwald, and Rosenmeyer 1963, 51). As West says (1992b, 285) in his recent, brief treatment of this fragment, the tempo presumably was quite rapid, and pointing indicates an upbeat (*arsis*) on the first and third of the basic five notes of the measure, written as 3/8 + 5/8 in his transcription.

Text and Translation

Lines 338–44 constitute the central portion of the antistrophe in the second set of choral lyrics. The speakers are women of Argos, sympathetic toward Electra and her brother Orestes, but with little understanding or insight—a typical Euripidean chorus. Electra is devotedly caring for Orestes during his extreme illness; the matricide, about to go on trial for his crime, proves repellent in his lucid moments and (to the chorus) pitiable when he raves.

The papyrus arranges the lines in an order generally thought incorrect; the result seems impossible to translate convincingly. For that reason, the translation given here is based on the line arrangement in the Oxford Classical Text edition: 338, 340 *ho megas olbos,* 339, 340 *ou monimos em brotois* to 344. The first portion of the antistrophe has been included as well; it provides a needed context for the central lines. As before, boldface is used for the Greek words and syllables with musical notation, and precise indications of accentuation are provided for the notated portions.

332	*iō Zdeu,*
333	*tis eleos, tis hod' agōn*
334	*phonios erchetai*
335	*thoazdōn se ton meleon, hōi dakrua*
336	*dakrusi sumballei*
337	*poreuōn tis es domon alastorōn*
338	**matéros** *haima sas, ho s'* **anabakcheúei;**
340	**ho mégas ólbos** *ou monimos* **em brotoîs:**
339	*katolophuromai katolo***phúromai.**
341	**anà** *de laiphos hōs*
342	*tis* **akátou thoâs tináxas** *daimōn*
343	**katéklusen** *deinōn ponōn* **hōs póntou**
344	*labrois ole***thríoisin en** *kuma***sin.**

334. The comma after *erchetai* in the Oxford Classical Text is incorrect.
340. **em** for **en.**

332	Help, O Zeus!
333	What piteous creature have we here? What is this
	obsession

334 with murder
335 that spurs you on, poor man? For you, tears
336 upon tears fall in a mingled stream
337 when we come into the house of those spirits who
                                    claim vengeance
338 for your mother's blood, that drives you to
                                    Bacchic madness.
340 Great prosperity does not last long among men:
339 I cry in lamentation, cry in lamentation. . . .
341 Back and forth, like the sail
342 of a swift skiff, it is shaken by some avenging spirit
343 that overwhelms it with fearful sufferings
344 in the raging, deadly billows of the deep.

Pitch Key

The modality cannot be determined. The vocal notation has g, a, *b* or b♭, b♭ or b, d′, e′, and *f′* or f′ (italicized notes are raised by a quarter tone); this sequence resembles that of the (supposedly) Damonian *harmonia* given by Aristides Quintilianus. The signs for all of these except the first occur in both the chromatic and the enharmonic versions of the Lydian *tonos;* that for g is diatonic only. There are three instrumental notes, f or f♯, b♭ or b, and g′. The first two are inserted in line 343, once after *kateklusen* and a second time after *ponōn*. The third, g′, separates line 339 from line 338, 338 from 340, and 340 from 341. Then, in line 344, it reappears within a word, dividing *olethrioisin* unevenly in two. Concerning these aulos notes West feels confident "that they were intended to sound simultaneously with the following word, possibly continuing as a drone throughout the phrase" (1992b, 206). The first of his two suggestions is much more convincing than the second. He further contends (207) that the recurrences of instrumental f♯ and b natural in 343 seem to indicate that "the two auloi here diverged to blow the chord of a fourth." The assumption that there were two auloi is gratuitous; so also the belief in a "chord." If the claim was meant to apply to the two separate pipes of the usual aulos, the notion is tenable; but two instruments are not likely to have been involved.

As for genus, the instrumental notes too may be either chromatic or enharmonic. Since no accidentals occur, we cannot make an informed choice. Pöhlman (1970, 81) has chosen chromatic but admits that greater clarity was the only ground. He sees the possibility of a mixed scale such as can be found in the Delphic hymns. Gombosi (1950, 110 n.1) conjectures two enharmonic tetrachords, though Pöhlmann presents this hypothetical *tonos* as a mixture of two enharmonic and one diatonic.

Melodic Form

More often than not, the fragmentary melodic sequences stay within a range represented by the lower tetrachord plus the anomalous diatonic g. The most active area spans only a major or minor third, g a b (b natural or flatted, whether by chromatic or by enharmonic increments). When the melody goes higher, d' and e' are the only notes used except for a single appearance of f' in line 340. At the very end of the text and notation, the sequence a' b♭' e'' . . . g' has an unexpected leap. All other high notes are separated from those of the lower tetrachord. For the first two lines of the papyrus (339, 338), such isolation may be due simply to lacunae; after that, interjected instrumental notes set them off. These interjections, however, usually punctuate stepwise sequences. Once they intervene between b♭' and g' (343 *-as ti-*); the only larger interval in which they figure is a' to d'' (340 fin. *-tois* to 341 *a-*).

If any feature can be singled out as especially noticeable in this lamentably incomplete *melopoiïa*, it is the apparent emphasis on the *puknon* or pycnum, the cluster of semitone (or quarter-tone) "movable" intervals within the tetrachord, b and b♭. The composer has juxtaposed them four times: 339 **-phu**romai, 340 **em brotois,** 342 **-katou,** and 343 **kateklusen.** In this last instance, it is approached from the g below, not the a. If, like Winnington-Ingram, one takes the genus to be enharmonic rather than chromatic, the setting here provides powerful evidence to counter the hypothesis that the enharmonic microtone was only a "passing-tone" variation on the pitch of the fixed or "standing" note immediately below it. West (1992b, 194) suggests that such emphasis on the inner interval sequence of the pycnum may have been "typical of music in the enharmonic genus, with the undivided semitone."

Mesē of the Lydian *tonos,* d, occurs only twice as an independent note (it forms the second element of the setting for 343 **hōs**), at the beginning of line 340 and of line 341. The tonic of this melody must be sought elsewhere, and so little remains as to make any certain identification impossible. Yet we should note the ways in which the anomalous diatonic note g, Lichanos Hypatōn, has been employed. Of its four occurrences, just one might be said to emphasize a, Hypatē (cf. Winnington-Ingram 1968;35, on the second Delphic hymn). The other three do not remotely qualify it as tonic; but on five occasions the instrumental notation indicates that the aulete is to play a g—at what pitch, we do not know. This last point remains to be explained.

Accent and Pitch

There are three questions here. They have been answered to the satisfaction of all but a very few scholars. The first is whether the relative pitches of the vocal notation correspond to those of the text in any significant degree. Clearly, they do not. The antistrophe contains four violations of the "rule of accent"—a rule constructed largely on the basis of archaizing, Graeco-Roman texts with musical notation— together with three instances in which it is observed, or appears to be observed. While this does not constitute either proof or disproof, the burden of proof lies with those who claim to see correspondence.

The second question has grown out of the first and concerns strophic correspondence. Did the Hellenic poet-composer repeat in an antistrophe the melody that he had devised for the strophe, even though it could not possibly fit the new words, with their new sequences of tonemic accent? The alternative would have been a composition of the type called *durchkomponiert* in German, "through-composed"—that is, with fresh melodic invention throughout. Allied with the second question, and once again derivative, is a third that tends to be forgotten: Did the original setting, that of the strophe, follow the pitch accents of the text?

Pöhlmann (1970, 79, 82) has answered both of these questions. Beneath the vocal notation of the *Orestes* fragment he places the Greek text of the relevant portions of both strophe (322–28) and antistrophe. Instances of violation or again of observance prove to be almost exactly as numerous for the strophe—three on each count. Pöhlmann concludes, justifiably, that the composer of this choral lyric laid out his melody for the strophe without regard for word accent, then transferred it to the antistrophe; West concurs (1992b, 285). The burden of proof rests where it lay before.

When we speak of strophic correspondence, we must give the adjective full weight. The archaizing attention to word accent so evident in the compositions of Mesomedes and Limenius proved possible only because their Graeco-Roman hymns and paeans were nonstrophic. As Pöhlmann notes (1970, 82), this archaism extends from the Delphic inscriptions to the Christian hymn discovered at Oxyrhynchus, but it does not characterize the notated fragments of tragic drama that have survived.

A final point. To speak of archaism is permissible, since the pitch accents that marked Hellenic Greek gave way increasingly to the dominance of stress during the Hellenistic period. By the third century, they were in danger of being forgotten. It was then that the grammarian Aristophanes of Byzantium reduced to order the welter of existing accentual systems. In their place he established the simplified arrangement of two basic pitch signs—acute and grave, combining to form the circumflex—that has remained in use ever since.

To students of Greek music, few things can be more touching than the desire of so many to see in the *Orestes* papyrus a genuine, credible echo of the singing and aulos playing heard by Athenian theatergoers in 408 B.C. The papyrus has now been discussed for a hundred years; throughout all that time, a poignant concern with establishing its Hellenic authenticity has never been lacking.

Virtually no possibility exists that the wish can be granted; insurmountable difficulties bar the way. Chief among them is the absence of any evidence that Hellenic Greeks had a written system of musical notation in general use, together with the probability that they depended instead on cheironomy. Alongside these considerations we must place three others, scarcely less daunting: the "occasional" nature of both music and drama in the fifth century, the subsequent development of the concert audience, and the concomitant rise of professionalism.

The first of these has the greatest significance. Western culture has conditioned many of us to believe in the sacredness of the original setting. Such a way of thinking had no place in ancient Greece, where a kind of music flourished that had, and still has, its affinities primarily with the music of non-Western peoples. We may well take as credible the account that Athenians captive in Syracuse sang lyrics from Euripides' tragedies, for the melodies had been part of their own experience (compare the classical view of history as what the oldest survivors could remember); but the *melopoiïa* of a tragic poet was not regarded as specially privileged. If the two score surviving fragments of ancient Greek music teach any lesson that has relevance here, it is that in the Hellenistic and Graeco-Roman periods a text could and did receive a fresh setting. As for the earlier centuries, according to Nettl (1964, 230–31) nonliterate cultures are the ones in which such re-working may take place. It is dangerous, and stultifying as well, to think of Hellenic music as an annex of *Altertumswissenschaft,* somehow exempt from the influences and tendencies that ethnomusicologists have made increasingly clear for music the world over.

The concept of an audience is central to the second consideration. Yet even to use the term *audience*—from the Latin *audire,* "to hear, listen to"—gives a false impression of attendance at dramatic or musical events during the Hellenic period. The earliest known concert hall, said to have been erected by Pericles, bore the name *Ōideion;* the name, significantly, derives not from *akouein,* which parallels *audire* in meaning, but from *aeidein,* "to sing." The Odeon, accordingly, was a "singing place." (Contrast Greek *akoustērion,* "lecture hall," and its Latin rendering, *auditorium,* both from the late Graeco-Roman period.) But it was a separate place from the theater, where musical competitions had previously been held. This separateness well exemplifies the conditions that would give rise to a new phenomenon: the concertgoing audience, no longer involved, but instead listeners, waiting to be entertained. They demanded novelty, and the new settings that we have mentioned called for the use of notation, aide-mémoire scores meant only to help the performer.

The third consideration, that of professionalism, is exemplified by the guildsmen of Dionysus taking over the group performance of drama and liturgy, and by individual performers too—the recitalist with his anthology of tragic arias, the mime artist drawing interpretations from the more sensational aspects of mythology. For what either of these developments could mean, we need only turn to Suetonius' descriptions of Nero as *artifex.*

The *Orestes* papyrus is valuable because it can be dated to the end of the third century B.C. This assures that the music is Hellenistic, quite separate from Graeco-Roman efforts to ape antiquity. Nothing, however, can justify the assumption that it has preserved the melodizing of Euripides. What we have here may be one of the countless resettings of tragic lyrics made by the aulete or by the music coach (*didaskalos*) in a group of *technitai Dionusiakoi,* for presentation by one of the "tragic teams" made up of three *tragōidoi* and their *aulētēs* (Pickard-Cambridge 1968, 283–84; see Pöhlmann 1976, 69).

An alternative exists, though it must be thought less probable. This scrap of text and notation may have served a concert singer as the score for an aria; the limited stock of monodies could never have sufficed to meet the demand. Such a use would have represented aulody (*aulōidia*), singing to the accompaniment of the double pipes, which enjoyed a brief vogue in the sixth century. It was banished from the public competitions, however, almost as soon as it had gained entrance to them. According to Pausanias (10.7.8), its "profound gloominess" provided the reason; his phrase seems an apt description of the passage from the *Orestes*. We cannot know; but we should abandon the wishful thought that time and chance have placed in our hands the music making of Euripides.

The Song of Seikilos

These verses are usually dated to the first century A.D., on epigraphical evidence. They are inscribed on a memorial stele found at Tralles (Aïdin), a small city of Caria about fifteen miles east of Magnesia. Four verses are arranged in seven lines.

Meter

The meter is chiefly iambic. Verse 1 is an iambic metron, with highly unusual syncopation; 2 is aristophanean (- ⌣ ⌣ - - ⌣ - -); 3 and 4 are two iambic metra, the second and fourth iambs syncopated. See West 1982, 165; 1992b, 186, 280, 301–2.

Text and Translation

1 *Hóson zêis, phaínou,*
2 *mēdèn hólōs sù lupoû.*
3 *pròs olígon estì tò zên;*
4 *tò télos ho chrónos apaiteî.*

1 The reading *euphrainou*, "be cheerful," in Halaris 1992 (see the discography) has no warrant.

1 While you live, shine forth:
2 don't be sad at all.
3 We have only a little while to live;
4 time demands the end [of life] in repayment.

By the first century A.D., pronunciation no longer followed the Hellenic norms embodied in the system of transliteration usually followed. (As in our transliteration of other late texts, however, zeta is given above as *z*, not as the Hellenic *zd*.) For our purposes, most of the changes have no importance; but the post-Hellenic leveling of vowels and diphthongs resulted in a succession of identical or similar sounds that give a different coloring even to this short text. All of the following words or syllables (not including portions in parentheses) were pronounced more or less to rhyme with English "see": 1 *zêis*; 2 *mē̄(dèn)*, *su*, *lu(poû)*; 3 *i* in *oligon* and *estì*, *zēn*; 4 *eî* in *apaiteî*. Thus one can perceive a schema of assonance that links the final syllables of lines 3 and 4. It parallels, and in a sense carries on, the effect of *-ou* at the close of both 1 and 2. The diction and syntax of the Song of Seikilos are notably simple; perhaps such simplicity lent itself to the clinching effect provided by jingles at the line ends.

Pitch Key

This is Ionian, with e, f♯, g, a, b, c♯', d', e'; a Phrygian modality has often been thought to coexist with this. Pöhlmann (1970, 56) finds the choice of *tonos* "unexpected": he refers to the failure to use Lydian, which at some unknown point had gained a clear ascendancy over Dorian (Anderson 1966, 145, 274 n.74); it dominates the (presumably) Hellenistic exercises of Bellermann's *Anonymus* and the Graeco-Roman hymns of Mesomedes. Since the latter can be securely dated to A.D. 117–138 (Hadrian's reign), they come from approximately the same period as the funerary melody commissioned by Seikilos. Why, then, the choice of Ionian?

Several factors may have had a bearing on the choice. Only a few miles separated Tralles from the southern borders of Ionia; and Ionian had for five centuries been associated partly with mourning. In the *Suppliant Women* (69), Aeschylus' chorus claim to be "fond of lamenting in Ionian melodies [*nomoisin*]." Varied and apparently conflicting attributions of ethos were made to this *harmonia* (or *eidos*, or *tonos*), however; we conjecture at our peril (for extended discussion, see Abert 1968, 86–91). Isobel Henderson (1957, 370) makes the point that "the opening fifth CZ, if it is intelligible at all, must surely be a main progression between fixed notes—whereas in the *tonos* C and Z are movable notes." This leads her to question as perhaps unhistorical "the interpretation of Greek music in terms of theoretical octave-structures," and to conjecture that "a particular range of signs" indicated "not an absolute pitch, but a special temperament of intervals." In his examination of the scale and pitch key of this composition, West concludes that "the shape of the scale must be more significant than the notation" (1992b, 186).

Melodic Form

The composition opens with a leap of a fifth. This violates the "rule" that in any word an unaccented syllable should not be set to a higher note than the accented syllable—a rule otherwise strictly observed throughout this composition. Since several other fragments open with the same clash, it may well have been thought permissible in an anacrusis.

The melody proceeds stepwise from measure 2 almost to the end of measure 4. Then we have prominent use of intervals of a third, linked and given variety by brief stepwise sequences. No attention is paid to tetrachordal structure. Lines 2–4 all show an ascending-descending movement, and in their opening notes both 3 and 4 might be interpreted as ways of fleshing out the bare fifth with which the melody opens, and within which almost all of the melodic movement takes place up to the closing cadence. On five or six occasions, a long vowel or diphthong has the extended rhythmic value shown by a triseme (duration of three eighth notes): 1 *zēis* ♩., cf. *phai-* ♪♪♪, *-nou* ♩.; 2 *-pou* ♪♩; 3 *zēn* ♪♩; perhaps 4 *-tei* ♪♪♪. All of these have the triseme mark over the Alypian notation letter or letters, except for 1 *phai-* and 4 *-tei*. In the latter instance, the stonemason ought clearly to have included it. Pöhlmann, showing undue caution, merely suggests it in the critical apparatus. The same holds true for *phai-*, which West (1982, 165) explicitly identifies as a triseme sung on three notes. (He also finds resolved trisemes, ⌣ – or ⌣ ⌣ ⌣, in the melody.) Henderson (1957, 371) correctly points out that "a uniform time-scheme" of twelve rhythmic units has been "imposed on irregular verses" by the music. As for the irregularity, the four lines (chopped into six on the stele) contain five, seven, eight, and nine syllables respectively—we note the smoothly increasing line lengths. They are leveled out initially into nine, eleven, eleven, and eleven metrical units and finally into the "perfect" artificial uniformity of a dozen rhythmic units apiece.

The larger questions that surround this melody have called forth controversial attempts to answer them. For Henderson (1957, 371), the forced uniformity of the rhythmization constitutes evidence that "breeds of music alien to the orthodox tradition" existed in the "superficially Hellenized world" of Seikilos. Fischer (1953) proposed modern parallels and earlier survivals (Gregorian chant, German folk song); along with many others, Pöhlmann (1970, 56) remains unconvinced. Recent years have seen the argument of Beaton (1980, 10–11) that the affiliations of Seikilos' song lie with Turkish popular melodies. He makes his case strongly and may have solved the puzzle. Such an origin would explain the distinctiveness of this little *Grablied,* and possibly its popularity as well. It makes a different impression from the other fragments that have survived; and this sense of a difference may be due to the fact that, with few if any exceptions, they either come from the "establishment" world of liturgy or are settings of lyric texts performed in concert as solo arias. We have the texts of a number of folk songs, but not a single musical setting. To assess fully the qualities that set off this melody from Tralles is, therefore, a task that we are not equipped to undertake.

As for popularity, the Song of Seikilos has no rival. It may be termed the only piece of Greek music to have held the interest of others besides classical philologists. Some nineteenth-century Englishmen sang it before dinner, in lieu of a grace. Admittedly, we do not know to what extent this attachment has been occasioned by the words, with their comfortably bourgeois moralizing. As poetry, the work is embarrassingly banal; as music, it does not lack a certain charm even to our ears, especially in the buoyant notes of the opening. Perhaps the reason we are comfortable with it is that it comes closer than any other ancient Greek melody to the simple, foursquare structure of European folk song, so that the pentatonic cadence at the close—natural enough in context—proves startling. Henderson (1957, 370) finds the "diatonic banality" of the melody disconcerting; but Beaton (1980, 10) points out that this is just what one should expect. The text, at any rate, hardly rises above the level of doggerel.

Solomon (1986), armed with the panoply of Aristoxenus' rules for melodic progression, has subjected this little ditty to an exhaustive analysis. Unfortunately, the rules waver between the prescriptive and the merely descriptive. Also, as we have seen, the status of Seikilos' song as Greek music appears insecure to begin with; indeed, one of the most incisive critics in this field has little use for the work as music of any kind.

A valid analysis of the musical fragments remains to be achieved. We must await someone who, like Harold Powers on the music of India, possesses a theoretical mastery of modal melodization in an essentially monophonic musical culture. Only then can we hope to have a system that might, for example, stand alongside Schenker's triad-based scheme for Western music from Bach to Brahms.

Bibliography

Earlier bibliographies of ancient Greek music are listed in Winnington-Ingram 1981. To these may be added Ōki 1981, based on *L'année philologique* and perpetuating its omissions. On Mathiesen 1974, see my review.

Abert, Hermann. 1968. *Die Lehre vom Ethos in der griechischen Musik.* 1899. Reprint, Tutzing: Hans Schneider.

Adam, James, ed. 1938, 1929. *The Republic of Plato.* 1902. Reprint, Cambridge: Cambridge University Press.

Ahrens, Christian. 1976. Volksmusik der Gegenwart als Erkenntnisquelle für die Musik der Antike. *Die Musikforschung* 29: 37–45.

Aign, Bernhard Paul. 1963. Die Geschichte der Musikinstrumente der ägäischen Raumes bis um 700 vor Christus: Ein Beitrag zur Vor- und Frühgeschichte der griechischen Musik. Ph.D. diss., Johann Wolfgang Goethe-Universität, Frankfurt am Main.

Allen, Thomas W., W. R. Halliday, and E. E. Sikes, eds. 1980. *The Homeric Hymns.* 1936. Reprint, New York: Benjamins.

Anderson, Warren D. 1966. *Ethos and Education in Greek Music.* Cambridge, Mass.: Harvard University Press.

———. 1974. Review of Mathiesen 1974. *The Musical Times* 115, no. 1581: 949–50.

Athanassakis, Apostolos N. 1976. *The Homeric Hymns.* Baltimore: Johns Hopkins University Press.

Bachmann, Alberto. 1975. *An Encyclopedia of the Violin.* 1925. Reprint, New York: Da Capo.

Baines, Anthony. 1957. *Woodwind Instruments and Their History.* New York: W. W. Norton.

Balfour, Henry. 1976. *The Natural History of the Musical Bow.* 1899. Reprint, New York: Longwood.

Barbera, Charles A. 1983. Review of Lord 1982. *Review of Politics* 45: 616–20.

Barker, Andrew. 1982. The innovations of Lysander the kitharist. *Classical Quarterly* 32: 266–69.

——, ed. 1984a. *Greek Musical Writings*. Vol. 1, *The Musician and His Art*. Cambridge Readings in the Literature of Music, ed. John Stevens and Peter le Huray. Cambridge: Cambridge University Press.

——. 1984b. Review of Mathiesen 1983. *Ancient Philosophy* 4: 255–62.

——. 1987. Text and sense at *Philebus* 56a. *Classical Quarterly* 37: 103–9.

——, ed. 1989. *Greek Musical Writings*. Vol. 2, *Harmonic and Acoustic Theory*. Cambridge Readings in the Literature of Music, ed. John Stevens and Peter le Huray. Cambridge: Cambridge University Press.

Bate, Philip. 1969. *The Flute: A Study of Its History, Development, and Construction*. London: Ernest Benn.

Baud-Bovy, Samuel. 1967. L'accord de la lyre antique et la musique populaire de la Grèce moderne. *Revue de la musicologie* 53: 3–20.

——. 1983. Chansons populaires de la Grèce antique. *Revue musical* 69: 5–20.

Beaton, Roderick. 1980. Modes and roads: Factors of change and continuity in Greek musical tradition. *British School at Athens* 75: 1–11.

Becker, Heinz. 1966. *Zur Entwicklungsgeschichte der antiken und mittelalterlichen Rohrblattinstrumenten*. Schriftenreihe des Musikwissenschaftlichen Instituts der Universität Hamburg, vol. 4. Hamburg: Musikverlag Hans Sikorski.

Bélis, Annie. 1984a. Auloi grecs du Louvre. *Bulletin de correspondance hellénique* 108: 111–22.

——. 1984b. Un nouveau document musical. *Bulletin de correspondance hellénique* 108: 99–109.

——. 1986. L'aulos phrygien. *Revue archeologique* 1: 21–40.

——. 1988. *Kroupezdai, scabellum*. *Bulletin de correspondance hellénique* 112: 323–39.

Bernert, E. 1950. Plagiaulos. *RE* 20: 1998.

Blacker, Carmen. 1986. *The Catalpa Bow: A Study of Shamanistic Practices in Japan*. Cambridge, Mass.: Unwin Hyman.

Blümner, Hugo. 1969. *Technologie und Terminologie der Gewerbe und Kunste bei Griechen und Römern*. 4 vols. 1879–1912. Reprint, Hildesheim: Georg Olms.

Bodley, Nicholas B. 1946. The auloi of Meroë. *American Journal of Archaeology* 50, no. 2: 217–40.

Böhme, Robert. 1953. *Orpheus: Das Alter des Kitharoden*. Berlin: Weidmann.

Bowra, Cecil M. 1930. *Tradition and Design in the "Iliad."* Oxford: Clarendon Press.

——. 1961. *Greek Lyric Poetry*. 2d ed., rev. Oxford: Clarendon Press.

——. 1966. *Heroic Poetry*. London: Macmillan.

Brandt, Paul. Pseudonym; see under Licht, Hans.

Burrow, T. 1973. *The Sanskrit Language*. 1955. Reprint, London: Faber and Faber.

Bury, John B. 1945. *A History of Greece to the Death of Alexander the Great*. 2d ed. London: Macmillan.

Calame, Claude. 1977. *Les choeurs de jeunes filles en Grèce archaïque*. Rome: Ateneo & Bizzarri.

Campbell, David A. 1964. Flutes and elegiac couplets. *Journal of Hellenic Studies* 84: 63–68.

――, ed. and trans. 1982a. *Greek Lyric.* Vol. 1, *Sappho and Alcaeus.* Loeb Classical Library. Cambridge, Mass.: Harvard University Press.

――, ed. 1982b. *Greek Lyric Poetry: A Selection of Early Greek Lyric, Elegiac, and Iambic Poetry.* 1967. Reprint, Bristol: Bristol Classical Press.

Carey, Christopher. 1991. The victory ode in performance: The case for the chorus. *Classical Philology* 86: 192–200.

Černý (Czerny), Miroslav K. 1990. K vzniku a stáří staročeských hudebních notací (Zur Entstehung und Deutung der altgriechischen Notenschrift; summary in German). *Listy filologické* 113: 9–18.

Chailley, Jacques. 1979. *La musique grecque antique.* Collection d'études anciennes. Paris: Société d'édition Les belles lettres.

Chantraine, Pierre. 1968–1980. *Dictionnaire étymologique de la langue grecque.* Paris: Klincksieck.

Cirlot, Juan Eduardo. 1991. *A Dictionary of Symbols.* 2d ed. Translated by Jack Sage. New York: Philosophical Library.

Comotti, Giovanni. 1972. L'endecacorde di Ione di Chio. *Quaderni Urbinati di Cultura classica* 13: 54–61.

――. 1977. Words, verse, and music in Euripides' *Iphigenia in Aulis. Museum philologum londiniense* 2: 69–84.

――. 1983. Un antica arpa, la magadis, in un frammento di Teleste (fr. 808 P.). *Quaderni Urbinati di Cultura classica,* n.s. 3: 57–71.

――. 1989. *Music in Greek and Roman Culture.* Translated by Rosaria V. Munson. Ancient Society and History Series. Baltimore: Johns Hopkins University Press.

Comparetti, Domenico. 1898. *The Traditional Poetry of the Finns.* Translated by Isabella M. Anderton. London: Longmans, Green.

Conway, Geoffrey S. 1972. *The Odes of Pindar Translated into English Verse.* London: Dent.

Daremberg, Charles Victor, and Edmond Saglio, eds. 1877–1919. *Dictionnaire des antiquités grecques et romaines.* Paris: Hachette.

Davies, M. 1982. The paroemiographers on *TA TRIA TŌN STĒSICHOROU. Journal of Hellenic Studies* 102: 206–10.

Deiters, Hermann. 1870. *De Aristidis Quintiliani Doctrinae harmonicae fontibus.* Bonn: Carl Georgi.

Delatte, Louis. 1938. Note sur un fragment de Stésichore. *L'antiquité classique* 7: 23–29.

Denniston, John D. 1934. *The Greek Particles.* Oxford: Clarendon Press.

Diels, Hermann, and Walther Kranz, eds. 1956. *Die Fragmente der Vorsokratiker.* 8th ed. Berlin: Weidmann.

Dodds, Erik R., ed. 1944. *Euripides: Bacchae.* 2d ed. Oxford: Clarendon Press.

――. 1957. *The Greeks and the Irrational.* Boston: Beacon Press.

Dover, Kenneth J. 1973. Classical Greek attitudes to sexual behavior. *Arethusa* 6: 59–73.

Drerup, Engelbert. 1921. *Das Homerproblem in der Gegenwart: Prinzipien und Meth-*

oden der Homererklärung. Homerische Poetik, ed. Engelbert Drerup, vol. 1. Würzburg: C. J. Becker.

Düring, Ingemar. 1945. Studies in musical terminology in 5th century literature. *Eranos* 43: 176–97.

———. 1955. Review of Lasserre 1954. *Gnomon* 27: 431–36.

Dyer, Robert R. 1964. On describing some Homeric glosses. *Glotta* 42: 121–31.

Edmonds, John M., ed. and trans. 1963–1967. *Lyra Graeca.* 3 vols. 2d ed. Loeb Classical Library. 1922–1927. Reprint, Cambridge, Mass.: Harvard University Press.

Eitrem, Samson, Leiv Amundsen, and Reginald P. Winnington-Ingram. 1955. Fragments of unknown Greek tragic texts with musical notation. *Symbolae osloenses* 31: 1–87.

Erlmann, Veit. 1983. Marginal men, strangers, and wayfarers: Professional musicians and change among the Fulani of Diamaré (North Cameroon). *Ethnomusicology* 27: 187–225.

Evans, Arthur J. 1921–1935. *The Palace of Minos.* London: Macmillan.

Evelyn-White, Hugh G., ed. and trans. 1936. *Hesiod; The Homeric Hymns and Homerica.* Loeb Classical Library. 1914. Reprint, Cambridge, Mass.: Harvard University Press.

Fischer, Wilhelm. 1953. Das Grablied des Seikilos, der einzige Zeuge des antiken weltlichen Liedes. In *Amman-Festgabe,* edited by Johann Knobloch. Innsbrucker Beiträge zur Kulturwissenschaft, 1: 153–65. Innsbruck: Selbstverlag des sprachwissenschaftlichen Seminars der Universität Innsbruck.

Freeman, Kathleen. 1948. *Ancilla to the Pre-Socratic Philosophers.* Oxford: Blackwell.

Gentili, Bruno. 1979. *Theatrical Performances in the Ancient World: Hellenistic and Early Roman Theatre.* London Studies in Classical Philology, vol. 2, ed. Giuseppe Giangrande. Amsterdam: J. C. Gieben.

Georgiades, Thrasybulos Georgos. 1958. *Musik und Rhythmus bei den Griechen: Zum Ursprung der abendländischen Musik.* Rowohlts Deutsche Enzyklopädie, no. 61. Hamburg: Rowohlt.

Gerson-Kiwi, Edith. 1981. Cheironomy. *The New Grove Dictionary of Music and Musicians* 4: 342–47.

Gill, Dominic, ed. 1984. *The Book of the Violin.* New York: Rizzoli.

Gombosi, Otto J. 1950. *Tonarten und Stimmungen der antiken Musik.* Copenhagen: Ejnar Munksgaard.

Görgemanns, Herwig, and Annemarie Jeanette Neubecker. 1966. "Heterophonie" bei Plato. *Archiv für Musikwissenschaft* 33: 151–69.

Gundert, Hermann. 1935. *Pindar und sein Dichterberuf.* Frankfurter Studien zur Religion und Kultur der Antike, vol. 10. Frankfurt am Main: Vittorio Klostermann.

Guthrie, William K. C. 1956. *The Greeks and Their Gods.* Boston: Beacon Press.

Haas, Gerlinde. 1985. *Die Syrinx in der griechischen Bildkunst.* Wiener Musikwissenschaftliche Beiträge, vol. 11. Vienna: Böhlau.

Halporn, James W., Martin Ostwald, and Thomas G. Rosenmeyer. 1963. *The*

Meters of Greek and Latin Poetry. The Library of Liberal Arts, no. 126. Indianapolis: Bobbs-Merrill.

Havelock, Eric A. 1963. *Preface to Plato.* Oxford: Basil Blackwell.

Heath, Malcolm. 1988. Receiving the *kōmos:* The context and performance of epinician. *American Journal of Philology* 109: 180–95.

Heath, Malcolm, and Mary Lefkowitz. 1991. Epinician performance. *Classical Philology* 86: 173–91.

Henderson, Jeffrey. 1975. *The Maculate Muse.* New Haven: Yale University Press.

Henderson, M. Isobel. 1957. Ancient Greek music. In *The New Oxford History of Music,* edited by Egon Wellesz, 1: 336–403. London: Oxford University Press.

Henderson, M. Isobel, and David Wulstan. 1973. Ancient Greece. In *Music from the Middle Ages to the Renaissance,* edited by F. W. Sternfeld, 1: 1–58. New York: Praeger.

Hickmann, Hans. 1956. Handzeichen. *Die Musik in Geschichte und Gegenwart* 5: 1443–51.

———. 1958. La chironomie dans l'Egypte pharaonique. *Zeitschrift für ägyptische Sprache und Altertumskunde* 83: 96–127.

Hornbostel, Erich Maia von, and Curt Sachs. 1914. Systematik der Musikinstrumente. *Zeitschrift für Ethnologie* 46: 553–90.

Huchzermeyer, Helmut. 1931. Aulos und Kithara in der griechischen Musik bis zum Ausgang der klassischen Zeit. Ph.D. diss., University of Münster. Emsdetten (Westphalia): H. & J. Lechte.

Hudson, Lee. 1980. Between singer and rhapsode. *Literature in Performance* 1: 33–44.

Janssens, A. J. 1941. De Muziekpsycholoog Damoon van Oa. *Tijdschrift voor Philosophie* 3: 499, 506, 649–712.

Jebb, Richard C. 1892. *Sophocles: The Plays and Fragments. Pt. 5, The Trachiniae.* Cambridge: Cambridge University Press.

Kassler, Jamie C., and Jill Stubington, eds. 1984. *Problems & Solutions: Occasional Essays in Musicology Presented to Alice M. Moyle.* Sydney: Hale & Iremonger.

Kenyon, Frederic G. 1932. *Books and Readers in Ancient Greece and Rome.* Oxford: Clarendon Press.

Kirk, Geoffrey S., and J. E. Raven. 1971. *The Presocratic Philosophers.* 1957. Reprint, Cambridge: Cambridge University Press.

Kitto, Hugh D. 1950. *Greek Tragedy: A Literary Study.* London: Methuen.

Landels, John G. 1960. Ancient Greek musical instruments of the wood-wind family. Ph.D. diss., University of Hull.

———. 1963. The Brauron aulos. *British School at Athens* 58: 116–19.

———. 1964. Fragments of auloi found in the Athenian Agora. *Hesperia* 33: 392–400.

———. 1966. Ship-shape and *sambuca*-fashion. *Journal of Hellenic Studies* 86: 69–77.

———. 1968. A newly discovered *aulos. British School at Athens* 63: 231–38.

Lasserre, François, ed. 1954. *Plutarque: De la musique.* Bibliotheca Helvetica Romana. Olten: URS Graf-Verlag (reviewed by Düring 1955).

Lawergren Bo. 1982a. Acoustics and evolution of arched harps. *Galpin Society Journal* 94: 110–29.

_____. 1982b. Acoustics of musical bows. *Acustica* 51: 63–65.

Leaf, Walter, ed. 1900. *The Iliad.* 2d ed. London: Macmillan.

Lentz, Tony M. 1989. *Orality and Literacy in Hellenic Greece.* Carbondale: Southern Illinois Press.

Lesky, Albin. 1966. *A History of Greek Literature.* Translated by James Willis and Cornelis de Heer. New York: Thomas Y. Crowell.

_____. 1983. *Greek Tragic Poetry.* Translated by Matthew Dillon. New Haven: Yale University Press.

Levin, Flora R. 1961. The hendecachord of Ion of Chios. *Transactions of the American Philological Association* 92: 295–307.

Licht, Hans [Paul Brandt]. 1974. *Sexual Life in Ancient Greece.* Translated by John Henry Freese. 1932. Reprint, New York: AMS Press.

Lindsay, Jack. 1963. *A Short History of Culture.* New York: Citadel Press.

List, George. 1963. The boundaries of speech and song. *Ethnomusicology* 7: 1–16.

Lomax, Alan, Edwin E. Erickson, and Joan Halifax. 1968. *Folk Song Style and Culture.* Publication No. 88. Washington, D.C.: American Association for the Advancement of Science.

Lord, Albert B., ed. 1954. *Serbocroatian Heroic Songs.* Vol. 1. Cambridge, Mass.: Harvard University Press.

_____. 1975. *The Singer of Tales.* 1960. Reprint, New York: Atheneum.

Lord, Carnes. 1982. *Education and Culture in the Political Thought of Aristotle.* Ithaca, N.Y.: Cornell University Press (reviewed by Barbera 1983).

Maas, Martha. 1974. On the shape of the ancient Greek lyre. *Galpin Society Journal* 27:113–17.

_____. 1975. Back views of the ancient Greek kithara. *Journal of Hellenic Studies* 95: 175.

_____. 1992. *Polychordia* and the fourth-century Greek lyre. *Journal of Musicology* 10: 74–88.

Maas, M., and Jane M. Snyder. 1989. *Stringed Instruments of Ancient Greece.* New Haven: Yale University Press.

Macran, Henry S., ed. 1974. *ARISTOXENOU HARMONIKA STOICHEIA: The "Harmonics" of Aristoxenus.* 1902. Reprint, Hildesheim: Georg Olms.

Maehler, Herwig. 1963. *Die Auffassung des Dichterberufs im frühen Griechentum bis zur Zeit Pindars.* Hypomnemata: Untersuchungen zur Antike und zu ihrem Nachleben, vol. 3. Göttingen: Vandenhoek & Ruprecht.

Malm, William P. 1967. *Music Cultures of the Pacific, the Near East, and Asia.* Prentice-Hall History of Music Series. Englewood Cliffs, N.J.: Prentice-Hall.

Marrou, Henri Irénée. 1946. Melographia. *L'antiquité classique* 15:289–96.

_____. 1964. *A History of Education in Antiquity.* Translated by George Lamb. New York: Sheed & Ward.

Marzi, Giovanni. 1973. Il papiro musicale dell' "Oreste" di Euripide (*Pap. Vindob. G.* 2315). In *Scritti in onore di Luigi Ronga* 315–29. Milan and Naples: R. Ricciardi.

Mathiesen, Thomas J. 1974. *A Bibliography of Sources for the Study of Ancient Greek*

Music. Music Indexes and Bibliographies, ed. George R. Hill, no. 10. Hackensack, N.J.: Joseph Boonin (reviewed by Anderson 1974).

———. 1981. New fragments of ancient Greek music. *Acta musicologica* 53: 14–32.

———, trans. and comm. 1983. *Aristides Quintilianus: On Music in Three Books*. Music Theory Translation Series. New Haven: Yale University Press (reviewed by Barker 1984b).

Michaelides, Solon. 1978. *The Music of Ancient Greece: An Encyclopaedia*. London: Faber and Faber.

Monro, David B., ed. 1963, 1964. Homer: *Iliad*. 1884, 1888. Reprint, Oxford: Clarendon Press.

Morgan, Kathryn A. 1993. Pindar the professional and the rhetoric of the KŌMOS. *Classical Philology* 88: 1–15.

Moutsopoulos, Evanghélos. 1959. *La musique dans l'oeuvre de Platon*. Paris: C. Klincksieck.

Murko, Matija (Matthias). 1919. Neues über südslavische Volksepik. *Neue Jahrbücher für das klassische Altertum* 43: 273–96.

———. 1929. *La poésie populaire épique en Jougoslavie au début du xxᵉ siècle*. Paris: Honoré Champion.

———. 1951. *Tragom srpsko-hrvatske narodne epike*. Zagreb: Jugoslavenska akademije znanosti i umjetnosti.

Myres, John F. 1967. *Who Were the Greeks?* 1914. Reprint, New York: Biblo and Tannen.

Nettl, Bruno. 1964. *Theory and Method in Ethnomusicology*. London: The Free Press of Glencoe.

Nilsson, Martin P. 1927. *The Minoan-Mycenaean Religion and Its Survival in Greek Religion*. London: Humphrey Milford.

Norwood, Gilbert. 1945. *Pindar*. Berkeley and Los Angeles: University of California Press.

Ōki, Hiroyasu. 1981. *Répertoire de littérature musicale de la Grèce antique: 1958–1978*. Yokohama: Hiroyasu Ōki.

Page, Denys L., ed. 1962. *Poetae Melici Graeci*. Oxford: Clarendon Press.

Paquette, Daniel. 1984. *L'instrument de musique dans la céramique de la Grèce antique: Études d'organologie*. Université de Lyons 2: Publications de la Bibliothèque Salomon Reinach, vol. 4. Paris: Broccard.

Pearson, Lionel. 1977. The dynamics of Pindar's music: Ninth Nemean and third Olympian. *Illinois Classical Studies* 2: 54–69.

———, ed., trans., and comm. 1990. Aristoxenus: *Elementa rhythmica*. Oxford: Clarendon Press.

Phaklaris, Panayiotis. 1977. CHELUS. *Archaiologikon deltion* 32, pt. A: 218–33.

Pickard-Cambridge, Arthur W. 1946. *The Theatre of Dionysus*. Oxford: Clarendon Press.

———. 1962. *Dithyramb, Tragedy and Comedy*. 2d ed., rev. Oxford: Clarendon Press.

———. 1968. *The Dramatic Festivals of Athens*. 2d ed., rev. Oxford: Clarendon Press.

Pintacuda, Mario. 1978. *La musica nella tragedia greca*. Cefalú: Lorenzo Misuraca.

Plumley, Gwendolen A. 1966. *El Tanbur: The Sudanese Lyre or the Nubian Kissar.* Cambridge: Town and Gown.

Pöhlmann, (Friedrich) Egert, ed. and comm. 1970. *Denkmäler altgriechischer Musik: Sammlung, Übertragung, und Erläuterung aller Fragmente und Fälschungen.* Erlanger Beiträge zur Sprach- und Kunstwissenschaft, vol. 31. Nuremberg: Hans Carl.

——. 1976. Die Notenschrift in der Überlieferung der griechischen Bühnenmusik. *Würzburger Jahrbücher für die Altertumswissenschaft,* n.s. 11: 53–73.

Pugh-Kitingan, Jacqueline. 1984. Speech-tone realisation in Huli music. In *Problems and Solutions,* edited by Jamie C. Kassler and Jill Stubington, 94–120. Sydney: Hale & Iremonger.

Reinach, Théodore. 1904. Tibia. *Dictionnaire des antiquités grecques et romaines* 5: 300–332.

Renfrew, Colin. 1972. *The Emergence of Civilisation: The Cyclades and the Aegean in the Third Millennium B.C.* London: Methuen.

Richter, Lukas. 1967. Zum Stilwandel der griechischen Musik im 5./4. Jahrhundert v.u.Z. *Forschungen und Fortschritte* 41: 114–16.

——. 1968. Die neue Musik der griechischen Antike. Pt. 1, Die literarische Überlieferung; pt. 2, Die Tondenkmäler. *Archiv für Musikwissenschaft* 35: 1–18, 134–47.

Riefenstahl, Leni. 1974. *The Last of the Nuba.* New York: Harper & Row.

Riethmüller, Albrecht, and Frieder Zaminer, eds. 1989. *Die Musik des Altertums.* Neues Handbuch der Musikwissenschaft, ed. Carl Dahlhaus, vol. 1. Laaber: Laaber-Verlag.

Roberts, Helen. 1974. Ancient Greek stringed instruments 700–200 B.C. Ph.D. diss., University of Reading.

——. 1979. The technique of playing ancient Greek instruments of the lyre type. *British Museum Yearbook* 4: 43–76.

Rose, Herbert J. 1960. *A Handbook of Greek Literature.* New York: E. P. Dutton.

Rubio, David. 1984. The Strings. In *The Book of the Violin,* edited by Dominic Gill, 37–43. New York: Rizzoli.

Rycroft, David K. 1981. Gora. *The New Grove Dictionary of Music and Musicians* 7: 535–36.

Sachs, Curt. 1940. *The History of Musical Instruments.* New York: W. W. Norton.

Samoïloff, A. 1924. Die alypiusschen Reihen der altgriechischen Tonbezeichnungen. *Archiv für Musikwissenschaft* 6: 383–400.

Sanden, Heinrich. 1957. *Antike Polyphonie.* Heidelberg: Carl Winter.

Schadewaldt, Wolfgang. 1965. *Von Homers Welt und Werk: Aufsätze und Auslegungen zur homerischen Frage.* 4th ed., rev. Stuttgart: K. F. Koehler.

Schäfke, Rudolf, trans. and comm. 1937. *Aristeides Quintilianus: Von der Musik.* Berlin: M. Hesse.

Schlesinger, Kathleen. 1970. *The Greek Aulos.* 1939. Reprint, Groningen: Bouma.

Schliemann, Heinrich. 1878. *Mycenae.* New York: Scribner's.

Schneider, Marius. 1946. *El origen musical de los animales-símbolos en la mitologia y la escultura antiguas.* Barcelona: Instituto Español de Musicologia.

———. 1957. Primitive music. Translated by Stanley Goodman. *The New Oxford History of Music* 1: 1–82.

Sieveking, Ann, and Gale Sieveking. 1966. *The Caves of France and Northern Spain: A Guide.* Philadelphia: Dufour.

Simmel, Georg. 1967. The stranger. In *The Sociology of Georg Simmel,* edited and translated by Kurt H. Wolff, 402–8. New York: Free Press.

Smyth, Herbert W. 1963. *Greek Melic Poets.* 1906. Reprint, New York: Biblo and Tannen.

———. 1968. *Greek Grammar.* 1920. Reprint, Cambridge, Mass.: Harvard University Press.

Snell, Bruno, ed. 1955–1989. *Lexikon des frühgriechischen Epos.* Göttingen: Vandenhoeck & Ruprecht.

Snyder, Jane M. 1981. The web of song: Weaving imagery in Homer and the lyric poets. *Classical Journal* 76: 193–96.

Solomon, Jon. 1986. The Seikelos inscription: A theoretical analysis. *American Journal of Philology* 107: 455–79.

Southgate, Thomas L. 1915. Ancient flutes from Egypt. *Journal of Hellenic Studies* 35: 12–21.

Stanford, William B. 1967. *The Sound of Greek: Studies in the Greek Theory and Practice of Euphony.* Sather Classical Lectures, vol. 38. Berkeley and Los Angeles: University of California Press.

Sternfeld, F. W., ed. 1973. *Music from the Middle Ages to the Renaissance.* Praeger History of Western Music, ed. F. W. Sternfeld, vol. 1. New York: Praeger.

Thimme, Jürgen, ed. 1977. *Art and Culture of the Cyclades in the Third Millennium B.C.* Translated by Pat Getz-Preziosi. Chicago: University of Chicago Press.

Thomas, Rosalind. 1989. *Oral Tradition and Written Record in Classical Athens.* Cambridge Studies in Oral and Literate Culture, vol. 18. Cambridge: Cambridge University Press.

Vorreiter, Leopold. 1972. Münzen und Musik im antiken Mytilene. *Münzen- und Medaillensammler* 12: 1347–53, 1375–88.

———. 1975. The swan-neck lyres of Minoan-Mycenean culture. *Galpin Society Journal* 28: 93–97.

Wace, Alan J., and Frank H. Stubbings, eds. 1969. *A Companion to Homer.* London: Macmillan.

Webster, Thomas B. L. 1958. *From Mycenae to Homer.* London: Methuen.

———. 1970. *The Greek Chorus.* London: Methuen.

———. 1972. *Potter and Patron in Classical Athens.* London: Methuen.

———. 1973. *Athenian Culture and Society.* Berkeley: University of California Press.

Wegner, Max. 1949. *Das Musikleben der Griechen.* Berlin: Walter de Gruyter.

———. 1963. *Griechenland.* Musikgeschichte in Bildern, ed. Heinrich Besseler and Max Schneider, vol. 2, pt. 4. Leipzig: VEB Deutscher Verlag für Musik.

———. 1968. *Musik und Tanz.* Archaeologia Homerica: Die Denkmäler und das frühgriechische Epos, vol. 3, chap. U. Göttingen: Vandenhoeck & Ruprecht.

Wegner, Ulrich. 1984. *Afrikanische Saiteninstrumente.* Veröffentlichungen des Museums für Völkerkunde, Berlin, n.s. 41, sec. Musikethnologie V. Berlin: Museum für Völkerkunde.

Wellesz, Egon, ed. 1957. *The New Oxford History of Music*. Vol. 1, *Ancient and Oriental Music*. London: Oxford University Press.

Werba, Erik. 1940. Die Rolle und Bedeutung des Sängers bei Homer und Pindar. Ph.D. diss., University of Vienna.

West, Martin L. 1971. Stesichorus. *Classical Quarterly* 21: 302–14.

———. 1973. Greek poetry 2000–700 B.C. *Classical Quarterly* 23: 179–92.

———. 1974. *Studies in Greek Elegy and Iambus*. Untersuchungen zur antiken Literatur und Geschichte, vol. 14. Berlin: Walter de Gruyter.

———, ed. 1978. *Hesiod: Works and Days*. Oxford: Clarendon Press.

———. 1981. The singing of Homer and the modes of early Greek music. *Journal of Hellenic Studies* 101: 113–29.

———. 1982. *Greek Metre*. Oxford: Clarendon Press.

———. 1983. *The Orphic Poems*. Oxford: Clarendon Press.

———. 1984. Music in archaic Greece. In *Actes du VIIᵉ Congrès de la Fédération internationale des associations d'études classiques*, edited by János Harmatta, 1: 213–20. Budapest: Akadémiai Kiado.

———. 1992a. Analecta musica. *Zeitschrift für Papyrologie und Epigraphik* 92: 1–54.

———. 1992b. *Ancient Greek Music*. Oxford: Clarendon Press.

Winnington-Ingram, Reginald P. 1928. The spondeion scale. *Classical Quarterly* 22: 84–91.

———. 1932. Aristoxenus and the intervals of Greek music. *Classical Quarterly* 26: 195–208.

———. 1958. Ancient Greek music 1932–1957. *Lustrum* 3: 5–57.

———. 1968. *Mode in Ancient Greek Music*. 1936. Reprint, Amsterdam: Hakkert.

———. 1970. Music. *Oxford Classical Dictionary*, 705–13.

———. 1981. Greece. I: Ancient. *The New Grove Dictionary of Music and Musicians* 7:659–72.

Discography

The recordings listed here vary greatly in merit. Most of the earlier ones are too brief to be of much use, although the two items in the *New Oxford History of Music* reflect the scholarship of M. Isobel Henderson, an Oxford classicist. From the same period, J. Murray Barbour's profound knowledge of scale structures lends weight to the conjectures in the Musurgia collection. See the review of this recording by R. P. Winnington-Ingram in *Gnomon* 31 (1959): 499–502. During the last two decades, the musical remains have suffered mistreatment by professional musicians with little scholarship and less judgment. Paniagua can indeed claim a few successes (see above, p. 171), but he lapses repeatedly into the bizarre; details in Jon Solomon's review, *American Journal of Philology* 102 (1981): 469–71. Like Paniagua, Halaris has no command either of text (see above, p. 223) or of context. His efforts are mentioned here only for the sake of completeness; they should be strictly avoided. Two recent attempts at a comprehensive treatment are another matter: the achievements of Professor Bélis, in particular, augur well for her undertaking. Andrew Barker has now reviewed both of these recordings in *Skutala Moisan* 2 (1995): 15–20. Finally, the newly released compact disc by the members of the Empire Brass Quintet contains an arrangement for brass and percussion of the First Delphic Hymn. They maintain that the work is anonymous, a folk song from a period before the appearance of notation. One does not know whether to laugh with Democritus or weep with Heraclitus.

First Delphic Hymn. On the album *Passage, 138 B.C.–A.D. 1611.* Empire Brass Quintet. Telarc 80355. 1995. Compact disc.

First Delphic Hymn (not complete, but supplements MSS 54). Palestrina Choir. Victor 20896. 78 rpm.

Hymn to Calliope; First Delphic Hymn (not complete). J. E. Butt. MSS 54. 78 rpm.

Musique de la Grèce antique (contains all the fragments edited by Pöhlmann 1970). Gregorio Paniagua and Atrium Musicae de Madrid. Harmonia Mundi HM 1015. 1978. 33 rpm. Harmonia Mundi HMA 190.1015. 1979. Compact disc.

The Song of Seikilos; First Delphic Hymn (accompanies the *New Oxford History of Music,* vol. 1). D. B. 21485 and D. A. 2006 on *His Master's Voice,* Historical Series. Arda Mandikian. Victor LM 6057. 1957. 78 and 33 rpm.

The Song of Seikilos; First Delphic Hymn; Hymn to Helios. On the album *The Theory of Classical Greek Music.* Theory Series, A, no. 1. Musical examples played on a specially tuned harpsichord by Robert Conant. Commentary by Fritz A. Kuttner, assisted by J. Murray Barbour. Musurgia Records. 1955. 33 rpm.

The Song of Seikilos; First Delphic Hymn; Second Delphic Hymn; Invocation of Calliope and Apollo; Christian Hymn (partial listing of contents). On the album *Music of the Ancient Greeks.* Philip Neuman and De Organographia. Pandourion Records U.S.A., PRCD 1001. 1995. Compact disc.

The Song of Seikilos; First Delphic Hymn; Second Delphic Hymn; Orestes Fragment; Invocation of Calliope and Apollo; Christian Hymn; Bellermann's Anonymous; Trumpet Call Setting (Bélis 1984b; see above, p. 203) (partial listing of contents). On the album *La musique grecque antique: de la pierre au son.* Annie Bélis and Ensemble Kérylos. Available from Kérylos, 37 Avenue de Strasbourg, F-57070, Metz, France. 1993. Compact disc.

The Song of Seikilos; Hymn to Helios. On the album *2000 Years of Music.* Hans Joachim Moser and chorus. Decca 20156. 78 rpm.

The Song of Seikilos; Hymn to Helios; Hymn to Nemesis; Hymn to the Muse; Orestes Fragment; Ajax Fragment; First Delphic Hymn; Second Delphic Hymn; Christian Hymn (partial listing of contents). On the album *Music of Ancient Greece.* Christodoulos Halaris and instrumental ensemble, vocal soloists. Orata Orangm 2013. 1992. Compact disc.

Index